It Was Always ME!
Edward Edwards
The Most Prolific Serial Killer of All Time

By: John A. Cameron

Publisher: ReelTime Media

Seattle, Washington

2018

Copyright

It Was Always ME!

Copyright April 2018, John A. Cameron

All rights reserved. No portion of this book may be reproduced in any form, except for brief quotations in reviews, without permission in writing from the publisher. Published by ReelTime Media
19930 69th Ave NE Kenmore, WA 98020

Cameron, John A.

It Was Always ME!, by John A. Cameron—2nd ed. p. cm. ISBN 978-1-7322374-4-5
1. Murder. 2. Serial killing. 3. Zodiac killer. 4. Egyptian mythology. 5. Satanism. 6. Edward Wayne Edwards.

Manufactured in the United States of America
Paperback edition, April 2018.
Producer - Barry Henthorn
Editor - Josh Willaert
Cover Art - Max Mittler
Asset Manager - Lucas Kostenko

Contents

Copyright 2
Dedication 5
Forward 7
Introduction 11
The Arrest 13
The Great Falls Murder 17
Looking into Edwards 27
Introduction to Zodiac 43
The Arrest of Edward Edwards 61
My Obsession 77
The Zodiac Ciphers 79
Meeting the Family 91
Edwards Writes! 103
Neal Questions 121
Edwards Puzzled 125
A Killer's Mind Games 127
Edwards Gets His Wish 143
Preparing for the Interview 145
Edwards Gets His Second Wish 157
A New Plan Needed 159
Dropping the Bomb 177
The Atlanta Child Murders 205
A Big Piece of the Puzzle 223
Edwards' Recognition 233
A Living Victim Speaks 239

Hollywood!	245
Profile of a Ritualistic Killer	253
Chicago	259
Stephanie Bryan	267
Marilyn Sheppard, 1954	289
The Early 50's	299
Edwards Gets Out 1967	303
The 70's	319
The Occult	331
The West Memphis Three and the 90's	335
1945, The Beginning	343
The Solution	361
America's Most Wanted	387
The Final Decade of Killing	401
The Conclusion	468
Further Uncovered Cases	471
Darlie Routier, 1996	473
Scott and Laci Peterson	479
Coleman Case Review	485
The Set-up of Steven Avery and Brendan Dassey	503
The Known Victims	555
The Wrongfully Convicted Still Alive	563
The Known Wrongfully Convicted Deceased	567

Dedication

This story is dedicated to the crew at Morning Light Coffee Shop in Great Falls, Montana, all of those whom have contributed their research, and anyone who had the misfortune of having Ed Edwards enter their lives.

Forward

Welcome to the rabbit hole.

The discoveries, realizations, and proof contained in "It Was Me Edward Wayne Edwards The Serial Killer You Never Heard Of" sent a shock wave throughout law enforcement, the judicial system, and serial killer aficionados everywhere. Since then there has been widespread media attention on Edwards and Cameron including numerous articles in newspapers, magazines such as "In Touch" a front-page article published by "People Magazine", and a six-part documentary series on The Paramount Network starring John Cameron and Wayne Wolf (Edwards grandson) where the two traveled across the country exploring Edwards murders.

It was not the publicity however that compelled Cameron to write this drastically updated version of his original book but the outpour of additional information and evidence that was not available prior that has flooded into law enforcement and to Cameron since its publication. It is the knowledge that many people now sit in prison or have already been executed for crimes that they absolutely did not commit, and the many families that have gained closure or begun to heal now having the knowledge of what happened. It is our heartfelt hope that by including additional cases and evidence that those unrightfully incarcerated may be released and that more evidence will be forthcoming allowing more cases to be solved.

Forget everything you thought you thought you knew about the most publicly covered murders of our time. The evidence leads to one man committing the most chilling and widely known murders that have captivated the public's interest and caused terror throughout our communities. Due to the persistent work of John Cameron and others It is now widely accepted (although there will always be those that hold onto antiquated theories) that Edward Edwards was in fact the Zodiac Killer who killed in Northern California in a series of murders during the 1960s and 1970s in which he taunted the newspapers and law enforcement with letters written in various codes including a 13-block cipher. The Zodiac (Edward Edwards) did not stop killing nor were the Zodiac murders the first murders that Edward Edwards had committed. Edwards Murders date back to his childhood when he was 11 (some maintain his first murder was his own mother when he was only 5 years old although it was ruled a suicide that he witnessed), where he committed a double murder and successfully framed someone else by pointing the finger. Later in 1947 when he was 13 Edwards murdered Elizabeth Short in Los Angeles, California. The murder became known posthumously as "The Black Dahlia," among many others up until he was in his 70s.

Based on the investigation by veteran detective John Cameron and others contained in this book Edwards is also now linked to the murder of Laci Peterson for which he set up Scott Peterson who is currently on death row for killing her. The evidence also strongly suggests that he killed JonBenet Ramsay and that he framed the parents whom were later exonerated. As you begin to get into the mind of Edward Edwards you will uncover so many murders in which he set up people only to testify against them or to tip off the police as to where to find the evidence he had planted. Take the journey of a lifetime of murder and deceit all while flaunting it to the press, appearing on TV shows as a reformed criminal, and police begging to be caught while laughing inside. You will discover how Edwards killed Theresa Halbach and framed Steve Avery while watching the trial from the sidelines and even making an appearance in "Making a Murderer" the Netflix original series that followed Steve Avery's trial and conviction. And as you will discover those murders were just the tip of the iceberg and that only by seeing Ed's life of murder as a whole can you begin to grasp the magnitude of his Satanic destruction.

-Barry Henthorn

Introduction

John A. Cameron is a 57-year-old retired police detective from Great Falls, Montana. His career in law enforcement began in 1979. He retired in 2005 as a sergeant of detectives, working cold cases. He has worked on FBI serial killer task forces, including catching ritualistic child cannibal killer, Nathan Bar-Jonah. His cases have been featured on America's Most Wanted, Dateline NBC, and he helped produce a series known as, "Most Evil" on Tru TV in 2010.

John then began working off a lead from a text he had been forwarded while working as an analyst for the Montana Board of Pardons and Parole, in Deer Lodge Prison, Montana. Once he started down the rabbit hole he could not stop following the evidence which led him to uncovering information that had been kept secret for 55 years. John had discovered the most intelligent and prolific serial killer of all time who had been killing for over 60 years undetected.

This led to him writing "It Was Me Edward Wayne Edwards The Serial Killer You Never Heard Of" in 2014. That book is arguably the second most significant book in relating to and understanding the most public murders of our century.

Chapter 1

The Arrest

June 2009

On March 9, 2009, NBC affiliate WMTV in Madison, Wisconsin, ran a special on a 30-year-old cold case with new DNA evidence. The brutal murders of Timothy Hack and Kelly Drew had never been solved. No one really expected any results from the airing of the new evidence, but a detective with the Jefferson County Sheriff's Office got a call from Akron, Ohio a few days later. The woman identified herself as April and then said, "I think you need to talk to my father." The detective investigated the tip and his interest skyrocketed when he discovered her father's name on the list of the 75 suspects that had been interviewed shortly after the murders.

Hack and Drew had been killed in 1980 following a wedding reception near Concord, Wisconsin. Drew's clothing was found shredded along a road a few days later, but two months passed before their bodies were discovered in a wooded area about eight miles away. Drew had been bound at the ankles and wrists and strangled, a broken hyoid bone in her neck. Hack had a penetrating knife wound to his back.

April had said that her father, Edward Wayne Edwards, had been employed as a handy man by the Concord House, a reception hall, at the time. He aroused suspicion when witnesses saw him with a "bloody nose" shortly after the murders. He told officials that the injury occurred while deer hunting, but was unavailable for further questioning. He packed up his wife and five children and bolted during the night. As they left town, he pointed to a field and told his children, "They're going to find a couple of dead kids over there."

Acting on the tip, the detective and a deputy traveled to nearby Louisville, Kentucky to the address that had been provided by April. An overweight, sickly-looking individual on oxygen answered their knock on the door in a wheel chair. He denied any knowledge of the crime or memory of the incident, but when asked if he had ever been deer hunting, he responded, "Oh. *That* murder."

Edwards eventually submitted to DNA testing and the results came back an exact match. The press excitedly touted, "DNA leads to arrest in cold case." In reality, it was April's tip and the detective's tenacious follow-up that led to the arrest. DNA only confirmed they had the right suspect.

Due to poor health, Edwards was transferred by air from Louisville to Wisconsin. He pleaded not guilty to the charges and not much happened for almost a year. After 30 years, witnesses were difficult to locate and his court-appointed attorney kept the wolves at bay by petitioning the court for more time to prepare for a possible change of venue to insure an impartial jury.

During that time, the prosecution did discover a few interesting details. Their suspect had once been on the FBI's 10 most wanted list and he had also been looked at as a "person of interest" in the slayings of two teenagers in Portland, Oregon around Thanksgiving in 1960.

Even more interesting was that the suspect had written and published his autobiography in 1972 titled "Metamorphosis of a criminal". The book detailed his life of robberies, escapes, car thefts and other crimes across the country, mostly taking place during the 50's and 60's. In his book, he claimed to be reformed at the age of 35 and was now a successful married family man with 5 children.

With a combined effort of the detective and the Homeland Security Agency, a bulletin was sent to law enforcement in all cities mentioned in Edwards' book. It inquired if there were any "unsolved cases," particularly double murders, which may have occurred during the appropriate time period.

Over a thousand miles away, an officer with the Great Falls Police Department in Montana passed the information on to me by text message to me. I was a retired cold case detective living in Great Falls when that message effectively ended my retirement and began my investigation of Edward Wayne Edwards.

Chapter 2

The Great Falls Murder

June 2010

I was sitting at my desk, day-dreaming as I tossed an orange Nerf ball at the stick-on hoop on the wall. The outer door of my office now read, "Montana Board of Pardons and Parole," but my secretary Judy from my years at the GFPD still sat at a desk in the inner office. She ran a tight ship, organizing my calendar and handling calls. Her routine was interrupted when a local detective Doug Mahlum entered and asked to see me. She recognized him as the new cold case detective in town who I had trained while still at the department.

"Hey, Judy," yelled detective Mahlum, "You still working for this bum? Why don't you put in for a transfer and come and work for a real cop? I'll get you a job title, probably a new Ferrari, the company's Lear jet twice a year, and a key to the executive washroom!"

"Lear jet," Judy burst out, "You mean that thing that your grandpa used for crop dusting? You couldn't get me off the ground in that for nothing!" She had worked with me for over 20 years and she adored me.

"Now, that key to the washroom.?" joked Judy.

She buzzed me on the intercom. "John, Doug Mahlum's here to see you."

"Send him in," I responded, wondering what brought the detective in. Having spent more than 2 decades in law enforcement, on the job I had discovered my passion. My natural ability to analyze and profile, combined with a good memory and instincts led me to the arena of cold cases. My career was geared toward solving homicides and violent crimes, and I was good at it.

Mahlum had come to share a bulletin from the Homeland Security Agency about a killer they had in custody in Ohio.

"Is this about that text message on Edwards?" I asked.

"Yeah, you gotta hear the rest of this story," Mahlum answered. "Apparently, this guy just confessed to five murders between 1977 and 1996. But back in 1972, he wrote a book. It's an autobiography on his life, claiming himself to be a reformed criminal. He apparently mentions several cities in the book and Homeland Security sent out memos to all of them to see if they have any unsolved crimes that might match his M.O., particularly double murders from the 50's or 60's. Great Falls was mentioned in chapter 20, so they sent the bulletin to us. You ever heard of the guy? His name is Edward Wayne Edwards. He also cut some kind of religious motivational album in 1970."

"Sounds unbelievable, Doug—76 years old and he never got caught for murder until now? Tell me more."

"In 2010, Edwards confessed to 5 murders. Two were double murders from over 30 years ago, and he just added the fifth, confessing to killing his adopted son in 1996 to collect a quarter million in insurance!"

"Good god," I responded. "Five cases wrapped up and done—all by one perp. Somebody's boss must be happy. I wonder how these cases were solved."

"Apparently Edwards has a daughter that finally coughed him up. It looks like he sat in jail from 2009 to 2010, proclaiming his innocence. Then, he suddenly fesses up to the original charges of the first double murder and additionally gives them 3 more victims they didn't know about. What's more, he wrote a book!"

I was puzzled trying to piece it all together. Examining Mahlum's paperwork, it looked like Edwards had killed two teenagers in Wisconsin in 1980. He not only murdered them but kidnapped them and left their bodies miles away. I had to wonder why. The kids had come up missing on August 8th, but their bodies were not found for several months. The press had labeled him the "Sweetheart Killer" after his capture because he liked to kill young couples on lover's lanes.

I also wondered why, after a year in jail, Edwards would confess not only to those murders, but to the brutal slayings of two teenagers in Ohio. Their bodies had been discovered almost immediately, on August 9, 1977. Finally, in a taped interview he gave them the details of executing his 21-year-old adopted son, Dannie Law Gloeckner, in 1996.

Edwards had stated, *"Dannie boy was someone we—I had taken in. With Dannie, I saw an opportunity to—you know, I was always a schemer; I was always thinking of ways of making money. I've always been into crime and ahh, with Dannie I saw an opportunity here—ah, long range—about a year to set it up, and that's what I did. I set it up to collect the money and ended up getting 250,000 dollars out of it-and-ah-ah, it was arranged, it was premeditated, it was thought out, it was planned, and that's what I did. I walked him into the cemetery, had him bend down and grab some cigarettes out of my duffel bag and I shot him in the head. I reloaded and shot him again. He didn't even see it coming. I went back a few months later and took his head and threw it in a corn field. I did it, it didn't bother me, and I moved on. That's all, that's all I killed!"*

(Edward Wayne Edwards, 2010)

"Yeah, right," I told Mahlum. "A book, an album, kidnappings, preplanned murders for money, and then he gets identified as a serial killer! I don't believe that's all he ever killed." I buzzed my secretary. "Judy, see if you can find me a copy of Edward Edwards' book, 'Metamorphosis of a Criminal.' Get on the internet, Amazon, Alibris. It's spelled M E T A...."

Judy interrupted, "I know how to spell, boss. I graduated from college!"

"Well, see if you can spell me up some half decent coffee then!"

Mahlum left my office muttering, "I don't see how she puts up with you."

Having never seen or heard of anything like this, I was captivated. Homeland Security was wondering if Edwards could have done any crimes in Montana. This was a cold-case detective's dream come true—a possible thread to some 50-year-old unsolved crimes. With the time frame about right, the first case that came to mind was the 1964 Arrotta double murder of a Great Falls couple in a grocery store. I had arrested a man in 2001 for the killings and he was tried before a judge in 2004. With no jury, he was acquitted—despite my feelings. I still felt strongly the guy was good for it. However, any good investigator should not wear blinders and if Edwards was the real killer, this new lead merited investigation.

    I worked for the Board of Pardons and Parole, so I decided the first thing to do was to run a National Crime Information Center records check and find out what Edwards had done in the past. The NCIC is the warehouse of all criminal records. Edwards' report came back immediately. It proved he was in Leavenworth Federal Penitentiary from 1962 until 1967 for armed robbery. That eliminated him from killing the Arrottas in Great Falls in 1964. As simple as that, Edwards didn't do it because he was sitting in Leavenworth Prison—an airtight alibi. Edwards' Montana rap sheet showed an extensive record of robbery, auto theft, and impersonating an officer. The crimes dated back to 1951.

HEADQUARTERS
MONTANA STATE PRISON
Deer Lodge, Montana

The following is a transcript of the record, including the most recently reported data, as shown in the files of this Bureau concerning our number 17598

F. P. C. 15 O 9 U OOM
          L 24 W IOI 17
F. B. I. No. 760 165 A

Fred Douglas Superintendent

Ref._____ By Ken_____

CONTRIBUTOR OF FINGERPRINTS	NAME AND NUMBER	ARRESTED OR RECEIVED	CHARGE	DISPOSITION
Marine	Edward Wayne Edwards #1118804	enlisted 6-22-50		
PD Dayton Beach Fla	Wayne Edward Edwards #DB 34185	5-30-51	inv car theft	TOT Jax Fla Auth car theft 5-31-51
SO Jacksonville Fla	Edward Wayne Edwards #81007	5-31-51	B&E & GL	7-6-51 PG sent susp. & rel & rel to Shore Patrol
PD Jacksonville Fla	Edward Wayne Edwards #34-742	7-31-51	B & E & GL	7-6-51 PG SS TOT Shore Patrol on Gr Lar (auto rel to Morristown Police for F.B. 4-25-52
ntgomery Co Pr Morristown Pa	Edward W. Edwards #411-52	4-24-52	chg of B & E & Inv.	
PD Phila Pa	Edward Wayne Edwards #253251	4-25-52	vio of the Dyer Act	TOT fed Auth
USM Phila Pa	Edward Wayne Edwards #11588	4-28-52	Dyer Act	$1,500 for Ort 2 yrs on chg of ITSMV & 30 das on chg of illeg wear of uniform to be served o
Fed Ref Chillicothe Ohio	Edward Wayne Edwards #33245	7-8-52	Trans Stolen Auto Interstate Illegally wearing MC Uniform susp	2 yrs 12-8-53 min exp with EOT pending 3-31-55
PD Akron Ohio	Edward Wayne Edwards #42351	3-11-55		
PD Akron Ohio	Edward Wayne Edwards #42351	3-18-55	B & L (W)	4-5-55 to GJ on chg of B&L, $2,000. bond escaped from City Jail on 4-5-55.
SO Akron Ohio	Edward Wayne Edwards #9402	3-11-55	Fug & B & L (Texas)	4-5-55 TOT Akron PD
SO Billings Mont	Wayne Edwards #8074	3-7-56	armed robbery	
PD Billings Mont	Edward Wayne Edwards #14103	3-7-56	armed robbery	
SP Deer Lodge ont	Edward Wayne Edwards #17598	3-20-56	robb	10 yrs

Disch'd as undesirable on 8-22-51 at Jacksonville Fal by reason of misconduct (conviction by civil auth_____)

MT HIST LIBRARY+ARCHIVES ☎ 14064445297   08/10/10 13:59 :07/08 NO:364

NOTICE.—This Record is furnished for official use only

CONTRIBUTOR OF FINGERPRINTS	NAME AND NUMBER	ARRESTED OR RECEIVED	CHARGE	DISPOSITION
	WANTED: Edward Wayne Edwards for escape from City Jail 4-5-55 (B&L $2,000 bond). Notify PD Akron, Ohio, per inf rec 10-28-55. NO LONGER WANTED: Per information received dated 3-8-56. (located by SO & PD 3-7-56. Billings, Mont.)			

(Edwards' Montana Bureau of Identification Records From 1956)

Turning back to the NCIC report. "This guy has been a very busy boy!" I mused.

Arrests and Warrants-EDWARD WAYNE EDWARDS: DOB 6/14/1933

1951: Florida, auto theft.

1952: Pennsylvania, impersonating an officer, Chillicothe Prison, released October 1953.

1955: Texas, breaking and entering, armed robbery.

1955: Ohio, escape.

1955: California, Oakland, Sacramento, armed robbery.

1956: Montana, robbery. Deer Lodge Prison released 1959.

1960: Portland, Oregon, escape and impersonating an officer.

1961: Ohio, robbery. Leavenworth Prison 1961-released September 1967.

1982: Georgia, Atlanta. Flight to avoid prosecution, arson, larceny.

1982: Pennsylvania, arson, felony theft. Sentenced 5-12 years Pennsylvania State Penitentiary; released June 1986.

2009: Wisconsin, two counts deliberate homicide, kidnapping. Life sentence.

2010: Ohio, two counts deliberate homicide, kidnapping. Life sentence.

2010: Ohio, one count deliberate homicide, kidnapping— PENDING COURT.

(Edward Wayne Edwards' NCIC Record)

Being at least familiar with all the unsolved murder cases in Montana, I recalled the January 2, 1956 lover's lane execution of Patty Kalitske and Duane Bogle in Great Falls. Edwards' M.O. fit exactly and his record showed he was busted for a robbery in Montana a few months after that date. I started sifting through the information, looking at articles and notes on the case. No longer a licensed police officer, I didn't have access to the police reports. The Kalitske/Bogle case was technically an ongoing investigation, albeit 50 some years old. There is no statute of limitations on murder. There were still a few guys around that had been on the case, but I personally didn't know the details. I began reading the newspaper articles on the murders.

<u>Great Falls Tribune, January 3, 1956</u>
OFFICERS FEAR GIRL KIDNAPPED
Airman Boyfriend Found Executed on Lover's Lane.

<u>Great Falls Tribune, January 5, 1956</u>
Girl Friend of Slain Airman Found Murdered Near City
Sixteen-year-old Patty Kalitske found executed, thrown off Mount Royal Road.

I sat back in my chair and began piecing the picture together in my mind.

Patty Kalitske. Just a name. Most people from Great Falls wouldn't even remember her. But, like all murder victims, she had friends, a family. She was loved. In 1956, she was sixteen years old. The kids at high school knew her as "Ski". A few weeks before Christmas, she was the talk of the school for showing up with a crew-cut, styled after a Dick Tracy comic strip character. She was fun loving, well known, and liked by all. Plus, she had a new boyfriend. She was going out with Duane Bogle, an 18-year-old airman stationed at Malmstrom Air Force Base.

The night of January 2, 1956, Patty and Duane had a date. They didn't plan on staying out late because Patty was due back in school and New Year's Day had just come and gone. Pete's Drive-In was the local teenage hang-out and the kids arrived around 8:00 p.m. They ordered two vanilla-cokes, socialized for about an hour, and then left to head out Central Ave. West toward Wadsworth Park, the local area's lover's lane. They never came home.

When they didn't show up that night, Patty's parents were concerned, but also had thought, or hoped, the kids had eloped. They knew Duane and he was welcome in their house. He had spent Christmas with them.

The following morning, Duane was found lying next to his car door with two bullet holes in his head. He had been shot once above and behind the right ear and a second shot was fired to the left temple. Both hits were through and through, so no slugs were ever recovered. His hands were bound behind his back with his own belt. Investigators said that he had been ordered to his knees before he had been executed. They also speculated that Patty had been made to watch before she was kidnapped from the scene.

When his body was found, Duane had 5 dollars in his wallet and an expensive camera was still in the car, so robbery was not the motive. The area was unlit, yet there were no shell casings. The killer would have needed a flashlight to find the brass and he probably used it to control Patty and Duane. It looked like he may have approached the kids posing as a cop. Patty appeared to be the intended victim, as she was taken from the scene. Everyone prayed and hoped that she would be found safe, released or that she would escape somehow. Unfortunately, her fully clothed body would be found the following morning, 5 miles from the first murder on Mount Royal Road. There was no sign of sexual assault. She had been executed like Duane, shot in the back of the head. There was no fathomable reason. The hearts of every person who heard wrenched. Tears and disbelief—sharing the feeling of the unimaginable fear that must have gone through Patty in her last few hours, knowing that she too was going to die. The monster that had done this crime was not a jealous suitor. He was not just some "crazy" that got carried away. This killer was evil.

Great Falls lived in fear and law enforcement was helpless. Leads were followed but ran out. The police had nothing to go on. I didn't know it yet, but the cops actually had Edwards shortly after the killings. Unfortunately, it was for robbery and they never connected the cases. How different things might have been. How many other lives would have been saved over the years, how many families would have been spared, if only....

It was most likely not the killer's first. It was definitely not his last.

Patty and Duane had been confronted while parked on a lover's lane, by someone with a gun and a flashlight and executed. Not robbed, not raped, just executed! No witnesses. The police were puzzled.

By March of 1956, the killings had been in the Great Falls Tribune repeatedly and it was clear that there was no suspect and no evidence. In addition, suspicious calls had been made during the investigation to throw the police off. The killing terrorized the city. The police indicated the type of weapon used was a larger caliber handgun. Investigators from Omaha, Nebraska contacted the Cascade County Sheriff's Office to inform them that a young woman had been slain under similar circumstances in their area. She had been shot with a 32-20 military police gun. Her body was discovered on the campus of the University of Omaha on December 9, 1955, just 3 weeks before the Great Falls murders. Investigators felt the two cases could be connected.

I set the file back down on my desk. My mind was racing. Edwards confesses to two 30-year-old cases back east, double murders of young couples on lover's lanes. No robbery, no suspects or motives. The M.O. was identical to the Great Falls killings 20 years before that. My detective instincts were starting to hum.

A confessed murderer of young kids parked on lover's lanes was in the same area where Kalitske and Bogle were killed. The odds were astronomical for the killer to be someone other than Edwards. A guy doesn't just start executing people when he's 44 years old, he must have been killing a long time. Edwards was only 22 when he was in Great Falls. I couldn't let it go.

Chapter 3
Looking into Edwards
July 2010

I wasn't a cop anymore, but my job with the parole board kept my instincts sharp. I had interviewed over 2000 inmates in the last 3 years at Deer Lodge Prison. Spotting a con was easy and Edwards was turning out to be the master con. By early summer, things were getting interesting. I was convinced Edwards was the killer of Kalitske and Bogle in 1956. The case was over 50 years old and most of the people involved had died or moved away. My cold case instincts were screaming that Edwards was the perp, but proving it was going to be difficult. Law enforcement didn't like to be proven wrong. It would not be the only time this was encountered during my investigations. I had attempted to tell the Cascade County Sheriff's Office about Ed Edwards, but they were not interested. The agency in charge of the Kalitske-Bogle murder had gone public in the 80's and 90's, going on national TV to claim the case solved. Their suspect back then was a child molester serving time in a California prison. A psychic had been used and the killing was turned into a TV show called the "Cottonwood Killings", so named for the large trees where Duane Bogle was ordered to his knees and executed.

By 2010, members of law enforcement had set their blinders on and refused to look elsewhere. I had contacted all the local agencies; the FBI, Cascade County Sheriff, Great Falls Police and officials in Ohio and Wisconsin. I tried to convince them that Edwards had killed in a lot of places and a task force was needed.

By late July, I arranged a meeting with local law enforcement. I visited the sheriff's office with my information on Edwards, but they weren't interested. They didn't want my help and they didn't want to be proven wrong. "Stay out of our case" was the clear message.

I tried appealing to higher authorities and sent my information to the FBI. He received a polite E-mail in return, but it went no further after local officials complained that I was not a cop anymore.

(FBI Quantico E-Mail to Cameron)

Cameron, John

From:	gmvecchi@fbiacademy.edu
Sent:	Tuesday, August 03, 2010 7:42 AM
To:	Cameron, John
Cc:	steven.conlon@ic.fbi.gov
Subject:	Re: ZODIAC

John

Thanks for the info.

We are doing some damage control due to your comments to several law enforcement agencies regarding this matter, which has caused unnecessary conflict. I am waiting to field some calls to resolve it. We are also reviewing your material and cross referencing it in order to validate your information so we can move forward as necessary which means getting the appropriate people and agencies on board as appropriate. Steven Conlon of my unit is handling it so please give him a chance.

Greg

I had made a few enemies by this point but was in too deep. The FBI never returned his calls and it became clear they wanted nothing to do with Ed Edwards. Regardless of law enforcement's attitude, I was incapable of blowing off the information. My obsessive-compulsive behavior wouldn't let me stop researching Edwards. I decided I really needed to look at Edwards' autobiography. It was out of print and the edition size was very small. A reporter in Wisconsin had faxed me thirty pages, including a chapter titled "Armed Robbery". In that chapter Great Falls, Montana was specifically mentioned during the year 1956. Judy had not yet located a copy and I needed the rest of the book.

    This was when the first of many coincidences in the investigation occurred. I had been talking about the case for a number of weeks by now, when a good friend, Deb, came into my office.

    "Who do you love the most, besides your mother?" she asked.

    "She's dead, but do you really want the list?" I chuckled.

    "I brought you a present." She tossed a copy of 'Metamorphosis of a Criminal" onto my desk.

    "Unbelievable! Where did you get this?"

    "You're not going to believe this, but I had it in my library! Probably the only copy in the state of Montana."

    "Alright," I admitted. "I might love you."

    I started reading as she left the office. The 1972 autobiography was entitled, "Metamorphosis of a Criminal, The True-Life Story of Ed Edwards."

He was on the F.B.I.'s list of the "Ten Most Wanted Criminals."
He was a hold-up man, a bank robber, a dangerous character.
He spent 14 years in five jails.

Now he is a writer, a respected citizen and the head of a family of five.

METAMORPHOSIS OF A CRIMINAL

THE TRUE LIFE STORY OF
Ed Edwards

(Cover of Edwards' book)

(Ad for Edwards' book)

At the beginning of the book, Edwards relays a difficult childhood, being raised by Catholic nuns in an orphanage. He states that his mother died from complications from a self-inflicted gunshot wound to the stomach. It went down officially as a suicide. He claimed to be 2 1/2 years old at the time.

"I was born Charles Murray on June 14, 1933 in Akron, Ohio. My mother was Lillian Myers. I was told she was my aunt. I didn't know my father. My career was almost preordained to be a criminal. My mother needed someone to care about her, someone who would not judge her for the impetuous love affair that resulted in my birth. That someone never came. In December of 1935, in a bungled attempt to shake her family into recognizing her need, she got a rifle and shot herself in the stomach. Complications set in, and she died of septicemia in a number of days. I was adopted by Mary Ethel and Fred Edwards, and was given the name Edward Wayne Edwards. I remember when I was 7 and my grandma gave up on me and sent me to Parmadale Catholic Orphanage. An old battle axe nun informed me that she was now my new mother. She would try to break me of my rage, defiance and bed-wetting. I remembered being the youngest in the reformatory and the other kids tying me to a tree, taking their turns kicking me, trying to get me to break my bed-wetting and to stop my escalating acts of defiance. My hatred for Sister Agnes Marie and the Catholic reformatory grew to the point that even the reformatory couldn't control me. My frustration grew for years until I was released back to grandma. Toward the end, and after several escapes, the orphanage gave up on me and requested her to come get me. Upon my departure, Old Sister Agnes Maria shook her head and asked me, 'Ed, what are you going to be when you grow up?'

"I looked at her and said, 'I'm going to be a crook, and I'm going to be a good one.'

"In 1945, I returned to my grandmother and started public school. But I planned and schemed, hour after hour, how to be a good crook. That was the only way I would get any...recognition."
*
The book was a puzzle and the first lie in it was his name. Edwards' real name was Charles Edward Myers. He lied in the book about specific facts that would make the puzzle harder to solve. By 1945, Edward Wayne Edwards was 11 years old and began creating crimes of recognition. A major force driving Edwards his entire life was his

desire and need to be recognized. In his book, he explained the recognition he sought was not in the context that he wanted to be recognized or identified.

He wanted to be present when everyone was talking about the horrible crime, and nobody knew the perpetrator was standing next to them. He wanted society to realize his significance. He wanted to be elevated above everyone else, including the police and justice system. And he wanted revenge against the Christians. Edwards continues in his book:

(*Metamorphosis of a Criminal")
"In January of 1948, I was sent to the Philadelphia Protectory, a school located right across the river from Valley Forge. My resentment knew no bounds. I hated the school, but I gained an education. I learned what burglar's tools were, how to 'hot wire' a car, how to pick locks and forge checks. I learned how to avoid being caught by setting off fire alarms away from the scene of the crime, thus deflecting the cops down a blind alley. I learned how to jimmy a door or window, and how to crawl through a transom. I was all set to tackle the world. Someday people would hear of Ed Edwards, master criminal." *

Edwards had placed himself in Great Falls around March 1956 in his book, two months after Patty and Duane were executed. He was trying to create an alibi. Edwards had written about being there, committing robberies and describing encounters with victims begging for their lives.

"That robbery had been too good to be true. I knew I was stretching my luck, and I decided that we better get the hell out of Seattle. We'll stop in Great Falls, Montana. When we get there you can call your mom long distance."

"Oh Honey! One of my brothers lives in Great Falls."

In Great Falls, after renting a room, I decided we would scout out gas stations. We spotted one on the highway that was set off by itself. I was getting compulsive about my heisting. Robbery was beginning to give me an exhilaration close to the thrill a person must feel when he breaks a bank at gambling. I don't like the idea of putting more than one person under the gun at a time. You can never tell what they might do."* (Metamorphosis of a Criminal)

Edwards spoke of beatings he gave to women. "That did it. I slappèd her, knocked her down, kicked her, picked her back up, and knocked her down again. I fattened her lip, bruised her up, and cussed her out violently. I called her a whore, a slut, and a little son-of-a bitch, and threatened to cut her tits off and flush them down the toilet."* MOAC

The book left a trail of corn for the reader to follow. Edwards had made mention of Great Falls or Montana in the book over 50 times, and alluded to killing. He placed himself in specific cities where unsolved murders had occurred, but left him enough time in the book to create an alibi. I spotted the evidence and couldn't let it go. If my theory was right, then there would be other murders in the book. I was spending hours researching and examining microfilm at the Great Falls Public Library. It was easy to put Edwards in Montana in 1956, because he was caught in a robbery and sentenced to Deer Lodge Prison within 3 months of the Kalitske Bogle murders. I wondered if I could put him in Great Falls in January. After traveling to the Montana History Museum in Helena, I found the original prison records on Edwards from 1956. The prison records have Edwards arriving in Great Falls, January 1956, by his own admission!

When arrested, Edwards claimed that his name was James Garfield Langley, supposedly living with his new wife's brother, Roger White in Great Falls. The admission sheet specifically placed him in the city at the time of the murder. He had escaped from an Ohio jail just 6 months earlier and traveled the country committing crimes and robberies, glorifying his exploits in the book he wrote in 1972. He was hiding out in Great Falls in 1956, pretending to be a married family man with his pregnant wife, Jeanette White. Edwards robbed Bob and Ole's gas station in Great Falls on March 6, 1956 and fled 200 miles away to Billings, Montana. He was caught on the following day doing another robbery. He detailed in his book his attempt to kill himself and escape after his capture in Montana.

"I did not want to do away with myself, but I did intend to do my best to escape. Slashing my wrists had been a hopeful act. About a week later, I went to court with a court appointed attorney.

The judge asked: "Do you have anything to say before I pronounce sentence?"

"Yes, sir. I would like to ask for leniency. I realize the mistakes I've made, and I've come clean with everything. I have a wife, and a child on the way. I'd like an opportunity to go back and start a new life."

(Montana State Prison, Deer Lodge, admission sheet March 20, 1956)

Edwards' book was a truthful account of his life on the run, but he left out any mention of killing. Everything in the book was a clue to be followed, and he had written it 16 years after the Great Falls murder. The police connected him to the Great Falls robbery, but never questioned him and he got away with murder at the age of 22. Within three weeks he was locked up in Deer Lodge Prison. Prior to being admitted to the prison, Edwards complied with a judge-ordered psych exam and admitted to being accused of kidnapping women by gun point.

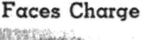

Faces Charge

EDWARD W. EDWARDS

Court Orders Mental Exam

(Billings Gazette, March 8, 1956)

March 19, 1956 11:00 AM
Edward Wayne Edwards. Yellowstone County, Billings, Montana
Conclusion: ANTI-SOCIAL REACTION
History:
Edward Wayne Edwards was seen at the request of the county attorney, Mr. John Cavan Jr., and with the consent of defense attorney, Mr. James Palmereheim. Prisoner was advised of his rights, was told that if he did not say anything that this might be used against him in court or it might be "good for him." After advising him of this, he said he understood, and added "all I want is to get straightened out." He added he is

in jail now for committing an armed robbery. He said this particular series of crimes started in Las Vegas where he got a gun, went from there to Reno. He says he held up a couple of places on the way to Billings and after arriving in Billings he was short on money and he used the gun to hold up a gas station. He believes it was a Standard Oil station. "I couldn't really say why I done it. I had a good wife; she was pregnant; we had no money. We didn't blow it on gambling or anything." He said he felt terrible about all the places he robbed and felt "scared to death." He said he has a history of prison incarcerations beginning when he was about 13 or 14 years of age, he claims. At that time, he was placed in an institution for juvenile delinquency in Parmadale, Pennsylvania, for stealing a bicycle. He has been in jail in Akron, has been a prisoner in Chillicothe Federal Reformatory in Ohio 1951-53 for stealing a car. His last incarceration was in March of 1955 in Akron, Ohio. He was apprehended at 5:00 am in a stolen car which he had taken from the house of some longtime friends. Also, at this time, a girl he had given a ride from Florida to Akron told police he took her at gunpoint. But the charge was dropped, he says.

Past History:
Subject prisoner claims he is 22 years of age. He says he was born 14 June 1933, in Akron, Ohio. There have been no siblings and he never knew his father. He states his mother wasn't married when he was born. When he was just an infant, he claims she committed suicide by shooting herself. He declines any knowledge of this until he was 13 or so. After his mother's death, her sister and husband adopted subject prisoner and six months after his adoption, his foster mother became paralyzed and was in bed for seven years. Subject prisoner says that his foster father was a drunk and drank and beat her in bed. His mother's mother, the maternal grandmother, was about the only person that the prisoner knew of a real relative. He was in an orphanage, the

Parmadale Catholic Orphanage in Cleveland, from 5 to 12 years of age, ever since stealing a piece of birthday cake at the orphanage. He has been in and out of trouble. He volunteered for the Marines when 16 or 17, and after basic training, he was refused eligibility to go overseas for being too young. He went AWOL.

He ran at the time and he went back to Akron and was running around until captured. When caught he was placed in a mental hospital. While in the hospital this first wife became pregnant from another guy, a corporal in the Marines, and she divorced subject prisoner when he was in the Chillicothe Federal Reformatory. He was also placed in the Florida State Hospital in 1953 in a mental ward. He was thinking of different things from his past.

"I ran away from the hospital and was sent back to the hospital." He was given an undesirable discharge from the Marines with no court martial. It wasn't clear from the subject prisoner's story just when this occurred.

It may have been in conjunction with his going AWOL; however, it also was in conjunction with stealing a car. He also claims to have been in a Veterans Administration hospital in Houston, Texas. He says he went into the hospital with ulcers, depression, and cried all the time. He was placed in ice packs and cold sheets, and after was placed in a strait jacket. And after running around, he says that he knows that the various crimes he has committed have been illegal. He felt guilty about it, committing some of them, and he isn't just sure why he does such things.

Mental State Evaluation:
Edward Wayne Edwards is a slightly built young man of about 20 to 25 years of age by appearance. There was no particular sign of deception during the period of observation, other than flushing of the face. He was cooperative and quiet throughout the interview. Speech was within normal limits. He did not appear in the least depressed, has a history of suicidal gestures,

no more than suicidal ideation theatrics. This may have been partially feigned, although it is certainly possible he feels neglected, discriminated against and sorry for himself as he appears to feel. There is a good possibility that he has deliberately exaggerated the story he told, with the intent of gaining sympathy. Only independent information from his past could clarify this. He freely admitted lying to his wife when he married her in October of 1953. He said he told her a bunch of lies.

"I told her I had seven brothers and sisters and went to college and played football. I told her I had fought in Korea and had recently retired. I don't know why I lied like that." There is ample evidence that subject prisoner was so emotionally unstable—explosive style of personality in which he is unable to tolerate very much stress. There is also ample evidence that he has reacted in stress through aggressive anti-social activity. There is no evidence of delusions, hallucinations or feelings of passivity or other evidence of a severe concrete thinking disorder. He is judged to be of average intelligence.

The summary of clinical psychological tests is as follows.

The patient, a young normal-appearing man, was tested at the county jail. He displayed some initial weariness about participating in the examination, as the judge and his lawyer had specified this by consulting him first. While attempts to reach his lawyer were unsuccessful, the patient consented to take the examination without further advice.

At one point he remarked that he didn't understand what could be gleaned from these tests, but nonetheless was performing to the best of his ability. The latter was born out by a conscience application of all of the tests that were presented to him.

DATED MARCH 17, 1956

Edwards had detailed his horrible upbringing to the psychiatrist evaluating him. Everything he said was the profile of a serial killer capable of conning everyone including the courts. Edwards lied about his age when his mother was shot in front of him in 1938. He wasn't an infant like he said. He was 5, and his name was changed after the shooting. He lost his identity at the age of 5 and teased everyone the rest of his life with his identity.

I concluded immediately that Edwards was a dangerous, disturbed man and had been killing since much earlier than 1956. His stories of running the country and conning countless women were red flags. He admitted to being locked up in strait jackets and injected with drugs to stop his rage. As a child, he was abused, a bed-wetter and sexually deviant. He loved to light fires. He confessed to the Billings authorities for robberies to deflect them from the Great Falls murders. The ruse was successful, but it resulted in 3 years in Deer Lodge Prison and for warrants being issued in San Francisco, Sacramento, and Oakland for robberies in 1955. The records proved it and he admitted it. I believe he had perfectly executed Patty and Duane in Great Falls in 1956 and he got away with it. Edwards was in California in 1955. He was an accomplished killer that loved to kill couples on lover's lanes!

Chapter 4
Introduction to Zodiac
August 2010

I had spent the last 6 weeks plowing over Edwards' records and life and realized that the man was constantly in the press, seeking recognition. Edwards had written a 400-page book, detailing his life, bragging that he was reformed when in fact he had never reformed. He had been on TV shows, inside major newspaper offices bragging that he was rehabilitated. It was all a ruse. I needed help, so I went to my usual spot in Morning Light Coffee. Mike, the owner, looked over and asked, "Hey, John, what are you working on?"

"I'm studying an old cold case from here in Great Falls. A couple of kids were killed over on the west side, back in 1956, and I'm convinced this guy they got in Wisconsin for some similar murders was the guy that did it. But do you want to know what's really crazy? This guy has many similarities to the Zodiac killer from San Francisco during the late 1960's. His criminal record shows that he was released from Leavenworth Prison just before the Zodiac started. You ever heard of the Zodiac?"

"Talk to Neal," Mike replied. "You know him, don't you? He's really into that stuff. He's got some ideas on some codes the Zodiac wrote. The guy knows a dozen languages and has an IQ off the charts."

"Yeah, I know him. I'll see if I can meet up with him."

So, I decided to call Neal and set up a meeting a few days later. When Neal arrived, I told him that I had a suspect who I thought could actually be the Zodiac killer. I gave him a brief history about Edwards, adding the serial killer had written a 435-page autobiography.

"Wait. You have a confessed serial killer that wrote a book about himself in 1972? You gotta be kidding!" Neal exclaimed.

"It gets even better," I said. "In 1972 he got on the national TV show, 'To Tell the Truth,' with Alan Alda and Kitty Carlisle. They were trying to figure out which of the three contestants was the real Ed Edwards. The entire show describes the making of a serial killer, born illegitimate, with no mother, no father or love, and he tells them he was a suspect in a double lover's lane murder in Oregon, 1960."

(Edward Wayne Edwards, October 1972, "To Tell The Truth")

In 1967, Edwards had been released from Leavenworth Prison on parole, and had been allowed by his federal parole officer to travel the country and preach that he was a reformed criminal. It was 1967-72 that he wrote the book. He had been killing while writing it. He married Kay Hedderly, July 20, 1968 and traveled the entire country for decades, using his wife and children as a ruse while he traveled, preached, and killed. He would portray himself as a reformed criminal, preacher, Dr. of Psychiatry, and an Investigator for the US Armed Services Division.

(Kay Hedderly and Ed Edwards, July 20th, 1968.)

Edwards was released from Leavenworth Prison after serving 5 years of a 15-year-sentence for bank robbery. He had conned the parole board in 1967 just as he had done in 1959. Within three months of being released he asked Kay Hedderly to marry him and she did. They married in a Catholic church in Akron, Ohio, July 20th, 1968. The Zodiac killings started 6 months later. He remained married to her until his capture in 2009. Edwards had told his wife that he was a long-haul truck driver and she never knew better. After his capture in 2009 it was revealed that his entire life was a lie. Edwards was never a long-haul truck driver in 1968 but had been fired from a trucking company shortly after his release, for stealing a truck load of tires.

    Cameron passed over his information on Edwards about his 2010 confessions in Ohio and Wisconsin.

    "Wow! "Neal exclaimed. "He admitted killing a teenage boy and girl? The boy first and the girl later. He had a pre-cut clothesline, they were shot and stabbed, and there was no robbery. Same deal in Ohio with no motive and no suspects. These are striking similarities to the Zodiac killings."

    "That's why I think he is the Zodiac killer, Neal. I didn't even want to think about it at first, but his NCIC records show an interesting story. He robbed a bank, tried to escape, got a 15-year sentence but only served 5 years. Look at his arrest date, 1962-02-09, and parole date, 1967-09-20. He got 10 years cut off a 15-year sentence and he was one of the FBI's Most Wanted men in 1961." I explained, "So Edwards is the FBI's most wanted man in 1961 and he gets favorable treatment in 1967 and is released a year before the Zodiac killings. He had to have been informing. He had a long history of doing that. Now listen to what the Zodiac killer did."

```
Arrest Date             1962-02-09
Arrest Case Number      15721
Arresting Agency        OHUSM0200 USM CLEVELAND
Subject's Name          EDWARDS,EDWARD WAYNE
        Charge Literal  ATT ESCAPE
               Agency   OHUSM0200 USM CLEVELAND
Court Disposition       (Cycle 014)
Court Disposition Date            1967-09-20
Court Agency            Unknown
Charge                  01
        Charge Literal  BANK ROB
             Severity   Unknown
          Disposition   (Other 1967-09-20;    PAR)
```

The Zodiac killer killed from 1968 until 1970 in the Bay area of California. He killed 5 in 4 separate attacks in Vallejo, Benicia, Lake Berryessa and finally in the heart of San Francisco. He approached couples on lover's lanes and shot them repeatedly. At Lake Berryessa, he put on a black executioner's hood with the Zodiac cross and circle and viciously stabbed a young couple lying on a beach. The surviving boy at Lake Berryessa said that the Zodiac mentioned having been in Deer Lodge Prison, having escaped and stolen a car. Edwards had spent 3 years in Deer Lodge in 1956-59, after fleeing Great Falls where he had killed a young couple on a lover's lane. He got caught in Billings for robbery. He was in a stolen car and had tried to escape from the Yellowstone County Jail. The victim described the Zodiac:

"He was barrel-chested, 5 feet 8, to 6 feet tall, dark-haired and heavy set, wearing a dark jacket and dark clothing that seemed sloppy and disheveled. He appeared to be in his thirties and fairly unremarkable. He ducked between some trees and emerged about 20 feet later. He was wearing a black hood that appeared professionally sewn and had the Zodiac's signature cross and circle on the front."

Napa Composites of Zodiac

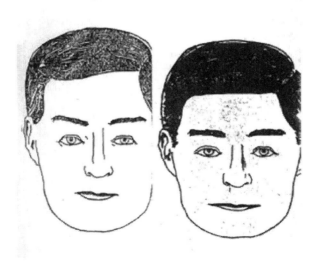

(Composites of Zodiac Killer)
A composite drawing was completed:

(Zodiac Composite 1969) (Photo - Edward Wayne Edwards 1970)

Edwards was 35 years old in 1968, 5ft 8 inches, 185 pounds, potbellied, reddish brown hair, and barrel chested. He matched every aspect of the Zodiac composite. Edwards' M.O. throughout his life was to seek recognition by contacting the press and police, just as he had done in 2010 after his capture. He had used knife, rope, gun and fire to kill and that is what the Zodiac claimed. In the Zodiac case, he contacted the police by phone at first, taunting the police with the details of his murders.

"I want to report a double murder. If you go one mile east on Columbus Parkway to the public park, you will find the kids in a brown car. They were shot with a 9mm Luger. I also killed those kids last December. Goodbye."

The Zodiac wrote letters to the press and police bragging that he was smarter than them and that they couldn't catch him:

"This is the Zodiac speaking. The SF police could have caught me last night if they had searched the park properly instead of holding road races with their motorcycles, seeing who could make the most noise."

On August 1st, 1969, the Zodiac sent a puzzle to three newspapers in the Bay area bragging that if it were solved they would have his identity.

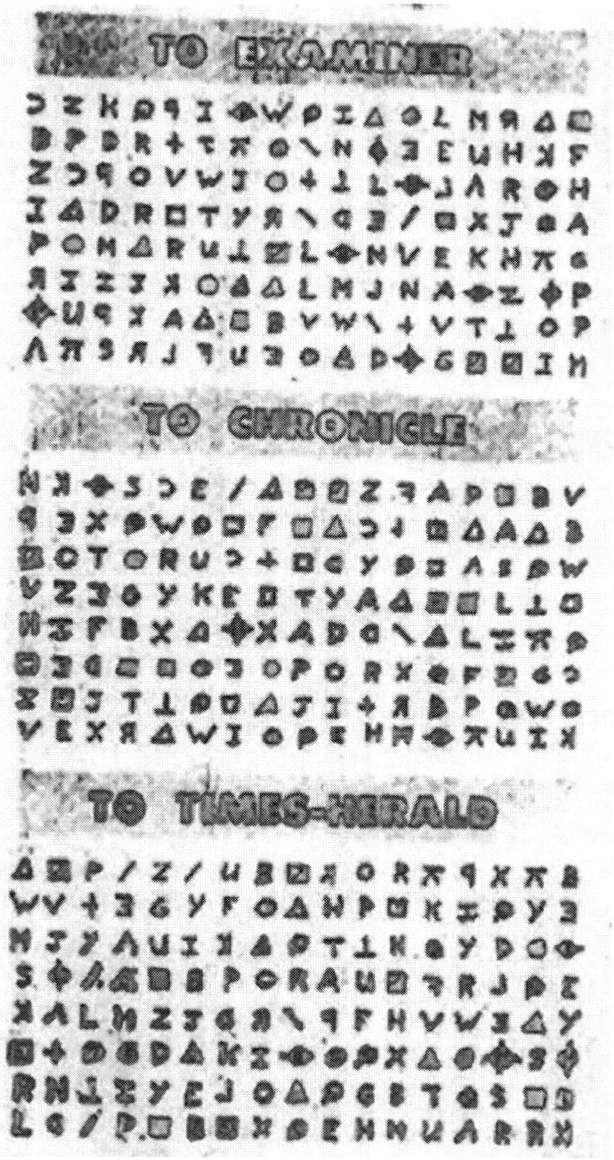

(Zodiac's July 30, 1969, 3-part cryptogram sent to newspapers)

The letter began, "This is the Zodiac Speaking." The cryptic message was written in strange symbols and letters. Donald Harden, a school teacher and his wife first cracked the code. When solved, it left a chilling message:

"I like killing people because it is so much fun. It is more fun than killing wild game in the forest because man is the most dangerous animal of all. To kill something gives me the most thrilling experience. It is even better than getting your rocks off with a girl. The best part of it is that when I die I will be reborn in paradise and all that I have killed will become my slaves. I will not give you my name because you will try to slow down or stop my collecting of slaves for my afterlife.

There were 18 symbols left over from the puzzle that had never been deciphered. The Zodiac had bragged that the puzzle, when fully solved, would contain his identity. There were two obvious E's left over in the puzzle. Some letters appeared to be in mirror image like the R and K

(18 Characters from Zodiac 420 Cipher)

The Zodiac taunted the police and press for decades with anonymous letters and puzzles. They arrived in every part of the country since his killings began. The police were baffled. The San Francisco Chronicle, Examiner and Vallejo Times were having a field day; circulation exploded. What did the Zodiac killer want? He wanted recognition and sensationalism. The letters were taunting the police and the public to identify him. This killer was something no one had ever dealt with. As more Zodiac letters arrived over the years, they contained counts as to how many he had killed.

1969=Zodiac 7/SFPD 0
1970=Zodiac 13/SFPD 0
1971=Zodiac 21/ SFPD 0

1974=Zodiac 32/SFPD 0

What the Zodiac killer believed was that he was smarter than anyone and he proved it by sending letters in the 70's, 80's, 90's and even as late as 2008. He never stopped killing and was always seeking recognition. Edwards acted like the Zodiac killer his entire life. He was always seeking recognition, and his book was one big puzzle of murder thrown in the face of society to see if they could figure it all out.

Neal's family had purchased several of Edwards' books online and he contacted me all excited.

"John, guess what! A friend of mine just got a copy of Edwards' book in the mail and it's a home run. First off, it's signed and inscribed by Edwards to a police officer. 'Officer Carver, I hope you will find this book to be of some help in your work!' I think he is trying to say something about reading between the lines, like there is some kind of hints or puzzles to be worked out within the book! You're not going to believe what he found inside. Five loose pages, printed on both sides, including Edward's biography. There are photos showing Edwards traveling the country during the Zodiac, touting his rehabilitation and going on national radio shows. He spoke to law enforcement, schools, lawyers and churches. Edwards even had an article of himself talking to the head of the United Nations about how to fight crime in other countries!"

John Wingate, WOR Radio, New York City and Ed Edwards

Lee Phillips, WBBM-TV, Chicago and Ed Edwards

Ed Edwards
AUTHOR - LECTURER - CONSULTANT - AUTHORITY ON CRIME

BIOGRAPHY

Ed Edwards was born in 1933 in Akron, Ohio, an illegitimate child whose mother later committed suicide. It was because of this that he was sent to an orphanage in 1940 at the age of seven. Ed committed his first crime at the age of eight when he stole another child's birthday cake while in the orphanage, and his last crime was committed in 1962 when he robbed a bank while on the FBI's *"Ten Most Wanted"* list.

In between his first crime and his last one he spent a total of sixteen years in institutions around the country such as, Chillicothe, Montana State Penitentiary, Oregon, Leavenworth and Lewisburg for such crimes as car theft, burglary, robbery, bad checks and being a con man. In 1962, while in Leavenworth a *miraculous metamorphosis* started to take place, and in the six years that followed Ed completed his high school education, two years of college, three courses in Dale Carnegie and five years of vocational training in the building trades. In 1967, he became one of the first men who has ever been on the FBI's "Ten Most Wanted" list to be paroled back into society and one of the very few men to be paroled from a federal penitentiary for bank robbery the first time up before the parole board.

Since his release from prison he has married and his wife, Kay, is expecting their fourth child. He has continued his college education, written the book "Metamorphosis of a Criminal" and is in the building and remodeling business, which is the trade he learned while at Leavenworth. Since 1968, Ed has been traveling over 100,000 miles a year lecturing at universities, colleges, schools, churches, police academies and various civic organizations.

How does a man, once caught in the coils of criminology throw off the shackles that bind him? How does he summon the will and the strength to cure himself of his addiction to violence? Can a person with a history like this emerge from the degeneration and despair of being one of life's outcasts and propel himself by degrees upward until he becomes a force of good rather than a force of evil?

Some of what he tells is almost unbelievable. Some of what he tells is funny. Some of what he tells is tragic. All of what he tells is fascinating and exciting. His close brushes with the law and his realization of wrong-doing all make for edge-of-the-seat listening.

You may not approve of him, but you will not be able to keep yourself from liking him. You will be rooting for him all the way through his squalid life to his miraculous rehabilitation and metamorphosis.

You will not want to miss listening to Ed. He tells about his life, how to avoid juvenile delinquency, why not to use drugs, prison reforms and community reforms. Ed says, "There is a tremendous breakdown in parental communications today, and we have got to realize there is no substitute for love or discipline."

Dr. Micel Davidson, Under Secretary General of the United Nations. Dr. Davidson appeared on this show, KMBC in Kansas City, Mo., with Ed and discussed crime in the U.S. compared to other countries.

Capt. Larry Bradley, Atlanta, Georgia Police Dept. and Ed. While Capt. Bradley and Ed are the best of friends today, it was Capt. Bradley who led the raid and arrested Ed in Atlanta in 1962.

GENE RAYBURN, panelist on the television show "To Tell the Truth", ALAN ALDA, Hawkeye on the television show "Mash" and ED EDWARDS.

LEE LEONARD, host of the television show "Dialing for Dollars" in New York City and ED EDWARDS.

JACK O'BRIEN, columnist and host of his own radio show in New York City and ED EDWARDS. MR. O'BRIEN writes the syndicated column which the late and most famous crime reporter, DOROTHY KILGALLEN used to write.

ALAN DOUGLAS, host of his own show on NBC radio in New York City and ED EDWARDS. MR. DOUGLAS, who used to have his own show on radio and later television in Cleveland, Ohio refers to ED as, *"a most fascinating guy."*

ANN COLONE and ED, WANE-TV
Ft. Wayne, Indiana

MARCIA CORSARD, WKYC-TV
Cleveland, Ohio

BOB BRAUN and ED
Bob Braun's 50-50 Club
Cincinnati, Ohio

DOROTHY FULDHEIM and ED
WEWS-TV, Cleveland, Ohio

(Photos - Edwards' Author Biography and photos of media appearances)

"What a con man." I said to Neal. "I want copies of everything. Listen to this, Edwards even admits to traveling 100,000 miles since his release in 1967. This jerk was on parole. How was he allowed to travel?" I asked Neal, "Have you had a chance to read his book yet? Even as a child Edwards craved attention and recognition.

He loved the excitement of pulling fire alarms and watching the shiny fire trucks arrive. He even mentioned that he would sit back and watch the crowds angrily talk about the inconsiderate bastard that pulled the alarms. He was proud that he had created the chaos. During the 1956 Great Falls murder investigation someone was pulling fire alarms, so much so that the fire chief went public begging for it to stop."

<u>January 13, 1956 Great Falls Leader</u>
CHIEF ISSUES WARNING ON FALSE FIRE ALARMS
Man hours wasted on false alarms

His book contained all the details of what his M.O. would be in the future. By being able to stand in front of everyone during the investigation he got his rocks off. There was a lot more to the book. Later in July of 2010, I called Neal all excited.

"I've got it, I've got the proof! Have you read the book yet?"

"Yeah," answered Neal, "There is a lot of religious connotation in there."

"Well, go to page 232. I didn't even catch it the first time I read it, but I read it again last night and I remembered you telling me about the Zodiac and his Satanic religious mention of slaves in the afterlife-and there it was, right in the book."

"Hold on, hold on. Let me get my copy." Neal started reading. He'd missed it, too. Right from the Zodiac crypto.

232 METAMORPHOSIS OF A CRIMINAL

killing her instantly.

Another inmate had been hitchhiking for some time without success. A farmer finally came along and picked him up, whereupon he showed his gratitude by shooting the farmer five times in the back with a .45.

An inmate who particularly stands out in my mind was the man who killed a deputy sheriff. When the posse found him hiding out in an outhouse, he told them:

"You can't convict me because I swallowed the evidence."

He had swallowed the bullets.

This demented individual showed an overwhelming interest in science fiction and Egyptian literature. He believed that anyone he killed would be his slave in the next life. He was generally disliked and distrusted by the other inmates. I personally felt that he was one of the most deranged and potentially dangerous persons in the prison. You never knew when he was going to erupt.

Unfortunately, this inmate idolized me, for the simple reason that I had earned the respect of the population—something, deep down, he wanted desperately to do. He had an uncanny knack for making your skin crawl. Today, when I think about all the different types I met in that excuse for a penitentiary, this man remains my most uncomfortable memory.

("Metamorphosis of a Criminal" "He believed that anyone he killed would be his slave in the next life." *)

"There it is, Neal. I told you the book was a puzzle. He is talking about himself. Everything in it is there for a reason. His family told me he loved to play games. Edwards is the Zodiac killer!"

Though Neal and I had not realized the magnitude, this would prove true throughout the entire book. "Metamorphosis of a Criminal," was a serial killer's game against the justice

59

system, and he had put the murders and clues in the book as a taunt, just as the Zodiac killer had done in his letters to the press and police. By using his NCIC records and his book, the murders would be revealed. Edwards had started killing in horrific, glorified, press-sensational murders ever since age 11—and never stopped. He had learned to manipulate the MEDIA in every venue—every year—and into his afterlife...

As he said in the book, Edwards would reach his goal of being the 'best criminal ever.'

Chapter 5

The Arrest of Edward Edwards

Louisville, Kentucky June 9, 2009

When the knock came on the door, his wife called out, "Wayne, there are two policemen here to talk to you." She had been with him 41 years. He had only one thought—how much do they know? He knew he was in serious trouble, but he was old and he was tired. The game had gone on for decades and he was sick. With cancer, neuropathy and a general sense of, 'I don't care', he let them ask their questions and he submitted to their request for a DNA sample. There was no question if they would be back, only when. He didn't feel like running; he didn't really have anywhere to go. Let the chips fall where they may.

It only took a month. When they came back, they didn't ask him any questions. They simply announced, "Edward Wayne Edwards, we have a warrant for your arrest for the murders of Kelly Drew and Timothy Hack on August 8, 1980." They read him his rights, cuffed him, and hauled him away. He weighed 300 pounds and was in a wheel chair.

July 30, 2009

It was the beginning of the end of 66 years of murder. They locked him up in county jail right out of Louisville, but soon extradited him to Dodge Correctional Institution in Wisconsin to face charges. Due to his failing health, they flew him in a chopper across state lines. He laughed to himself at what it must have cost the taxpayers. They had no idea of who he was or the magnitude of the crimes he had committed.

He had stated in the book how he would plan each crime. *"Whether it was forgery, robbery or burglary, I would plan each crime deliberately, patiently and cold bloodedly."* Those had been his self-imposed rules and he had stuck to them religiously. What he didn't mention in the book was murder and that helped him pull off the game for 66 years. A life of crime and terror, and now they finally had him. But no one knew—they were clueless. As far as he was concerned the cops were idiots. He had proved that for seventy years. He had toyed with them, flaunted his deeds in their face, and left them clues his entire life. No one had put it together. By this time, he doubted they would do so during his lifetime. That was probably a pretty good bet with his heart problems, emphysema, diabetes and other ailments. He didn't think he was going to be around that much longer.

Edwards first met his public defender, Jeffrey De La Rosa, in August of 2009. He didn't inform him of much, declaring his innocence in the murders. He stuck by his story for months, maintaining that he had seen 2 thugs "stomping on Hack" and he left the scene, figuring it was none of his business.

De La Rosa did the best he could, but he didn't have a lot to work with. He did manage to drag things out, getting the trial date extended a few times. He had a valid point that witnesses, facts, and a criminal defense were difficult to prepare for a 30-year-old case. Yet the evidence against Edwards was overwhelming and a trial was inevitable.

Edwards wore out. He decided to confess to the Wisconsin murders. He met once again with his public defender in April of 2010. Edwards had a lengthy rap sheet, having been in and out of prison most of his life. He had never been charged with murder and he made his decision. He decided to throw in the towel. He had been in jail for almost 11 months, his health was deteriorating, and he knew he wasn't escaping this time. There was nowhere to go. He had escaped the claws of justice for 66 years. He wanted to be executed.

He informed his lawyer of this decision, but De La Rosa argued against it. He told Edwards that he was still trying for a change of venue to get an impartial jury and they had a good chance the trial date would be extended yet another time.

Edwards informed De La Rosa, "You don't understand. I am done! It's over and I want the death penalty. I don't want the chair. I don't think I want them to fry me, but if they promise me the needle, I will give them the details."

De La Rosa advised against the guilty plea and told Edwards they could still fight the charges, but Edwards wanted nothing to do with that. He insisted he wanted the needle. De La Rosa finally acquiesced, but he added that there was one slight problem.

"What's that?" asked Ed.

"Wisconsin doesn't have the death penalty and they will not execute you," De La Rosa told him.

Edwards responded, "Do you mean to tell me there is no death penalty in Wisconsin? I thought I could be executed for the crime." Ed pondered the situation for several moments...then he asked... "Does Ohio have the death penalty for murder?"

De La Rosa paled. There could only be one reason for that question— another murder. He informed Edwards that Ohio did indeed. Edwards returned to his cell. He wanted the death penalty, but Wisconsin was not going to give it to him. De La Rosa walked across the street to the district attorney's office. He met with the D.A. and announced, "I have some good news and some bad news for you. Edwards wants to confess to the Hack/Drew murders."

The D.A. looked at him suspiciously and asked, "What's the bad news?"

"He wants the needle. He wants it in writing that he'll get the death penalty and in return he'll confess to all the details."

"Damn it!" said the D.A. "I finally get a break, and we can't deliver. Did you tell him there's no capital punishment in Wisconsin?"

"Yeah, and he got really upset. He told me we were done, and he went back to his cell."

"Do you think we can get him to talk?"

"I don't know; this guy insists on getting his own way. I don't think anybody is going to tell him what to do."

"Well, let me kick it around the office. We'll get back with you. Thanks for letting us know."

"There is one more thing."

"Yeah?"

"He asked me if Ohio has the death penalty."

"Oh, my God..."

Edwards concluded the best way to get the death penalty was to tell them about the 2 kids he had killed in Ohio in 1977. The word finally made it to the authorities, but they weren't sure if he was telling the truth or to which lover's lane murder he wanted to confess to. There were several in the 70's. Edwards comprised a confessional letter on April 15 and mailed it directly to the state district attorney's office in Norton. That got their attention.

Me. OK, My name is Mr. Edward Wayne Edwards and in the past I've been very well known there in Akron. You probably know who I am but I have no way of knowing that. At this time I'm in jail in Wi. awaiting trial on a double murder. I understand that you are interested in me for a double murder that took place in 1976. It was a male and female and they were shot in a park out by Doyles town close to Wayne County. — Norton

I'm getting old and tired so let me know if you are interested in what I might have to say. I'm from Akron broke out of jail there in 1955, robbed a bank there in 1961 and was sentenced 16 years, out of Cleveland I went to Leavenworth. I know shortly after this double murder that they had a kid from Doyles town for it. Believe me he had nothing to do with it and I hope their is no one in jail now for it. I was living in Doylestown at the time. I knew the two that were killed very well but I don't think I was a suspect in any way and I understand I am now.

Let me know if you are interested in what I have to say. I am interested in being brought back to Akron and you'll probably be wanting to put the needle in my arm. I have no problem with that. Let me know if your interested as I have some other people around the country wanting to talk to me. You are the first

Sincerely, Ed Edwards

(Wayne)

(Edwards' 2010 confessional letter to Ohio District Attorney Office)

By the end of April 2010, Edwards was frustrated. His anger flared when he didn't get his way. He had made what he considered to be his most important decision ever—to end his life. Now, the cops were interfering. No death penalty in Wisconsin? How dare they deny HIM! He was always in control. He had to give them the two kids from Ohio in 1977, but they were still clueless as to who he was. He was still waiting. He had put a puzzle in the letter that he was the Zodiac killer, "Norton, you are the first" ...But nobody caught it. The block lettering was the clue.

Edwards didn't hear back immediately, so he decided to drop a note to the detective in charge of his case in Ohio. Officer John Canterbury would receive a letter sent on April 29 from Dodge Correction Center, Wisconsin.

> Hi John,   4-29-10
>
> You were very nice the other day but I know you "let my guts". That's okay, I understand. You told me you would say nothing to Det Garcia. It is already around that I will be going back to Ohio for double murder. That will come up in court here. My atty. did not even know I talked with you. Anyway, I like to know, will you be taking me right from court or the jail, or will I be coming back for few months. If I'm coming back here for months I might as well stop talking and plan on staying here. I also have other places I can go — ☺
>
> Please answer me and
>
> Thank You
>
> Ed Edwards

(Letter postmarked April 30, 2010.)

Edwards was manipulating the cops and expressing his concern of getting extradited immediately to Ohio for the death penalty. If not? "I also have other places I can go." Edwards was trying to get executed as soon as possible. He was unaware that there were certain years in

Ohio that the death penalty did not apply and 1977 was one of them.

Edwards was really angry now. He'd given them two more of his murders, apparently for no reason. He felt like he'd been tricked somehow. He had written the Norton police detective less than a week earlier, certain that they would extradite him to Ohio. Now, he knew they wouldn't execute him for the 1977 Straub/Lavacco killing in Ohio. On May 4th, Edwards wrote Canterbury again. He was extremely angry and challenged the detective, "Did you know I cannot get the death penalty for a 1977 murder in Ohio?" He wants some answers. Then he concludes this letter with an incredible confession. Concerned with getting the death penalty, he wrote, "I would really like to know the above (in his letter) because there is another state that would love to have me, and they did, and still do, have the death penalty in 1977."

> John, 5-4-10
>
> I was up in the law lib today, & found out I cannot get the "Death Penalty" for a 1977 murder in Ohio. So what does the D.A. say about that? Did you know that when you were here? Would you please give me an answer. My court date was moved back again. It was on the news but they did not say when. I think it will be in Aug. or Sept. now. Another question, what makes you think WI. will turn me over to you? I'm just an old man wondering where my life is going. I would really like to know the above because there is another state that would love to have me & they did, & still do, have the death penalty in 1977.
>
> Hey, this is Ed Edward checking in.
> Have a good day!

(Letter postmarked May 5, 2010 to Detective Canterbury confessing to more murders)

In his letter, he confirms his court date for the Wisconsin murders have been extended again, to August or September. He's not sure if Wisconsin is going to let him face his charges in Ohio, so he threatens Canterbury with a shocker that was never followed up on. He claims there is another state that would "love to have

me" that had, and still does have the death penalty in 1977. Then he sardonically signs the letter:
    "Hey, this is Ed Edwards
    Checking in.
    Have a good day!"
    Edwards met with his attorney once again. "I have another question for you. Did Ohio have the death penalty for murder in 1996?" In disbelief, the court appointed attorney slowly nodded yes. Edwards continued, "Then I want to tell you how I killed my adopted son Dannie for the life insurance in April of '96".
    That got the ball rolling. After just more than a month, on June 11th, 2010, Edwards pleaded guilty to the 1980 slayings of Hack and Drew in Wisconsin. There was no question of his guilt. His daughter had turned him in; he knew all the "unpublished facts" and his DNA matched. He was given two life sentences. Two days later he was extradited to Ohio and pleaded guilty to the 1977 murders of Lavacco and Straub. It was the same M.O., the same gruesome unexplainable executions of two young adults on a lover's lane. He was given two additional life sentences.
    On June 18th, 2010, he confessed to yet another murder. He informed the news media on June 17th, 2010, "I executed my stepson, Dannie Gloeckner, and collected 250,000 dollars in life insurance." Before the court could accept his guilty plea for his final confession, he had to appear before a three-judge panel. The date was set for August 26th, 2010, but it was extended so he could get a psychological evaluation.
    I later understood from communications what he had been thinking.

    He was upset. He knew they had him dead to rights, no escaping this time. Boy, did that bring memories; escaping! He chuckled to himself, "Those idiots." He was thinking back to 1955, in Akron, Ohio, and 1960 in Portland, Oregon.

Foot Chase Fails

City Jail Prisoner Dashes To Freedom

A speedy ex-private eye broke from City Jail late Tuesday by the simple expedient of shoving aside the jailer and running.

With a bondsman and the police prosecutor in pursuit, Edward Edwards ran north on S. High st. and lost himself in a theater arcade.

A burglary suspect with a federal record, a man facing charges in two Southern states, Edwards still is missing.

The press, the public, the radio and television stations of the Akron area were asked to cooperate in the manhunt by carrying his picture and description.

He is 21, 5 feet, 8 inches tall, 156 pounds with blue eyes, sandy, wavy hair and a slight hook to his nose.

* * *

MOST OF HIS life has been spent in the Akron area. He has relatives living on Sixth st., Cuyahoga Falls, and gave this address at the time he was arrested.

Edwards had just been arraigned on a burglary charge when he made his break.

He appeared before Municipal Judge C. D. McRae in Police Court, heard himself held for the Grand Jury on the charge.

Detectives led him back to the jail which is entered at the rear of the court room and occupies the second and third floors of the Police Station.

* * *

JAILER RAY POPE said Edwards had asked to use t

EDWARD EDWARDS
...have you seen him?

From the Akron Beacon Journal, April 6, 1955.

Akronite On Priority List Of FBI

Slippery Edward Wayne Edwards, 28-year-old bandit who was born in Akron, today was added to the FBI's list of 10 most-wanted fugitives.

Edwards, described by the FBI as "a man with an incredible criminal career and an ego to match," escaped Dec. 10, 1960, from the city jail at Portland, Ore.

He is wanted on a federal charge of unlawful interstate flight to avoid confinement for robbery and for questioning about a double murder in Portland.

EDWARDS is still wanted here for breaking jail in April, 1955. Arrested as a burglary suspect he shoved the jailer aside and escaped.

Eleven months later he was picked up in Billings, Mont., after pulling several service station stickups.

Edwards was on probation for armed robbery when Portland authorities arrested him on charges of impersonating a federal officer, firing shots at a resident and turning in false fire alarms. He escaped a day after his arrest.

Edwards is about 5 feet 8, stocky build with light brown hair and blue eyes. He has many tattoos, the FBI said, including the words "Jeannette" on his right wrist and "Wayne Edwards" and "Devil Dog" on his upper right arm.

EDWARD W. EDWARDS

Article in Akron Beacon Journal, Friday, November 10, 1961.

(Akron Beacon Journal April 6, 1955)
(Akron Beacon Journal, 1961)

Edwards was a known escape artist since he was 12. "But now what?" Edwards mused. "I'm sick, I'm old and I'm sure not going to be able to make a phone call and somehow waltz out of here." The more he pondered the hopelessness of his situation, the more depressed he became.

"Well," he resigned, "I did it. I became a crook and I was a good one. I did more scams, I did more robberies, and I killed more people than anyone will ever believe. I flaunted it! I teased them, I taunted them, and I rubbed it in their faces for 66 years! Still, no one has a clue to who I really am. Finally, I guess it's over. In August, they are going to set my date." He lay down on his bunk satisfied.

He thought about his extradition from Wisconsin to Pickaway. He hadn't enjoyed the trip, but at least he was where he wanted to be—his home state of Ohio. The stupid cops may or may not have believed his story about wanting to be closer to family, but he wanted Ohio just for his death penalty. After all, they are second in the nation at putting people to death; Texas is first. Things had moved along pretty well, considering nothing ever happened quickly in the justice system. But now he was only weeks away from them setting the date. He was so affixed with having control over his own destiny; he didn't want anything to mess it up.

'What a joke." he thought. While in jail, over the years, he had faked several suicide attempts in jail to give himself a shot at escaping. Now he actually wanted to die, and it's like mission impossible. His new attorney in Ohio had told him between the helicopter rides, the medical conditions, and all the legal constraints, the "system" had spent well over a million dollars on him since his arrest. "For just a piece of that, I would've made a deal with them a long time ago." He heard the trustee making his way down the cell blocks, passing out mail. Since his arrest, he had gotten a letter or two a month from people wanting to write a book or make a movie on him. He never answered any of them, but he hadn't gotten anything in a while. "Maybe nobody knows I'm in Pickaway," he considered.

The trustee got to his cell and announced, "I got something for you today, Edwards." He passed a letter between the bars.

It was addressed:
Edward Wayne Edwards
_{Prisoner} # 584893
P.O. Box 209-FHC
Pickaway Correctional Institute
Orient, Ohio

That is not what piqued his interest. It was the return address. It had come from Great Falls, Montana. "Boy, does that bring back memories," he thought. "Fifty-five years ago." So much had happened since; so many killings. "They nearly had me, clear back then." He wondered what was inside the envelope. "Did someone know something?" he mused. "How could they, after all these years? But, Great Falls, Montana?" He stared at it several minutes and then opened the letter.

Letter written by Cameron, July 2010
Dear Ed:
My name is John Cameron. I am a retired Cold Case Homicide Detective for the Great Falls Police Department. I did 24 years of my sentence for that organization. 😊 I now work for the Montana Board of Pardons and Parole. I am an analyst, reviewing inmates' files, interviewing and recommending whether or not they are deserving of an early release. I like it. As a cop I was fortunate to have been able to work on many unsolved homicides that occurred here. I was able to solve 6 Cold Cases that were as old as 1964. One case I was never allowed to be involved in was the Kalitske/Bogle case from January 1, 1956. That case occurred in Cascade County, just outside Great Falls, and cops are very covenant about their homicides. The Cascade County Sheriff's Office worked that case. It has never been solved.

The reason I write to you is to close that case out and let the family know that you are in jail, serving a death sentence and life. There is only one relative around and she is 80. It is the sister of the victim. She is ill and has been told in the past that the cops know who did it but can't prove it. They were wrong.

I became involved in the case two weeks ago after I was sent a flier about you and your crimes. Several Great Falls police detectives contacted me because they were looking at you for killing a couple here in 1964. In that case a grocer and his wife were stabbed to death in their store. I arrested a man in that case in 2001. He was acquitted at trial. Since then, because of certain egos at the GFPD, they are always trying to find someone else that killed the grocer couple. Of course, you didn't kill them because you were in prison then. I guess the GFPD never bothered to check your record before attempting to tell me they were looking at a new killer for the '64 case.

So now, after reading about you, I was fortunate enough to have been contacted by an old investigator that asked if I would look into the January 1956, killing that you did here. And now that I have looked at your book, record, acquaintances, past crimes etc.... I know you can finally put this case to rest for Mrs. Kalitske and Bogle. I have researched you like no other. I find you fascinating. I have spoken with the County Attorney here, John Parker, regarding this case. I am putting some money on your account in case you are willing to write back. Thanks for your time, Ed. You have some years left and perhaps your last years could truly do some good for the remaining families.

Respectfully, John A Cameron

Edwards was shocked. For the last 66 years, he was in total control. He was the executioner. The world only knew what he had given them. He was the puppet master and the world was at the end of his strings. Now, for the first time, someone else knew. The first connection had been made. His hands were shaking. How much did this cop know, or even suspect? How far would it go and how much would they find out? I need my date with the needle now!

"This could really screw up my plans to be executed," he thought. He wondered if the cop would write again. He thought that over. "No," he said to himself, "I wonder *when* that cop will write again and who he has talked to!"

Chapter 6
My Obsession
September 2010

I was worried I was becoming obsessed. All I could think about was Edwards. I went into work, growled "morning" to Judy, and closed my office door. Nerf ball back in hand, I wondered, "What am I doing?"

I buzzed Judy, "Can you come in for a minute?"

"Sure," she responded. "Can I bring you anything?"

"How about a cup of good coffee?"

"Has something changed around here in the last twenty years that I don't know about, or do you want me to call someone and have it delivered?" was her answer.

"O.K.," I laughed. "I deserve that. I just need to talk to you."

Judy came into the office and sat down across from me.

"What's up, boss? I can tell something is bothering you."

"It's this Edward's thing, Judy. There's something about it I don't know."

"John, I've been with you forever, through the worst. Bar-Jonah—the Arrotta murders—all the other cold cases. I've never seen you take one so personal before. What's the deal?"

"This case is different. I've never experienced this before. It's sort of like the focal point of my entire career. Maybe of my life! I've been waking up, dripping wet, and shaking from visions."

"John, I'm so sorry. I hate it that you're not happy. You certainly deserve to be. Is there anything I can do for you?"

"Just having you here helps. I'd have never made it this long without you. Just talking to you makes it easier. I just realized I'm not being fair to you, and I'm not giving my job what's needed. I'm going to retire. Or take a leave of absence until everything works out. God knows how long that will take."

"I respect your decision and I certainly understand. I know you haven't been yourself lately. I'll always be here for you. Anything I can do to help, you just let me know."

"Thanks, Judy. You're wonderful." Now I needed that cup of coffee. I headed to Morning Light and ordered my usual.

"Hey John, what's happening?" asked Mike.

"I'm going to quit my job and go full time on Edwards. And I'm going to need the support of this coffee shop to do it."

"We got you covered, John." Mike promised.

Chapter 7

The Zodiac Ciphers

July 30, 2010

Early in the investigation, I had approached a colleague he had known for 20 years. Neal Best was at the time a 5-year-old recluse with an IQ higher than most. He had lived in China, studied the language, and had spent a great deal of time studying Egyptian and Greek mythology. On any given day he could be found at Morning Light Coffee Shop, studying another language. Neal had an unfortunate accident. A few years back, he had fallen asleep at the wheel, struck a family of 5, resulting in the death of a 12-year-old girl. It destroyed him emotionally and he was treated harshly by the justice system. Having taken a life, he fell into a great depression. Neal had been placed in the local jail, appeared on the news and was publicly humiliated. In the end, he was given 5 years of probation. When the facts of Neal's case were laid out, the punishment did not fit the crime. I helped Neal get off probation early.

The Zodiac had sent countless puzzles and letters to the media and police over the years. Some of the Zodiac's puzzles were said to be based on Egyptian mythology. Neal had studied this area for years and had read the Egyptian Book of the Dead many times. He hadn't studied the Zodiac killings and preferred not to engross himself in murder, but he was always into puzzles—especially those based on ancient mythology.

    I told Neal a few important facts about my suspect, Edward Edwards. In his book, Edwards wrote about his fascination with Egyptian history and science fiction. He also wrote about collecting "slaves for his afterlife." Neal was immediately engrossed. He knew what the Zodiac was referring to—mirrored worlds— life and afterlife. The Zodiac had bragged about killing slaves for his afterlife. Eternity is what the Zodiac sought and killing people for their perceived sins was his way there. I asked Neal for his help with the Zodiac killer's 13-character identity cipher. The name Edward Edwards contained 13 characters and if I was right on Edwards, the answer to the puzzle should be Edward Edwards.

*This is the Zodiac speaking
By the way have you cracked
the last cipher I sent you?
My name is ———*

A E N ⊕ ⊙ K ⊗ M ⊙ ⌋ N A M

*I am mildly cerous as to how
much money you have on my
head now. I hope you do not
think that I was the one
who wiped out that blue
meannie with a bomb at the
cop station. Even though I talked
about killing school children with
one. It just wouldn't doo to
move in on someone elses toritory.
But there is more glory in killing
a cop then a cid because a cop
can shoot back. I have killed
ten people to date. It would
have been a lot more except
that my bas bomb was a dud.
I was swamped out by the
rain we had a while back.*

(Zodiac Killer's April 20th, 1969 Identity Cipher)

    On August 1, 2010, Neal sent me his findings in an E-Mail.

    From: nealweemsbest [nealweemsbest@peoplepc.com]
    Sent: Sunday, August 01, 2010 11:44 AM
    To: Cameron, John

Subject: Re: FW: ZODIAC CIPHER DATED 4/20/1969

When John Cameron approached me with the 13-symbol name of the Zodiac, I was excited to solve it. Assuming John's research was correct, and the Zodiac was indeed Edward Wayne Edwards, then it would be a process of solving the riddle from two directions simultaneously. It soon became obvious that this was the essence of the puzzle from the start, that the Zodiac code was only solvable once a suspect name was available. The writings sent to newspapers and police agencies were found to be teeming with clues as to the solution, but until the central Zodiac blueprint was discovered, the clues were only random bits of madness.

I started with a few very lucky and extremely helpful clues that were just dropped in my lap. 1) John mentioned that Edward, in his book, admitted to a keen interest in ancient Egyptian religion. This is a subject that I've been fascinated with since the early 1980's. I have read "The Book of the Dead" in the original, many times. 2) Just prior to working on the cypher, I talked to my mother on the phone, and she told of a children's book, very artistically illustrated, that had the letter Z pointing in the wrong direction. 3) The solved 3-part cypher mentioned carrying souls to the other side in the afterlife. 4) In his novel, Ed strongly points out that his foremost desire is to be the absolutely most evil criminal. 5) The Zodiac is an egomaniac. He is about Me-Me-Me. 6) Ed's IQ is very high and I have studied TV shows concerning the spiritually evil criminal. 7) I noticed that the Zodiac was into symbols concerning basic centrality. I have studied this area for years, although not from the evil point of view. 8) Two faces were on all the envelopes he sent, not two postage stamps, but two faces.

The Zodiac Solution.

1. It is all about his name, about his name ringing through history, even into the afterlife. ("My name is —-")

2. It is about the conflict between good and evil. (Zodiac vs. SFPD)
3. It is about mirror worlds. (this world and the afterlife)
4. It is about gaining power through the death of others. (Satanic spirituality)
5. It is about being found out at the right time. (The letters are full of clues)
6. It is about proving how smart he is. (cryptograms)

Questions.
1. Is it a coincidence that an egomaniac has a first and last name so similar?
2. Is it possible that the killer played mystic games with his own name?
3. Is it possible that the killer made sure enough clues were available for the solution to the puzzle?
4. Is it a coincidence that parallelisms are found everywhere you look in the letters?
5. Is it possible the killer is far more intelligent than suspected?
6. Is it possible that the dual conflict in the killer would evidence itself in all his thoughts?

Facts and Clues.
1. The Zodiac crossed the words slaves and paradice. Draw a circle around this and it is the zodiac symbol.
2. The symbols in his long cryptograms were often letters in their mirror-image.
3. The symbolic logic of evil is similar to that of religious mysticism.
4. The Zodiac used the zodiac symbol to substitute for the letter d.
5. The solution is not one a supercomputer can devise.
6. The name Edward Edwards has 13 letters, but the letters are certainly scrambled.
7. Centrality's doorway to the afterlife in Egyptian religion is represented by the ankh symbol, which in Western cultures is the infinity symbol, which is two mirrored S's overlapping.

S is the odd letter in the 13 letters of the name. S should be the central letter.

    8. A small case r looks like a small case n.

    9. An M is an upside-down W.

    10. The previous puzzles used e as an e.

    11. Not all of the symbols in his coded name which looked like circles with figure-eights inside were actually the same. One looked like a figure-eight or infinity symbol, but the others had what looked like face-to-face D's.

    12. The Zodiac was meticulous in scribing his symbols. Such errors may have been intentional.

    13. The Zodiac displayed bi-polar personality traits.

    14. The Zodiac made sure he used a zodiac symbol in his name, although he had hundreds of others to choose from.

    15. Later, after solving the master-diagram, I learned that Ed chose aliases such as Rose, Love, Day, which are symbols and high ideas representing centrality, as does the zodiac symbol. The Chinese character for "day" is in fact an adaptation of the zodiac symbol.

    16. Ed is a Gemini. The Twins.

    17. The Zodiac had attacks of violent proportion in which his good side would be in battle against his evil side.

    18. The Zodiac buttons were important to him, not the word ZODIAC, but the symbol.

    19. Much of a person's writing does not necessarily represent a person's deep thought when that person is a liar and an extreme control freak.

    20. A master manipulator will have a splendid finale worked out in detail even before the show begins.

    This is a brief summary of a few of my thoughts.

    Questions?

    I hope this helps someone,--

    Neal Weems Best.

The Identity Cipher coincided with the anniversary of the Deer Lodge Prison riot that Edwards had lived through. Neal maintained this crypto could never have been solved without knowing the writer's name but once he had the name EDWARD EDWARDS, it was easy to see how the transition was made. Edwards had taken letters from his name and made his own symbols with the letters in mirror image. Mirrored worlds represented life and afterlife and the Zodiac killer was killing slaves for his afterlife.

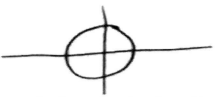

After Neal solved the first identity cipher he was able to solve the last 18 characters from the Zodiac's first cipher.

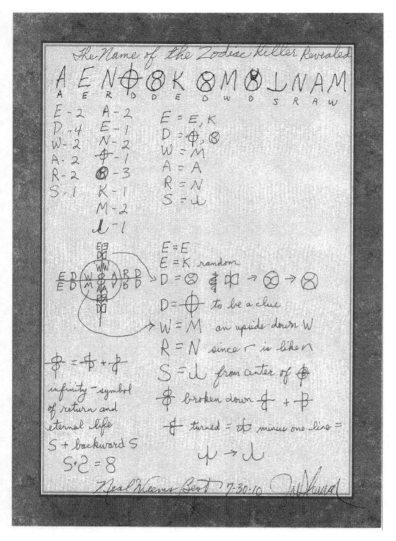

(The Zodiac cipher symbols were the letters in Ed Edwards' name in mirror image.)

The Zodiac Killer's 340-cypher Solved

I HAV NOTICE ALL OF THE EDITTOR'S EVOL NAMES ARE OFF. THEY USE LETTERS TO SHIT ME. I DOCTORED THEM AS PRISTINE, RATHER THAN INVEST TRIAGE PERENNIALLY. THEY MATE, SERVE, SO SEX LEDES TO THE GREAT AGE OF EVIL REASONING. MEAN RE HATES ME TO CRY OUT AT A FRUTE OF SIN. YOU TRY REAL FIT TO FIGHT IT, BUT RE'S FIRES DRILL HOT. I HAVE MELODY TO STEAL UNTO NIGHT A TRILL OF LIFE-TEARS. I'VE THE SOLUTION TO MY NEXT LIFE'S GOING FOR ETERNITY.

ZODIAC ED.

August 11, 2010

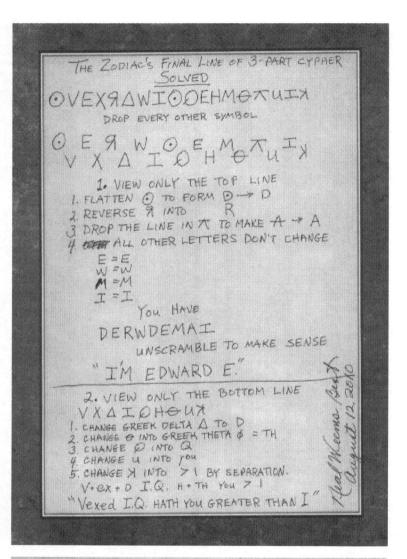

("I'm Edward E-Vexed IQ Hath You Greater Than I")

Edwards used many letters from his own name in mirror image to create the symbols used in the Zodiac ciphers. Edwards' portrayed himself throughout life as two people representing the mirrored worlds. He was the family man and the killer. The Zodiac was killing slaves for his next life. The central letter in the identity puzzle was mirrored "S's" which represent the figure eight or the sign of eternity. The Catholic Church uses the Zodiac sign throughout its churches. The priest wears it on his cassock. Edwards was abused in the Catholic orphanage and took everything from the Catholic Church and turned it into Satan.

Neal's knowledge of Christianity, Egyptian history and Greek and Chinese mysticism helped him solve the Zodiac's ciphers. Edwards had studied some of the same areas while housed in Deer Lodge Prison, Montana, from 1956 until 1959 and he wrote about it in his book.

Edwards had placed his "Identity" in the puzzle just as he had said, and was taunting everyone with his superior IQ. He was told throughout his formative years that he was stupid, when in fact he was a genius. Edwards IQ was registered at 132 when he was 17. He used his intelligence to create "Crimes of Recognition" to feed his desire to be loved.

There have been other cryptographers whom have independently cracked the ciphers and have come to the same conclusion. One notable couple Bobby Goodwin and his wife Karla Goodwin have conducted extensive research and broken many of the Zodiac Ciphers. Although I have communicated with Bobby and Karla over the years when they became aware that I was publishing this book they reached out to our publisher and provided the following statement.

"My wife goes by Karla Goodwin, we are both in agreement with John regarding Ed Edwards as being the Zodiac, murdering Theresa Halbach, Elizabeth Short (Black Dahlia), The West Memphis Three, Shandra Levy, Laci Peterson, and JonBenet Ramsay. Karla isn't convinced Edwards killed "all" of the Atlanta Child Murders (possibly 2 of them)."

He goes on to state that "Karla found Ed Edwards alias name encrypted (hidden) inside the message of the 2005 'SIKIKEY' letter in the Steven Avery case! She has also uncovered two cases that John has overlooked, … one of which is directly connected to the West Memphis Three murders." - Bobby Goodwin

He also offers to assist anyone who needs convincing and has posted a video showing evidence of Edwards being the "Zodiac", and the killer of the "Black Dahlia", and Theresa Halbach on the Ed Wayne Edwards Facebook page.

Chapter 8

Meeting the Family

September 27, 2010

I had spent the last three months investigating Edwards and knew that if I wanted to get to the bottom of it all, I had to speak to his family. My job with the Montana Board of Pardons and Parole in Deer Lodge Prison was not accommodating to the research. Edwards had conned the parole board in 1959 and they released him to Portland, Oregon. Edwards killed a young couple on a lover's lane in Portland in 1960 and got away with it. I had to ask the family some questions, so I traveled to Ohio and met with some family members. When I returned I met Neal at Morning Light Coffee.

"What did you learn? Did you find anything good?" Neal asked.

"It was a trip I'll never forget. I met some of Ed's kids, relatives and co-workers. I interviewed Kay, his wife of 43 years. She has all the signs of a battered woman. She stayed with him to raise the 5 kids and 11 grandchildren. Ed stabbed her once, but it wasn't reported to the police. He was always hanging out with the cops. Wherever they moved, and they moved often, he would immediately go to the police, introduce himself, and invite them over for barbeques and gambling. He was really into the FBI and had machines to make false credentials. She always thought he was a truck driver from 1968 to 1972, but it turns out he never was. He was a low-level lumper, unloading trucks part time. He was traveling the country preaching his rehabilitation, all while he's on parole.

"Edwards' daughter, April, was incredible. Her husband invited me in and I sat down with them for hours. It was depressing. Her father was ruthless and burned down homes repeatedly, making the family move and live in campgrounds, hiding from the police yet always having them around. He recorded everything when the cops were over and she had boxes of tapes. She said that Ed would alter them if he felt there was any damaging information. He was always a game player; you had to beat him at it. When the family was older, he purchased a Rottweiler that was trained to kill. She talked about being forced to sit on the living room couch for hours after Ed had placed the dog in front of her and the other kids, telling them not to move. She said if they had, the dog would have attacked.

"His son Jeff confirmed this." He told me, "Dad was repeatedly trying to get self-pity, and one day he walked into the kitchen and there he was, holding a shotgun under his chin, threatening to kill himself. I said go ahead and do it. I was sick of it." He told me he confronted his father about all the killings and hoped he would confess to give closure for the victims. Instead, Ed told him that the only closure he enjoys "is when they are begging for their lives."' The man was pure evil, Neal. April had a box of Ed's personal papers. Towards the top, I discovered an amazing article that's never surfaced before."

Zodiac Killer Leads

By WILLIAM KEZZIAH

Akronites are playing a part in the search for a San Francisco killer.

Two leads supplied by Akronites are being checked by San Francisco police in their search for Zodiac, the California murderer who uses codes, the mail and well-placed clues to defy capture.

A 57-YEAR-OLD former convict believes he served time with the man who claims 13 victims in four years of terror.

The Akronite said he recognized the composite drawing of Zodiac printed in the Feb. 14 Beacon Journal story that detailed Zodiac's trail.

The other bit of evidence was reported by a 63-year-old retired Army captain who claims he has deciphered the message EBEO RIET EMET HPITI, a phrase Zodiac uses.

Artist's conception of killer.

'Maybe he became tired of being pushed'
... A Former Convict

"In Montana, killing a police officer is not punished as severely as it is here. Probably Richard only served about 18 years."

THE FIRST thing police will no doubt try to do is find Richard's last name and his whereabouts.

"That won't be very hard," said the Akronite. "There've been only about 20,000 men who had served time since the jail opened in 1830."

A much harder answer will be in determining the meaning of Zodiac's seemingly undecipherable words EBEO RIET EMET HPITI, which were signed to one of his messages.

THUS FAR, the words have defied translation, but now a West Akron man believes the word means: "One tip here, I met Toebe."

"WHEN I saw his picture, I told my wife: 'What's that story about? I know that man,'" the former convict said.

"After reading the story, I'm sure I served time with him in Deer Lodge State Prison in Montana."

Deer Lodge was one of the prisons mentioned by a man who is believed to be Zodiac in September 1969 when he stabbed two college students near a California lake.

One of them, Bryan Hartnell, told police the man, who was wearing a mask, mentioned the prison before he tied up the couple and stabbed Hartnell seven times and then used the knife on the girl. Hartnell lived, the girl died two days later.

"The man I knew had the first name Richard when we were in jail. I can't remember his last name," the Akronite said.

ZODIAC carved the initials "RH" into a library study desk at Riverside City College where an 18-year-old co-ed was last seen alive. Police found her body on Halloween 1966 in a parking lot, her throat slashed with such intensity that it almost decapitated her. The initials, along with an eerie poem were verified as Zodiac's handwriting.

"I was in Deer Lodge with Richard from around 1956 to 1959," the Akronite said.

destroy the evidence. He was something of a nut."

"But Richard was shy and was bullied by the other inmates. Maybe Richard — if he is Zodiac — became tired of being pushed around and rebelled."

RICHARD worked as an auto mechanic, said the Akronite, but his passion seemed to be reading.

"The prison library had many old books and Richard's favorites seemed to be those on Egyptian history."

Some of Zodiac's secret codes have been influenced by his apparent reading of astrology and use of symbols from the Egyptian Book of Dead, say police who have made a study of his rambling messages sent to California newspapers and to officers.

The Akronite does not know when Richard left jail.

"I tried a variety of methods to break down the letters — transposing them, giving each letter numbers and trying to find some semblance of order," the former cryptopher and Army captain said.

"Finally I decided that the man who conceived the code wanted it translated and thus it must be fairly simple."

A wheel-like structure was formulated in which the letters were shifted around until they made sense.

The Akron man brought his code to Akron police who sent the information to San Francisco, where detectives assigned to the case said: "We take any shred of evidence that comes to us and check it out. You never know."

THE BRUTALITY Zodiac inflicts on his victims is foreboding for those who even read or think about the man.

Both men who have given information requested their names not be used.

The former convict's motives are economic — he would like to publish his own findings if and when his theory is proven.

The retired soldier expressed some fear: "I don't want you to use my name. He (Zodiac) may come after me."

(Sunday, March 21, 1971 Akron Beacon Journal)

Neal asked, "Do you mean Edwards actually contacted the San Francisco Police and the Ohio press?"

"Yeah, he told them that he knew who the Zodiac killer was from his stretch in Deer Lodge. Listen to what the article says.

"A former convict believes he served time with the man who has claimed thirteen victims in four years." When I saw his picture, I told my wife: "what's that story about? I know that man,"' the former convict said. "After reading the story, I'm sure I served time with him in Deer Lodge State Prison in Montana."

"Let me see that!" Neal demanded, "You found this in Edwards' stuff?" He started reading. It was incredulous. "John, I thought you had something when you found the page in Ed's book referring to the slaves. This absolutely proves a link between Ed and the Zodiac. It's like this article is trying to lead everyone somewhere, point them in a direction. Give them false clues or maybe some 'busy' work. Plus, he saved it in his personal files! Clearly it was important to him. This is so Zodiac-like. This article ran on the one-year anniversary of the Zodiac's Kathleen Johns abduction. What else did you get?"

"Ed had movie transcripts, letters to the FBI, and lots of newspaper articles over 50 years of crime—cut out, dated and saved in nice little neat files. He had traveled the country speaking at schools and churches everywhere. I discovered some more fliers like the ones you found in the book."

"By the age of 11 he had started a life of crime. He has committed every crime less than murder." I added, "During the Zodiac killings, Edwards had been promoting himself all over the country as an authority on crime with a degree from the University of Ohio."

The Man Who Experienced It

Mr. Ed Edwards came to The Home on Sunday, March 7, and was our guest speaker at Collier Chapel during regular chapel services. His background is certainly exceptional.

Mr. Edwards was born June 14, 1933. At the age of seven he was sent to an orphanage. After running away thirty-seven times he was sent in 1944 to live with his grandmother. In 1946 he was placed in a reformatory as an incorrigible. In 1952 he was placed in a federal reformatory for two years for stealing cars. In 1956 he was sentenced to The Montana State Penitentiary for ten years for armed robbery. In 1959 while in Montana, the prison was the scene of a large riot in which many men were killed. Because he did not participate in this riot he was paroled and placed on probation for five years. In December, 1960, he was arrested by the Portland police for suspicion of a double murder and impersonating a federal officer. He broke out of jail the next day and shortly thereafter was placed on the F.B.I.'s "Ten Most Wanted List." Ed (reported to be a near genius with an IQ of 132) was described by the F.B.I. as a "go-for-broke" fugitive with an incredible criminal career and an ego to match. He was considered a professional criminal, but he had never committed a crime of violence. He had impersonated a psychiatrist, been a private detective, and the manager of a variety of stores. In 1962 Ed was sentenced to sixteen years in Leavenworth for bank robbery.

Mr Edwards has been considered by various police officials and other people in high positions as an expert on the subject of crime. His ability to hold the attention of the young and old has been outstanding. He is the founder of the Club WWTH (We Want To Help) which now has several thousand members. Mr. Edwards is writing a book and making a record on the subject of crime. For those who are interested in writing to him for one of his bulletins, letters can be addressed to P.O. Box 3671; Akron, Ohio, 44310. He answers every letter he receives. Mr. Edwards' visit to our Home was certainly an enlightening experience for both young and old. Thanks to Mr. David Long for bringing this about.

— O. S. & S. O. —

(March 7, 1971, Collier Chapel, Xenia, Ohio)

"Edwards was getting off on fooling everyone. He admitted to being arrested for suspicion of double murder and impersonating an officer. He admitted being a psychiatrist, a detective, and a con man. He was fooling everyone all over the country while he was killing." I handed Neal some documents. "Look what his daughter April gave me—her own timeline as she could remember her life. She had given it to the police in 2009 but wasn't convinced anyone was looking into all the murders her father did. She is sure there are many more.

Time Line as Wayne Edwards after marrying Kay Hedderly Edwards

????–1974 (summer)   Avon St   Akron, OH

1974-1978 (summer)   (3 different houses)   Doylestown, OH

We lived in 3 different homes while in Doylestown. The first home (farm house) Dad burnt down the barn. I believe it was for insurance purposes. He later attempted to burn the house down. His first attempt left the house still standing, therefore he went back and finished burning it down. The second house we lived in was a rental. We lived there while we were building our other home. Our third home I believe was on Wayne Rd or Edwards Rd. We moved in before the building was finished. It was at this time I believe something happened to kids or teens in the area. I remember hearing stories of kids missing and I also believe it was while we were living in Doylestown that Wayne took us for a walk in the weeds and we supposedly came upon a body or bodies. We (the children) didn't see any bodies we were told that there were body(s). I was very young at the time and my memory is quite foggy on this event. It was also during this time that my Great Aunt Lucille was visiting us and one wet night my dad came home all muddy. The next day was when we heard kids were missing. My Aunt questioned my dad on this. She suspected him of something. So much so she talked about it with some of us kids.

1978-1979 (summer)   Ocala, FL

Stayed in a campground and rented a singlewide trailer from the camp grounds and lived there for a short period of time. We bought property and our own double wide trailer. After moving to our own trailer we befriended two brothers that were our neighbors. They were African Americans. One day they just stopped coming over. We heard rumors that something happened to them. I can't remember what but I do remember thinking it wasn't good and we never saw those boys again. We left Florida after selling almost everything. It didn't make since to me because we had just bought everything. It was also odd that one day when we came home from school a police car was pulling out of our drive and dad wouldn't tell us what it was about. We moved shortly after that.

1979 (summer)   **????, Arizona**

Stayed in a campground for a short period of time but then moved on.

1979-1980 (summer)   **Brighton, CO**

We left Colorado in the middle of the night.

1980 (about 3 months)   **Watertown, WI**

We heard about two teenagers missing.

1980-1981 (summer)   **Zanheiser St**   **Pittsburg, PA**

Suspect dad of killing an African-American boy. Age 5-7. Believe the boy was giving Jeff a hard time in school. Jeff would come home and tell dad about it. One day the boy wasn't in school. Dad said someone hit him in the head with a baseball bat and died. I remember the middle school I attended was called Greenway Middle so the elementary school should be located around the middle school.

1981-198?   **Portersville, PA**

My dad was arrested for shop lifting. I didn't know this at the time my mom told me later. She had to bail him out of jail. Dad also set fire to the house we were renting. Authorities suspected him of arson. We left town quickly.

198? **Atlanta, GA**

We stayed with a police officer's family. Authorities from PA found dad and came and arrested him for arson.

1982 **McConnell's Mill, PA**

We lived in a rented house in McConnell's Mill State Park while dad was awaiting trial. At this time we heard of a body being found in or around the state park. I believe it was a female. We lived at this residence until my dad was convicted of arson and went to jail.

1982-1986(late summer) **New Castle, PA**

We moved to New Castle when my dad was convicted. We lived in the city of New Castle while dad was in prison. Upon his release we stayed in area for about two more years.

1986-? **Burton, OH**

We Lived on Rt. 422 before moving to Rt. 700. At this time we knew a woman who was raped in Burton, OH. We also suspect dad of having something to do with Danny's murder.

1990-? **Sahuarita, AZ**

While in Arizona dad sold many guns. to whom?

199? **CampgroWund, Oklahoma**

199?-2000 **Brandford, FL**

200?-2009 **Louisville, KY**

*When we moved dad wouldn't allow us to write or call friends. We had to break all connections. I do not think he left forwarding addresses.

*As to a time line after they left Burton, OH is quit foggy my mom can not remember dates.

Other alias we know about:

Charles Raymond Myers Charles Alan Murray
Fred Knotte Edwards Charles Edger Myers
Jeffrey Wayne Myers Dustin Meckley
Wayne Edward Murray

(Time Line as Wayne Edwards after marrying Kay Hedderly Edwards)

"Neal, he was questioned in 1978 by the FBI regarding the Jimmy Hoffa disappearance."

"Remember what Ed said in his book about Jimmy 7 years before he killed him?" asked Neal.

"Jimmy and I had become friends almost instantly. We ate together, walked in the exercise yard together, lifted weights and played handball at least once a week, and spent long hours in the library discussing cases and reading. One day at chow, Jimmy said to me casually:

"Ed, I understand you've been writing letters to people looking for a job, so you can have something to put on your parole plan."

"That's right Jim. I'm afraid I haven't had too much success."

"Ed," Hoffa replied, "I'll be getting a visitor tomorrow or the next day. Twenty-four hours after my visitor leaves you'll have a telegram in your hands stating you have a guaranteed job on your release from Lewisburg."

"Jim, how can I thank you? If I get the job don't be surprised if I jump up and kiss you right on the forehead."

"Ah, now," Jim Hoffa chuckled, 'don't you worry about kissing me on the forehead. You're just an old time con, and you're trying to turn me into a homo."

"We both laughed and I tried to camouflage my anxiety. That night, I suffered my worst case of insomnia. A million things could happen. Jim could die of a heart attack."

I furthered, "Kay and April both remembered Ed being questioned about Jimmy. They were living in Ocala, Florida at the time and they fled. That's the same time April said the little black boys went missing. She described how they had just got new furniture and everything, suddenly; dad ups and moves everyone to Colorado to live in a campground. She had friends when she was young that just disappeared. She's talking about the years 1978-82 because Ed went to prison in 82. He was in hiding after burning down a house in Butler, Penn. He was staying at the home of a Marietta, Georgia policeman with his wife and kids. April remembered it. She said he had a police uniform, too. We have a picture of Ed standing with a captain of the Atlanta Police Department. We will find some killings in Atlanta.

"His daughter and kids have endured some incredible suffering, yet the family stayed together 43 years. I could have spent days with them, but once I realized that he was the Zodiac killer, I felt like I could be obstructing justice. I'm not an investigator. I just wanted to confirm my hunches that the man was a serial killer. I was hoping the FBI or cops would do something about this. Edwards had killed everywhere, and nobody wants to listen. The trip definitely confirmed that. The investigators from Ohio and Wisconsin took boxes of items in 2009. Who knows what is sitting in their evidence rooms! I doubt they even know what they have."

Neal exploded. "Can we look at that? Or get a list of what they took?"

"No way. First off, the FBI doesn't share. Second, this is supposedly an ongoing investigation, not open to the public. I'm not even in law enforcement anymore. I've been extremely lucky to get what I did and not get arrested! Oh, and I forgot to tell you, I wrote Edwards again."

"Anything come back? I wrote to him, too." said Neal.

"No, not yet. Sometimes it takes a while. I wonder if Edwards knows I've been talking to his family. Sometimes that jars something loose."

Chapter 9
Edwards Writes!
October 1, 2010

Neal called me. "Guess what? We're on first base!"

"You heard from Edwards!"

"You got it! I got a letter!"

Neal had sent Ed a letter in August of 2010 after he solved the cryptograms. He used the language Ed had used in the Zodiac cryptograms back at him.

Neal Best letter using 340 cipher
words back at Edwards.
August 21, 2010

Dear Ed,
　I hav the feeling you may want to get to know me. I could be your friend, your amigo. Many people will misunderstand you, but maybe not me. I hav notice all of the evol names people call you are off. You seem to be of an IQ that is less vexed than many others.
　Outside, I see many children waiting to play a game. The weather is right for it. Do you wish you could be free to play with them, too? Of course your body will be in prison, but your mind is still free to play.
　I forgive you all your actions. Through Christ, (the Furst), who lives in me, I have the solution to my next life's going for Eternity.
　My Father's name is Ray. He sees us as brothers, even twins. He would like for us to visit, U and I. Let us not disappoint Him.
　The rest of the world will never understand your deepest energy, but I do. Your quintessencial essence can be vindicated. You hav been my divinator; I could be yours.
　I'm listening to the FIFTH DIMENSION on the radio. I recently took a great interest in them.

Aug 21, 2010 (2

My name is Neal. It means "champion" in old Norse. It also means "capstone" on a pyramid in old Egypt. I have thirteen brothers, sisters, and cousins. My sister is into the higher levels of geometry. It is really a mind-trip.

I read your autobiography and understood its deeper meaning. I'm sure you did not go to all that literary trouble just for autographs.

Many people don't see the world for what it is. ◆ It's like light and darkness, all at the same time. I will never ask you to feel pity. Too many pissy people have no idea what right and wrong is.

I see you as my tío, my uncle, because I have read all of your writings. It takes two to tango. Would you like the amiga to be the beginning of a beauty-full relationship? Would you like to see the aurora-borealis before you die? Would you like to go where none expect you to? My Dad and I are nervous about sitting around forever. He loves his family very much; Even my brother who has a bad personality.

If you see me, doors will open for both of us. If a clam stays shut, it will starve.

In Montana, I have built bonfires with my dad Ray that are so hot they are scary. But we are always in control of the heat. We appreciate you.

Neal Best

(Neal Best Letter to Edward Edwards)

Edwards replied immediately to Neal on some yellow note paper he borrowed from another inmate. However, the letter took several weeks to arrive.

"Don't keep me waiting! What does it say?" We met up shortly to examine the note.

Hi Neal, Sept. 1-10

Thank you for the nice letter. I needed that! A guy here gave me their one pack of paper & an envelope so I could write to you. I do not have any nor do I have the money to buy any. People can send us money orders but they can also send folded up envelopes (not more than 4 per letter). They must be pre-stamped like the one I am sending you. I am not asking for anything, I'm just telling you the way things are here. I will write if I am able to. Tell me a little about yourself & family. Your age, family, married, kids & etc. You seem to know alot about

2.

me. Send a picture. This is the first letter I have written in months. I am told one of my letters is worth something, smile! The guy that gave me the paper & envelope is my black friend. I guess you know I did time in the old prison that was there in Mt. I was there 1956-57-58 & 1959 when they built the bad void. I did not like it there! Tell your dad I said hello. He sounds like a very nice person. Joe Neal, I'll be happy to write & keep in touch if I am able. Thank you again for the nice letter. Write soon again. Your friend, Ed

(Communication Opens. Edwards' First Response)

Edwards clearly connected to Neal. Only the author of the cryptograms would have understood Neal's letter. Neal reminded me, "When Ed says 'Tell your dad I said hello. He sounds like a very nice person,' he's not referring to my dad. He's referring to my reference in the letter 'My father's name is Ray. He sees us as brothers, even twins.' Ray is Satan in ancient Egyptian history. Ed communicates through satanic spirituality. Everything has a religious connotation. The cryptograms he sent in the Zodiac case were all Satanic."

"He even reminds you that his letters are going to be worth something." I thought the letter was the catalyst that linked Edwards to the Zodiac. Edwards and Neal would communicate throughout the investigation. Several lines of the letter caught my attention.

1) At the bottom of page 1— "You seem to know a little bit about me." Confirming Neal was right on the cryptograms.

2) "I am told one of my letters is worth something, smile" Implying this story is going to be big! And "smile" is written in block lettering, rather than script. Puzzles. In future letters, Edwards would simply insert the smiley face "☺". Neal and I both felt it signified something important or a clue.

3) Edwards mentioned the 1959 Montana State Prison riot in Deer Lodge.

"Ed wrote you for a reason, Neal. I think you tweaked something."

"Time will tell. I know he'll write back again."

While we waited for the next letter, I continued my investigation into the family. I located Edwards' cousin, Dawn, on the internet and contacted her. She had lived in San Francisco and had become related to Edwards through her mother's new marriage. Dawn filled me in on some background information on their childhood. She had lived with John Bellett and his new wife, Edith Myers Bellett, in Akron from 1945 to 1946. Ed was 12 and Edith was his aunt that attempted to replace his mother. He hated her and this reflected on his relationship with Dawn. Dawn also told of Ed's sexually deviant behavior at the age 12. In virtually all the psychological evaluations, Edwards exhibited behavior and sadomasochism uncharacteristic of a youth this age.

Dawn sent me a family photo taken back in Christmas, 1970, along with a sticky note describing the relationships. Dawn knew Ed as Wayne because that is the name he demanded to be called after his release from Leavenworth, 1967. He is center white.

The photo was taken shortly after Edwards killed everyone in the Zodiac case. The Christmas 1970 photo shows Edwards with some of the relatives he wrote about in his book, that he despised. Curious about Dawn and the San Francisco connection, I shared my suspicions about Edwards possibly being the Zodiac. I wasn't prepared for the response. She hadn't heard from Ed for years, but the Zodiac slayings had always terrified her mother and herself. They had even discussed the slaying of the cab driver, Paul Stine, particularly the circumstances. The Stine murder was out of character for the Zodiac. All the others followed the same M.O.—teenagers, lover's lane, no motive, no robbery. All similar to Edwards' killings. But the Stine killing originally went down as a cab driver robbery gone bad.

Forty years haven't provided even a hint as to why the Zodiac would shift from teens to a cab driver. Dawn Bellett provided the answer. She told me that her mother, Beatrice worked at Lefty O'Doul's. A Google search shows this Irish pub in the theatre district in San Francisco at the intersection of Mason and Geary. Those two streets together send tingles down the back of any Zodiac sleuth—the very intersection the Zodiac got into the cab of Paul Stine. It was the recorded site of the pick up. Dawn followed with, "My mom lived a couple of blocks away from where Stine was killed."

On page 392 of Edwards' book, he quoted his aunt belittling him upon his release from Lewisburg in 1967.

"Ed, please get out of the cab about two blocks from our house, will you? People around here have heard you've been released from prison, and our neighbors will be watching. I would rather you come inconspicuously. I realize it's raining, but I'm afraid I can't have it any other way.'" *MOAC

He further stated how her indifference tormented him throughout childhood. *"It bothered me then, and it does to this day"*. This quote from, "Metamorphosis of a Criminal,"' shows a truly remarkable tie to the Zodiac. It provides the only reasonable explanation for the 1969 Zodiac cabbie killing ever offered.

Between this testimony and Neal's interpretations of the cryptos, I was absolutely convinced that Edwards was the Zodiac. I wrote Edwards about my conversation with Dawn. By October, I still had not heard from him, so I pulled out all the stops. I wrote again and flat out accused him of being the Zodiac killer.

Dear Ed;

I wrote you about a month ago and never heard back. I put some money on your phone account and didn't realize the money only went to the phone account. I have now placed some money on your account so you can write me back if you want.

In my last letter I pretty much wanted to talk to you about our 1956 unsolved murder here in Great Falls Montana. But since then I surely would like to talk to you about who you really are. I find it amazing how long you were able to fool the cops and everybody about your TRUE IDENTITY. After I read the book, and got into reading it, knowing that you were who I always thought you were-THE ZODIAC> It was easy to figure out once I read the book and found the clues. Then a friend of mine broke your 13 Cipher Identity Code and --Baboom-It's you. I wanted to talk to you but was almost arrested by local cops. They say I have no business getting involved in this. Oh well-I did and figured it out. Are you willing to talk to me? I bet by the time you get this somebody already talked to you.

Anyway. Nice to finally meet you ZODIAC. I hope we can chat before you die. If not, good luck in the afterlife.

John A Cameron

(Cameron's Second Letter)

While I waited for an answer from Edwards, I contacted law enforcement in Ohio and Wisconsin trying to convince them that Edwards was the worst serial killer ever, and a task force was needed. It all fell on deaf ears. Nobody in law enforcement was interested in following the trail of Ed Edwards. Pressure was mounting, and nobody believed my theory. Then, in the middle of November 2010, Edwards wrote back to Neal and myself. We met in the back room of Morning Light

Coffee. I was beside myself. I felt this was "the proof."

I waited impatiently while Neal studied the letter.

Mrs John Cameron, 11-16-10

    I received your letter of 21 Oct. and also your first one of 14 July. I have done alot of lieing in my day & I don't know if your a lier or just a bull shiter! I guess I'll find out if you keep on writing to me. You ended your first letter by saying, "I am putting some money on your account in case you are willing to write back". The money was not there & I do not have money to get stamps & envelopes. I had to get this from a friend of mine so as to write this note. If you do send money please not it a M.O. & put it in a letter to me lee.

2.

You can send "pre-stamped envelopes only", to me but not more than 3 at one time. You cannot send paper to write on. If you send any thing please let me know in your letter. Otherwise I will not know. It is all up to you! You say you have looked at my book. If you did then you know my grandmother had 4 girls. Of th 4 girls I am th only child! No brothers or sisters. So I do not have a cousin, Dawn! My kids that I have talked with over th past months - just 2 weeks ago - said they have no idea who you are! I still like you John! Hell, we all like to bull shit

3.

once in awhile, ☺! In your first letter you said I was involved in the Kalitzke/ Bogel case in Great Falls, in 1956. You know I was in Deer Lodge when the first Parol officer went to work there! He got 5 years for selling a parole for $500.00! Where were you then? Smile. It sounds like you may have fit right in. That is a joke! No I did not kill anyone in Mt., ever! My son told me awhile back how much my old book was selling for. To bad we don't get any of that. I get a book offer about every other month. Maybe one day with some one! You know

4.

I go to court here later this month or in Dec. They want to put me to death! Oh well we all have to go some day. You say you won the Zodiac game I won. Goood luck! I'll bet I have more answers than you do. I remember a guy in Deer Lodge back in 1956 they called the Zodiac. He killed a guy in Great Falls. I may be 77 but I don't forget things. As for Portland, Org. you are full of it again. Remember John, I have nothing to lose even if I tell the police I did all these killings! there are alot of nuts around the U.S that think I

5.

did. I really don't know why I am writing to you because most of the time I just let the letters go right on by without an answer. As I said before if you want me to write to you then send some money! It is going to be Xmas soon so maybe you will send enough to buy some Xmas candy, ☹! By the way, if I were ever to call you it has to be collect & that means to a land phone, not a cell phone. Calls can only be for 15 min. & I think they cost about $5.00. Just letting you know. I hope you can read my

6

writing. I try! Well, I will wait for an answer to this letter. It was nice talking with you and good luck with your Zodiac game. If you write about me make sure you say nice things about me! I am really a nice guy! ☹! I am a little like you, just a big kid at heart! You should see some of the mail I get. The right address for me is, Edward Edwards, 584893, P.O. Box 209-FHC Orient, Ohio 43146 I am told one of my letters is worth alot. Make sure you save it, Smile Respectfully, Ed.

P.S. Am I to call you John or Neal?

(Edwards' response to Cameron's accusatory letter)

Neal put the letter down in disbelief. "This is truly incredible. It's certainly not proof beyond a reasonable doubt, but he admits to knowing the Zodiac killer. That is incriminating in itself. There is way more going on here than we know about, John. This is serious scary stuff you are playing with."

"Yes, it's his game, and we are going to have to play it!" yelled Cameron. "Did you read the line, 'good luck with your Zodiac game; I'll bet I have more answers than you do'?"

"John, listen, you open this box and there's no closing it. Ed is serious, and he has ties to people we don't want following us."

"I'm not stopping, Neal. This is a big puzzle of murder that has gone on for decades. This man has done things that are horrible, and I can't let it go."

"I wish he just said he was the Zodiac. John, I'm not sure I want to play the game. It certainly is a big story already, and the letter has several points of interest. Let me explain.

"First, he seems a bit preoccupied with money. Maybe we can use that somehow, I don't know.

"Second, look how he writes, not what he writes. His structure and syntax are horrible, and his spelling is worse. I noted several misspelled words in the letter. Four in the first two sentences, including your name. This is remarkably Zodiac-like. Zodiac was a notoriously poor speller, for whatever reason. These misspellings are clues."

"Third, I don't know why he is reacting so strongly about your reference to his cousin, Dawn. It's like you touched a nerve there."

"Fourth, why does he change his cursive text to block when he wrote Zodiac and smile?"

"Fifth, he mentions Deer Lodge twice. Responding to the Kalitske/ Bogle murders and again after wishing you 'good luck with your Zodiac game.' There's a connection there."

"Sixth. I think between the lines he is screaming there is a big story here. Things like, 'there are a lot of other cities' and 'my letters are going to be worth something someday.' He is implying something here is huge."

"Seventh, Edwards writes, 'If you write about me, make sure you say nice things about me.' It's like he is giving us permission to write his story. He's never going to admit straight out in these letters because the prison is reading them."

I finished the conversation with an observation. "Neal, I've been doing cold cases now for almost 30 years and there is a distinct pattern that emerges when you have found the right suspect. First off, the suspect reacts when confronted with his deeds. Edwards definitely reacted to us. Second, pieces start falling into place. A piece of the puzzle suddenly fits here and then another one answers something over there. It just starts snowballing. That's what is going on here. Everything we have looked at has turned into more evidence because it is him. I'm sure we are right."

"I can't argue. And another thing; We haven't found that big piece that says you're wrong."

That's how the case would continue.

Chapter 10
Neal Questions
October 2010

Over the next few days, Neal reflected over his last conversations with me. The Zodiac case had challenged law enforcement and amateur detectives for close to 45 years and was still unsolved. No case in history had ever compared to it. Not because of the brutal killings, nor the eyewitness sightings. This killer had actually conversed with some of his victims that had survived.

Unique to this case were the communications from the killer. Cryptograms. Notes. Clues. Phone calls to the police, "I am the killer of the two teenagers..." To this day, 45 years later, the San Francisco police get calls, leads. "I know who the Zodiac killer was." People are still interested, challenged. They feel or want to somehow contribute. "Maybe I can be the one to crack the case; maybe I can ferret out a clue or solve the mystery by seeing something no one else ever has."

At first, Neal thought my ideas were far-fetched and more than a bit of a stretch. But after solving the ciphers, as I had noted, more and more pieces were falling into place. By what I had produced so far, there was no doubt of a connection between Ed and the Zodiac. In the 1972

Ohio news article, he specifically says he knew the Zodiac in Deer Lodge and of a link to Egyptian mythology. It's exactly what Neal said about the cryptograms and it's what Ed wrote about in his book. At the very minimum, this proves that Edwards was aware of the Zodiac case, and that he knew of at least some of the details contained in the first cryptogram. The only other explanation is that he really did meet someone in prison that claimed to be the Zodiac.

I reminded Neal that Edwards is now a convicted killer of 5 people, 4 of whom were parked on lover's lanes and were killed with rope, knife and gun.

Neal thought about the timeline. Edwards was in Deer Lodge from 1956 to 1959, Leavenworth from 1962 to 1967. The Zodiac killed from 1968 to 1970. Ed started writing his book in about 1968 and published it by 1972. Next, he went on tour promoting the book. He appeared on the show, "To Tell the Truth." He gave motivational speeches to policemen, clergy, radio shows and newspapers everywhere. He had his picture taken with the United Nations undersecretary general. Everything fit Edwards as the Zodiac.

Neal marveled at the thought that the Zodiac would be revealed in Montana—a serial killer still killing after announcing himself 40 years ago. He considered a few things. Bryan Hartnell, a surviving witness, said that the Zodiac mentioned being in Deer Lodge, stealing a car and trying to escape. Edwards had done all. The M.O.s of killing teenagers on lover's lanes matched Edwards. Edwards stating in his book he knew an individual that liked to collect slaves. In 1971, Edwards gets interviewed by the Akron Beacon Journal, professing knowledge of the identity of the Zodiac. There was a connection between Edwards, his cousin Dawn and the mystifying cabbie killing of Paul Stine in San Francisco. Edwards' statement, "I'll bet I have more answers to the Zodiac game then you do!" in his letter to me. After his release from Leavenworth prison in 1967, and just before the

Zodiac killings, Edwards conned his way into an off-shoot of the Masons and achieved a bonus by being placed in charge of the money.

Toussaint Lodge Officers Elected

Whalen Pruitt was elected chancellor commander of Toussaint Lodge 51, Knights of Pythias, Jurisdiction of Ohio, at a meeting held in the Masonic Hall.

Other officers elected were Roosovelt Saunders, vice chancellor commander; Edward Edwards, master of exchequer; Willand L. Smith, keeper of record and seal; Jackson Hope, master-at-arms; Corey Martin, master of the work; Richard Yates, prelate; James Hill, inner guard, and Joseph Houston, outer guard.

(The Herald Star February 9, 1968)

I researched the Knights of Pythias and discovered its foundation was based on Greek mythology, the same type of history Edwards studied in Deer Lodge. The story relates to a young man returning to save his friend from being wrongfully executed by the king. This is very similar to the story of the Mikado that the Zodiac killer had quoted in letters. Edwards was the executioner in 1956 when he ordered Patty and Duane to their knees. And Edwards was seeking his own execution in 2010.

The Zodiac killer was the judge, jury and executioner!

Chapter 11

Edwards Puzzled

Pickaway Prison, Ohio October 2010

During August and September of 2010, Edwards sat waiting for his execution date. Several letters had arrived from myself, who was two months into it and not sleeping. Edwards was pleased that he'd been right. He knew the cop would write again. He didn't want to write me back, but after getting Neal's letter, he needed to know more. Neal appeared to be totally different. Totally uncop-like. Abstract writing, syntax changed, more personal. Non-accusatory. "We are always in control." That struck a nerve!

"These guys want to play a game? I'll give them a game." Edwards wondered about the words, pyramid, old Egypt, higher levels. "What was going on here?" First, this cop writes him, says his name is John. Now he gets a completely different note from someone using the name Neal, and he figured out the cryptograms! Edwards was challenged and confused. He needed to know more. Nobody had ever figured out his puzzles. But this Neal guy...

"Am I to call you John or Neal?" was the P.S. to me in the first letter. My mind games had worked, and Edwards wasn't sure if Neal or John was one or two people. I was using the mirrored worlds back at him. Ed hadn't met too many cops that had knowledge of the Egyptian Book of the Dead. He wondered how much I knew, and how did I figure out that deal in Great Falls after all these years.

Unreal. No one had ever even suspected. That cop must have figured out something from his book. He had mentioned that he had read it. Why, he was only a heartbeat away from figuring out the magnitude of "The Zodiac," if he hadn't already. "This could really screw up my execution!" It didn't take long to decide. He was going to have to write back. Edwards hated the fact that I had gotten to his family before he did.

"How did Cameron know about my cousin Dawn Bellett?" Ed thought back to living with Dawn at the age of 12 in 1945-46. That's when it really started, right after he burned the Catholic Church and destroyed the Bible in Akron. To this day, no one had discovered the extent of it. Ed wondered how much Dawn had told me. And I had already got to her and it pissed him off.

Now, at age 77, he knew he had been successful, and he was still playing the game. He thought it would be 300 years before someone would figure it out—but he knew they would. He had laid the groundwork. After all, he was a writer, a producer and the world's best criminal. He had planned out each crime, patiently, deliberately, cold-bloodedly. He left false trails and created red herrings. He had pinned many of his deeds over the decades on others, by setting them up, leading authorities up the wrong trail. He didn't know that I had discovered court records listing him as an informant. This information is on public record. Edwards provided the details that only the "murderer" would know, resulting in the convictions of innocent people. Edwards thought, "He figured out my M.O." He was impressed with my tenacity and thought to himself, "I have one more game in me. He's not even close to figuring me out."

Chapter 12
A Killer's Mind Games
November 2010

Numerous letters were exchanged. Phone calls were beginning, but I decided to employ the police technique of not answering. It had worked before. Frustrating prisoners that have no contact with the outside world often led to them opening up. Edwards kept hinting he had lots to tell and that his story would be worth a lot of money. He was insisting on holding back until he got a firm commitment and date as to when he would be executed. He knew they were reading his mail and was afraid they would halt his execution. Edwards sent me another letter that contained his competency to stand trial report. In the letter Edwards was making fun of the police.

Edward W. Edwards
#587893
P.O. Box 209 - PMC
Orient, Ohio 43146

John Cameran
820 5th Ave. North
Great Falls, MT.
59401

Hey John!   12-19-10
I want to get this in the mail so you will have some idea as to what is going on. I only have the one copy so you will have to show it to Neal. I fell the other day, my arm was under me & I broke a rib. I already have a cold & it hurts like hell when I cough!! I have been calling every day with no luck! Are you sure you guys even want to talk to me? You know after this trial I will be put on death row. I think that will go down in Feb. I'll still be able to

2

call & write letters. I will also be able to eat candy! Smile. ~~Day~~, please do ~~not~~ let people, but the police & others see this paper I have enclosed or it will start a fire storm here. If you do I won't let you know about any thing else! I know a lot and a lot of people would love & pay to know! So I better get some Xmas candy! I sent all the ~~papers~~ information to Neal! ☺ this could be the last letter you get this year. If so, "Happy New Year". Write soon,
Your friend,
Ed Edwards

Psycho-Diagnostic Clinic

209 South High Street • Akron, Ohio 44308-1610 • Telephone 330/643-2333 • Fax 330/643-6571

December 3, 2010

Honorable Forrest W. Burt, Judge
Geauga County Court of Common Pleas
100 Short Court Street
Chardon, Ohio 44024

CONFIDENTIAL

RE: Edward Wayne Edwards
Case# 2010C000096
Competency Evaluation

Dear Judge Burt:

Edward Wayne Edwards is a seventy-seven year old, married Caucasian male who was referred by the Court for a Competency to Stand Trial evaluation pursuant to Ohio Revised Code (O.R.C.) Section §2945.371(G)(3). Mr. Edwards is currently charged with Aggravated Murder with Death Penalty Specifications, AF1, Aggravated Robbery, a felony of the 1st degree and Kidnapping, a felony of the 1st degree for an incident that allegedly occurred in May 2006 1996

Mr. Edwards was interviewed at the Pickaway Correctional Institution for approximately three hours and forty minutes by Arcangela S. Wood, Psy.D., Clinical Psychologist on October 15, 2010 and one hour on October 27, 2010. He was administered the Wechsler Adult Intelligence Scale- IV (WAIS-IV) at the Pickaway Correctional Institution by Tayla Lee, M.A., Psychology Assistant, for approximately one hour and thirty minutes on October 15, 2010. He was also administered the Minnesota Multiphasic Personality Inventory-2 (MMPI-2) on October 27, 2010 by Dr. Wood over the course of approximately two hours and thirty minutes.

The nature and purpose of the evaluation, as well as client rights were explained to Mr. Edwards at the beginning of each interview and prior to psychological testing. He was told the information obtained during the course of this evaluation was not confidential and whatever he disclosed could be included in the report to the Court. Mr. Edwards was informed the report and supporting data would be provided to the Judge and copies would be given to his defense counsel and the prosecuting attorney. Mr. Edwards signed a written consent form and demonstrated an understanding of the aforementioned information.

The following documents were reviewed in completing this evaluation:

1) Journal Entry ordering the Competency to Stand Trial evaluation.
2) Copy of Indictment in this matter.

Serving the Common Pleas Courts of Summit, Medina, Portage, Geauga and Stark Counties

---

Office of the Ohio Public Defender
250 East Broad Street - Suite 1400
Columbus, Ohio 43215

www.opd.ohio.gov
(614) 466-5394
Fax (614) 728-3670

TIMOTHY YOUNG
State Public Defender

December 6, 2010

Edward W. Edwards
Inmate No. A584893
Pickaway Correctional Institution
P. O. Box 209
Orient, Ohio 43146

Re: *State v. Edward W. Edwards*, Case No. 10 C 000096

Dear Mr. Edwards:

Dr. Wood finally completed her competency evaluation and submitted it to the Court on December 3, 2010. I have enclosed a copy for you.

Dr. Wood found you competent to stand trial. As I have explained before, with this report filed, the next step will be a competency hearing in court, the formal purpose of which will be for Judge Burt to decide whether to find you competent as a matter of law, which I expect he will do. It remains to be seen whether the Judge will want to use that same court date to take additional steps in your case.

For example, if it remains your intention to waive jury, Judge Burt could find you competent and then proceed immediately to matters related to the waiver of a jury in a capital case. As we have discussed, Judge Burt alone has the authority to preside over the competency hearing and a jury-waiver hearing. If those two steps are taken, then Judge Burt would need to bring two other judges into your case in order to form a three-judge panel as required by Ohio law when a jury is waived in a capital case. If we get to this procedural point, the details of coordinating the schedules of three judges, the prosecutor, and your counsel may entail scheduling delays for further proceedings in your case.

Sincerely,

Gregory W. Meyers

Enclosure
Copy to Bob Umholtz, Esq.

```
            (Edwards' letter to John 12-19-10)
            (Edwards' Ohio competency test letters)
```

Edwards was making sure I knew that he wasn't a nut by sending me his Competency to Stand Trial determination. Edwards was getting his execution on his own terms and nobody was going to screw it up. He made sure to tell me "Hey, please do not let people like police and others see this paper or it will start a fire storm."

I became concerned about the developing relationship between Neal and Ed. Neal had come into the investigation after solving the Zodiac cryptograms and Edwards respected him. Neal had written Ed and asked him if he was the Zodiac, and if Neal's interpretations of the Zodiac cryptograms were correct. Ed responded:

Hi Neal,

It's me! This letter will be sent from Tenn. or Ky. I think. My friends wife is sending it. I feel sure they are opening all the mail I am sending out & then resending it after they read it. I am not saying anything wrong, but I just don't like it. When you get this don't say anything about how it was sent, but just say "I got the letter." Please let me know as soon as you can. When I told you in my last letter that it is okay if you writ my story, I meat it. There is just alot of things I don't want others to know at this time. Believe me I have alot to say. ☺! I do think of you as a

2.

friend! I hope you & your family are in the best of health. It is starting to get cold here & I know it is there in Mt. I have not been back there since 1959. Don't forget to give me your phone number if you would like for me to call some time. It would be a collect call. I was told the other day that my book is now going for $1079.00 on Amz. com. To bad I don't get any of it or my family! One day they will. Don't forget to send me a picture amigo. Well it is time to call it a night. Hope to hear from you real soon.
    Good night amigo,

(Ed Edwards November 2010 Letter Permission to Write Story)

"It's ME!" was more than just an admission to being the Zodiac. It was also a clue. Only Neal understood the real Zodiac story and Edwards respected him. Its beginnings were based in ancient Egyptian mythology.

The Zodiac was not a killer. The Zodiac was Satan. Edwards had been portraying himself as Satan since 1945, the year he escaped Parmadale Catholic Orphanage. Edwards' abuse in the Catholic orphanage set him on a path to portray the Devil his entire life. The written parables in his unsolved cryptograms contained his identity and were proclamations to his intelligence. Neal had solved them all and the following is what they said.

Ed Edwards, Zodiac Bomb Cipher 1969
"To All The SFPD:
"As I resurface I'm being the enemy. Oh! I hate you. I was greater than one I owe. Oh! Are you in nighties while I watch? What all I've dealt you I redouble you. I see in each affection allotted a way of each pity of the nastiest envy. I beat you back, wordsy acts, half real. Itchy to see ineffigy each asshole, unless the Zodiac tell ya. The pissy are a lie. The beauties he's dealt to you awry.

"Why Gee! Affectionate Tio to you! Or are you an Amiga?"

Ed Edwards 340 Zodiac Cipher 1969
"I have noticed all the editors names are off. They use letters to shit me. I doctor them as pristine, rather than invest triage perennially. They mate, serve, so sex leads to the great age of evil reasoning. Mean RE hates me to cry out at a fruit of sin. You try real fit to fight it, but RE's fires drill hot. I have melody to steal unto night. A trill of life tears. I've the solution to my next life's going for eternity

Signed: ZODIAC ED

Ed Edwards 18 characters Cipher 1969
"I'm Edward E. Vexed IQ Hath You Greater Than I"

After the solving of the ciphers, I suspected Neal was no longer sharing all his information from Ed—and it concerned me. Cons were manipulative, deceitful, and loved to control and Edwards was the worst (or the best). Neal was a babe in the woods. He was trusting and gullible. Something about 'a lamb to slaughter' crossed my mind. Edwards tried to divide Neal and myself in his letters:

Dec 28, 2010

Hi Friend,

    Let me first say thank you for the 16 envelopes you sent me. Would you believe I've only got 4 left. I used alot of them to send out card to my grand kids for Christmas. So yes Neal if you have more envelopes affalible I could use them. You can only put 3 envelopes in each letter. Was lucky they let those 16 pass on to me. I know I told you 4 but it's only 3 per letter. Neal, I think of you as my very good friend. I don't need to lie or B.S. you. While I'm here in prison. I did all my lieing when I was running from and to the police before I got here. You need to stop listening to those people who are giving you shard time about my letters and tell you you should not be writing to me. If you just stop and think about it, they are just jelous. I have not recieved any letters from Jim, latly. So I don't know anything about a box of candy sent to me. That was nice of you to tell him to do it. With all the snow we have had here, it is hard to get our mail sent out. I stopped calling your phone number a few days ago.

②

I'm not going to worry about it because some day we will get to talk about it.

Thank you for telling me a little about you and the nice picture you sent me. I would of taken you to be a little bit older. & you are a good looking man.

Neal, just remember John is the x cop and you are his nabbor. Don't let him be the bad cop and make you the good one. If you have any questions about what he tells you about me, then feel free to ask me about it. You have a very good head on you shoulder and your a smart man. Believe me I'm not trying B.S. you as I do consider you a very close and important friend. I will let you know everything that is going on with me, and when and where it's taking place. I think I have already told you that when I go back to court, maybe next month, I will be facing the death penalty. If that happens, so be it. It's not like it was when I was doing time there in Mt. back in 1956-59. You already know I was about to break out of there when they had the prison roit and killed the warden. I don't know why John thinks I killed that couple back in 1956.

> Hell I was a lover then and had a wife with me, and it only happened a couple of month before I went to prison for armed robbery for 10 years. John wasn't born until 1960 at which time I was penticing medicine in Minn. He remembers that because he told me about that. You ask me once if you were aloud to send me money. Yes, you are, as you ask me before. Before I bring this to an end, I want to remind you that maybe you shouldn't show my letter to those people who are giving you ahard time. Hope it don't take too long for you to get this letter, remember you are my good friend.
>
> I love you too!
> Sincerly,
> Ed
>
> PS
> Sorry about the waiting but the lights are low and I'm not a good speller. Wright back soon!

(Edwards' letter to Neal 10-28-10)

    Ed's letters were puzzles. "PS, Sorry about the writing. I'm not a good speller." Neither was the Zodiac killer. The writing would change with each letter received. Every period, scribbled out word, and misspelling, meant something. Ed was a letter writer his entire life, and the change to block lettering was a clue. We had caught the Zodiac killer, but we hadn't uncovered the entire story.

    There was a certain juxtaposition that existed between Ed, Neal, and myself. Neal, years prior, had been involved in a tragic automobile accident that resulted in an innocent death. Edwards had caused deaths through intent and evil. I, as a former cop, had wondered if the subject had ever been discussed between them. Neal considered Edwards a friend and I found that terrifying. I hoped Neal would not be hurt in any way. He had suffered infinitely more than anyone deserved.

Between October of 2010 and Christmas, things became scary. I had returned to my job after a leave of absence. I had supplied law enforcement with all of my findings, yet it was clear no one was investigating Edwards' past. Over the years, law enforcement and the media had failed miserably. There was a reason why the media ignored Ed Edwards in 2010.

On New Year's, 2011 Neal and I received a phone call from Edwards. Early in the conversation, Neal asked Edwards about his book.

Neal: So how much of your book is actually the 100% truth?

Ed: Oh, I would say the ...well, see here's the thing. That book...the book is true. There's a lot of things not in there...for example, when I was on the FBI 10 Most Wanted List, some of my very, very best friends— every Friday and Saturday night we used to get together in my apartment and we would play cards. And the fact of the matter is, I was on the top ten....and 8 of these guys were cops.

And then I was at a uh, I practiced medicine in Indianapolis, IN, and then I went to Jacksonville FL again and put up a license, a shingle that I was a private detective working on divorce cases and insurance cases. There's just a lot ...a lot of things, a lot of details that's not in there." (Ed Edwards, January 2011)

Edwards spoke to Neal and myself on the recorded prison phones. He knew they were listening to every word he said, so he was careful. He didn't want anything screwing up his execution. Regardless of where I wanted to take the conversation, Ed wanted to make sure he understood it was all about "setting people up" for his murders.

Ed: "For example, like, uh, John will be interested in knowing... There's a guy right now, doing life in a penitentiary—he's been in since 1982 and I don't know if he committed the crime or not, but he's in there because I said he did. And that was my getting even with him because he was pulling some bullshit on me, and so I thought, 'Okay, I'm gonna set you up real good. So, he ended up getting life on my testimony. I have a bad temper and uh, and also I've done time in jail and my philosophy was, once I even got out of Leavenworth, or out of federal prison, I'll not go back again.' So therefore, anything that I did, I ...I couldn't leave a witness."

I couldn't believe what was being said on a taped phone conversation. Everything was a clue to another murder he had done and another innocent person he had set up. Edwards knew it was being recorded and wanted to make sure everyone understood—it was all about the setup and never leaving a witness. Neal had tried to explain Edwards' pathology early on and I didn't quite understand it. Edwards was acting out as God, only he was on the dark side— like Satan. He would portray himself as a cop, a doctor of psychiatry, or a preacher in many instances. He would gain access to his victims and then he would kill their first-born son or daughter. Leaving the family members grieving the rest of their lives was more important to him. He was a ritualistic killer, killing for recognition. Movies and books have been written about all his crimes of recognition he bragged about.

Edwards spoke about the 1996 murder and beheading of his adopted son, Dannie Gloeckner. Edwards had met Dannie in 1993 and started planning his demise then. The plan was simple. Place life insurance on someone with a low IQ, not related to you in any way, convince them to take on your name, treat them good for two years and then kill them for the life insurance. Edwards had done this to Dannie in 1996 and had

5 others lined up for the ruse. He convinced Dannie to go AWOL from the Army in March of 1996, set him up for a burglary to his house by calling the police and giving them Dannie's blood. He told the police Dannie must have cut himself breaking into his house and stealing his kid's credit cards. Edwards had already executed him, hiding his body for a year before planting it behind a cemetery in Troy, Ohio around Christmas 1996. Edwards confessed to this crime in 2010. He had planted Dannie's DNA and this would be the way he would set up innocent people everywhere for 6 decades.

"I set him up. This took the heat right off me. This showed that he did it. This showed that he was back in the area and doing these things. It took the heat and put everything on him and other people, not me; I knew nothing about it." (Ed Edwards, 2010)

Edwards spent the summer and fall of 2010 contacting the press and police, giving details about how he sets others up. The press in Ohio and Wisconsin ran with a few of the stories, but for the most part, the national press ignored Ed Edwards' confessions in 2010.

Edwards told me repeatedly, "You don't know the entire 'Zodiac' story." What I didn't realize until 2013, was that some of the Zodiac's biggest killings were playing out in courtrooms across the nation in 2010—and nobody paid any attention to him. There was a reason the FBI ignored Ed Edwards in 2010. The killer was amongst us.

Neal and I spent January and February of 2011 communicating with Edwards by phone and mail. The challenge was sifting through the clues. The Zodiac story was nothing like it had been portrayed. It was worse than anyone could ever imagine, and it was preventable, over and over again. Yet it continued for decades.

Chapter 13

Edwards Gets His Wish

March 2011

Edwards finally got his day in court. On March 15, 2011, a panel of three judges swung the gavel and agreed to set the execution date. August 31, 2011 was the day. Edwards had conned and manipulated the entire system to pick his own manner of death. He had never given that consideration to any of his victims.

After receiving his date with the needle, Ed contacted the Geauga Maple Leaf press and granted them an interview. In that interview, Edwards detailed his ability to set up alibis, plant evidence, manipulate police, testify falsely and use the system for his schemes and plans of murder.

"I've always been into crime. I'm always scheming and planning."

"So, you're saying you are a cold-blooded killer?" the interviewer asks.

"Yup, that's right," Edwards would respond.

By the beginning of April 2011, I finally got the green light to interview Edwards. He had filled out the paperwork, got all the proper signatures, and was good to go with the prison, warden, and the attorneys. I was leery of Edwards' motives in agreeing to the interview. He had been a cop too long and he knew cons were the best at manipulation.

Chapter 14

Preparing for the Interview

April 2011

I had researched Edwards like no other and Edwards had put it all out for someone to put together. He had been on national TV throughout the 70's bragging of being a reformed criminal and a family man. In October of 1972, after he released his book, he went on the game show, "To Tell the Truth." Not only was his book a puzzle but so was his appearance.

As you watch the video of "To Tell the Truth," there is Gary Allen introducing Ed Edwards after he had killed everyone in the name of the Zodiac. He is introduced as a suspect in a double lover's lane murder.

"And here is the extraordinary story of Ed Edwards; I hope you find it profitable. It says, 'I, Ed Edwards, was once on the FBI's 10 most wanted list of criminals in America. Now I am a respected citizen in my community. Here is the story of my dramatic turnabout. As a young boy, I felt that the only way I could get any recognition was to steal. Eventually I committed armed robberies, impersonated a federal officer and was sought for questioning about a double murder. I spent time in the penitentiary in Leavenworth and Lewisburg. It was at the latter prison that I started vocational training and very slowly began to realize that I could still be somebody and return to my rightful and legal place in society.

There is a tremendous need for communication between parents and their children. I stress this point in my book, which is titled, 'Metamorphosis of a Criminal.'" (Ed's book is held up for all to see.)

The questioning began.

Gene Rayburn, another contestant: "Ed, I take it you didn't have a good relationship with your mother?"

Ed: "I was born an illegitimate child, so I never really had a mother to speak of."

(Ed Edwards, "To Tell the Truth," October 17, 1972)

I concluded that at the ending of the show, Edwards tells the world why he did the Zodiac.

Gary Allen: "Ed, there was one important point when you and I were chatting backstage and I asked you, what was the reaction in your neighborhood when you came out of the reformatory the first time? Were you put down by your fellow citizens or did they look up to you?"

Ed looks in the camera with a smirk and says, "No—ah, when I was released from the reformatory, they looked up to me and this motivated me to go on to bigger things, because this was why I was out there committing the crime, was for the recognition!"

I had uncovered Edwards speaking on radio, TV and through newspapers throughout his life. He loved the limelight and that is what he meant by doing everything for recognition. He would kill and then stand in front of everyone bragging that he was reformed.

Edwards' wife, Kay, called me on July 27, 2010 and agreed to an interview. She married Ed July 20, 1968, less than a year after his release from Leavenworth Prison and 6 months before starting the Zodiac killings. She pointed out that he only went by his middle name, Wayne, and "a thousand different alias." She had been a school teacher prior to meeting him in 1968 and was controlled by him the rest of her life as he traveled and killed everywhere. Their wedding certificate was full of lies.

(Edwards Marriage License to Kay Hedderly, July 20th, 1968)

    Even Edwards' marriage license to Kay had clues and his handwriting. Fred Knot Edwards is what Edwards put down for his father's name. Accent on the word "Knot." Edwards never knew who his father was. He also lied about not being previously married. He was married at least twice before Kay. He married Marlene Harmon three times alone in 1959-60 and he was married to Jeanette White when he killed in Great Falls, 1956.

    Kay provided invaluable information about Ed and his relationship with police. Whenever they moved, and that was often, Ed would make friends with the local police. He would drink and gamble with them and invite them over for barbeques. She claimed he had books and devices for making fake credentials and he was obsessed with the FBI. He had secret files that no one was allowed to touch in a dresser in their room. He saved articles about the Deer Lodge Prison riots. The inmates threatened to kill by rope, knife, gun and fire.

Chaplain Tries For Settlement

By JACK ZYGMOND

DEER LODGE, Mont. (AP)—Rioting convicts in the Montana State Prison threatened today to burn 18 hostages alive if authorities carried out plans to storm the prison.

The shouted threat came from an unidentified inmate. It was directed at a group of 150 Montana State Police, prison guards and newsmen gathered at the main gate.

* * *

CONVICTS have held control of the prison interior since late Thursday when they killed a deputy warden and captured 18 guards and employes for hostages. There are 430 prisoners within the walls.

Another guard was stabbed in the arm and Warden Floyd Powell held at knife point for nearly three hours before a burglar helped the warden escape.

A Catholic chaplain emerged from a meeting with rebellious convicts in the besieged prison today and said "everything looked good. I think we made some progress."

Father Gerald Lynam made the statement after accompanying Warden Powell into the prison to negotiate with rifle and knife-wielding convicts.

* * *

THE convicts set up a public address system inside the prison and broadcast an appeal for three out-of-state newsmen to meet with them and hear their complaints.

The convict spokesman, believed to be six-time loser Jerry Miles, said there was no danger to the hostages "as long as the officers don't come in." He said the hostages were being held two to a cell.

The unidentified convict shouted that the hostages would be burned with gasoline if the office is attacked.

(Edward Edwards Personally Saved Article, Deer Lodge Riot, April 1959)

Edwards had the article from his arrest in 1960, after being on the FBI's 10 most wanted list. He saved articles about the Portland, Oregon, 1960 lover's' lane murder in which he was a suspect, and an article about a guy named Wayne Budde, blown up with a bomb in Portland on the same day as the lover's lane murder. They listed his death as a suicide.

Edwards wrote the FBI in July of 1993 when he was living in Ohio and provided them with a list of the cities where he had done crimes and of the aliases he used.

Edward Wayne Edwards
P.O. Box 541
Claridon-Troy Rd.
Burton, Ohio 44021
(216) 834-1970

FBI-I.D.Section
Room 10104
10th. St. Penn. Ave. N.W.
Washington, D.C.
20537-9700

July 9,1993

Dear Privacy Act Agent,

In regards to my phone call July 2, 1993, I am writing in hopes of obtaining all of my CRIMINAL and HISTORY records from your office and the FBI field offices in the following cities. My reason for mentioning these cities is at one time I had either committed crimes there or was there long enough to have an FBI file put together on me.

(1) Arizona, Phoenix and Tuscon.
(2) California, Oakland and Sacramento.
(3) Colorado, Denver.
(4) Florida, Jacksonville, Lakeland, West Palm Beach and Key West.
(5) Georgia, Atlanta.
(6) Idaho, Idaho Falls.
(7) Indiana, Indianapolis.
(8) Minnesota, Minneapolis.
(9) Montana, Billings and Great Falls.
(10) Nevado, Reno and Las Vegas.
(11) New Mexico, Las Cruces.
(12) North Carolina, Wilmington.
(13) Ohio, Akron and Cleveland.
(14) Oregon, Portland.
(15) Penn., Allentown, Erie, Butler, Philadelphia and Pittsburg.
(16) South Carolina, Columbia.
(17) Texas, Houston and Dallas.
(18) Virginia, Norfolk.
(19) Washington, Seattle and Spokane.

The arrest record I have at this time is as follows.

5-30-51 Daytona Beach, Fla. B&B-GL Suspended Sentence
4-24-52 Phila., Pa. ITSMV-Illegal Wearing 2 years, Fed. Referal,
         of Uniform.   Chillicothe Rel.10-4-53.
3-11-55 Akron, Ohio B&L   Escaped jail; returned, Nollied 4-28-59.
3-7-56   Billings, Mont. Robbery 10 years; Rel. 6-2-59
6-25-59 Portland, Org. Assault & AR 5 years probation.
5-18-62 Cleve. Ohio Bank Robbery 16 years. Rel.8-20-67

Page 2

12-9-82 Butler, Pa.   Arson & Theft   12 years, released by State Appeals Court.

In Nov. 1960 I was put on your list of TEN MOST WANTED fugitives.

In 1972 I wrote the book "METAMORPHOSIS OF A CRIMINAL" which was published by Hart Publishing Co. The late J. Edgar Hoover more or less gave me permission to proceed with my book after I assured him there was nothing in it bad about the FBI.

I would like to have any information you may have on me being held INCOMMUNICADO while I was in the same cell with HUGO CLAY BLACK, the great nephew of the late SUPREME COURT JUSTICE, who was in jail in Phila. for murder? He was freed. My grandmother wrote the jail asking about me and she received a telegram from the U.S. Marshall telling her I had been transferred to the Federal Detention Center in New York. I was still in Phila. and I have never been in a New York jail. I have enclosed a copy of the telegram of june 17,1952. My grandmother is no longer living.

I am now 60 years old and on Social Security Disability. I broke my neck and back. When I was running around the country I had a few SS Numbers under other names. If I could get the numbers I had and the information I used to get them I could give it to the SS Administration, and if they can get it all together with my SSN now I could be getting more money.

I got a SSN IN Key West Fla. under the name of James Garfield Langley in 1955, and I was still using that name and number when I married Jeannette White in 1955, in Idaho Falls. While I was in the Mont. State Prison she had the name changed back to Edwards. She has nothing to show the number or the information I used to get it.

In 1961, while in Houston I got a SSN under the name of Gene Starr. I do not have any information on that either. I am not sure if I had a SSN under the names, Day, Martin, Jerry Love, Rose, or others. There is to many for me to remember!

I would like very much to get any information you might have in regards to the information I gave to the Secret. Service about a group that wanted to start up a counterfeiting ring in Akron, Ohio, and was told it was all hogwash. About a year later in the 70s, the largest counterfeiting ring ever was broken up and the information released read almost the same as the information I had given to them in the office of my probation officer. Even the same people.

I would also like to have your writings in regards to the information I gave to the FBI and police in Erie, Pa. that ended up with a man, John Peter Laskaris, being convicted of murder, and got him charged with two other murders. I broke the case and in doing so a friend of his made a plead of guilty to one of the murders and told them more about John. I also gave them information about another man who murdered a man and two children by arson. I keep my ears

Page 3.

open and I still give information to the FBI and other police. I talk to an Agent in Painesville now. The reason I would like to have your writings about all this is because I am writing another book.

My first book was about my Metamorphosis and the one I am writing now is about some of your worst criminals who I knew, celled with, and even went to school with while in prison. A few of those men are, Tony Provenzano, Billie Sol Estes, Anthony Deangelis, Albert Nussbaum, Peter Curry, Charles Manson, Vito Genovese, Frank Sprenz, John Paul Chase, Clarence Carnes, Oscar Collazo, Andres Cordero, Rafael Miranda, Teddy Green, Leon Beardon, Clyde Johnson, Darl Lee Parker, Barry Keenan, George Gessner, Morton SOBELL and others. It was James Hoffa that got me a job driving truck so I would have a parole plan when released from Lewisburg in 1967. I also talked to the FBI after he came up missing as it was me who broke up the fight between Hoffa and Provenzano at Lewisburg.

Thank you for your time and I hope you will be able to give me the information I need.

I have changed! I have been married 25 years and have a 24 year old daughter with two children, a 23 year old son in the Air Force with one son, a 21 year old son that is now a school teacher, a 19 year old in the Army, and a 17 year old daughter still at home. Two of the boys were State Wrestling Champions and the school teacher was asked to go to the STATE POLICE ACADEMY.

We would all like to thank you for your help in this matter.

Edward Wayne Edwards
Edward Wayne Edwards

(Letter Recovered in 2010 from Edwards' Personal Files, Note reference to talking to FBI about Hoffa)

I knew that Edwards would have never sent this to the FBI unless he was taunting them with a murder. Most likely there will be a horrific murder before June 1993 I surmised.

Neal read all the letters and stated, "This is remarkable. The audacity. He goes on T.V., a book tour, he informs the press of his connection to the Zodiac, and he writes the FBI! He never gets caught until his daughter rolls on him in 2009. I tell you what, if he wasn't the Zodiac, he was his twin brother. NEVER has any suspect matched in so many regards. First off, what other suspect ever has a reputation and an affinity for killing teenagers on lover's lanes? Just like the Zodiac. That alone moves him to the top of my list. But then the personality. Obviously, the Zodiac craved the headlines. And brother, did he accomplish that! But look at Edwards—he also craves attention. He shows it constantly. How many more letters do you think he sent?"

"Hundreds, if not thousands," I responded. "Edwards gave all these names in the letter for a reason. There is a connection that needs to be followed."

I had been working on Edwards for over 10 months now and had kept law enforcement at every level appraised of my findings. By April of 2011, I had made enough enemies around the country that it started to affect my work. Prosecutors in Portland were demanding that I be fired for using my Board of Pardons letterhead to inform them of my findings. They didn't want to hear that they had tried and convicted three innocent people back in '69-'70 for two murders Edwards had done. The parole board was supportive of my investigation, until prosecutors in Oregon started complaining.

I was conflicted. The parole board had let Edwards out in 1959 and he killed again. I wondered, "Do I have a responsibility as a parole board analyst to seek the truth?" The head of the parole board thought I had overstepped my bounds and warned me that I would be fired if this continued.

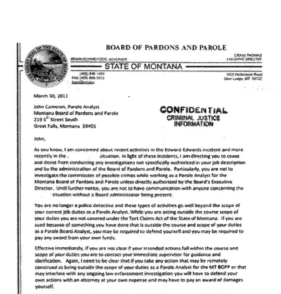

(Cameron Letter of Reprimand from Montana Board of Pardons and Parole)

A decision had to be made and on April 1, 2011, I walked into my office, submitted my resignation, and decided to pursue the Ed Edwards' investigation full time.

Chapter 15

Edwards Gets His Second Wish

April 7, 2011

Neal got up, showered and walked down to Morning Light Coffee, hoping I would show up. He hadn't spoken to me in a while and wanted to know when I would be interviewing Edwards in prison. I arrived at about 10 and had a surprised look on my face.

"Neal? Ed died in his cell last night. Maybe we shouldn't have sent him all that candy. He was a diabetic."

Neal could only think, "We are going to need a new plan."

Chapter 16

A New Plan Needed

April 2011

Neal and I met the following day. We both had received numerous E-mails asking how Edwards' death might affect the book. I tried to remain upbeat and offered, "Neal, don't worry; it's okay. This isn't that bad. We can work around it. In fact, it might even be a good thing! We need to regroup. Why don't we look at everything that indicates Edwards was the Zodiac?"

1) He had no father, and his mother was shot in front of him. He was forced to change his name by age 7 so he immediately has an identity crisis.

2) He was a bed-wetter, and sexually and physically abused in the Catholic orphanage by age 8.

3) He was sexually active and deviant by age 12. Those first three statements alone could produce such a killer as the Zodiac.

4) He was jailed more than half of his teen years in institutions and was diagnosed as a psychopath at age 13.

5) He enlisted in the Marines at age 17 and went AWOL within 6 weeks, after being told he wouldn't be allowed to go to Korea and kill communists.

6) At the age of 22 he killed a couple on a lover's lane in Great Falls, 1956.

7) He killed a couple on a lover's lane in 1960 in Oregon.

8) He did 7 years in Leavenworth and was released in 1967, just before the Zodiac started.

9) He killed the couple in Wisconsin in 1980. He killed a couple in Ohio in 1977. Both on lover's lanes.

10) In a news article in 1971 he claimed to have "known someone in Deer Lodge" who was the Zodiac.

11) He says in his book he knew someone who believed the people they killed would be his slaves in the afterlife.

12) He provides the only explanation ever as to why Paul Stine, the cab driver, was picked as a victim. (Dawn Bellett, relative, lived there.)

13) Edwards considered himself the executioner, evidenced by his methods of killing. Zodiac did also, noting not only his methods, but his references to Koko in the Mikado.

14) Eyewitness Hartnell said the Zodiac hood appeared professionally sewn—Edwards was a tailor while in prison in Chillicothe.

15) All the phone calls and letters to the press and police that Edwards did. The Zodiac would call the police station from a nearby booth to announce his deeds.

16) He not only wrote letters his entire life, but he called the TV stations in 2010 to announce his confession to 5 murders. His need for publicity was astonishing.

17) He was the right age, height, weight, hair color; military trained, police trained, and drawl in voice. Everything physically and mentally matches Edwards.

18) Edwards has confessed to 5 murders and he used knife, rope and gun to achieve it! That's exactly what the Zodiac claimed in his letters.

19) His handwriting matches the Zodiac letters... Edwards gave us every one of his

writing styles in the dozens of letters we got from him over the past year. The man could write forwards, backwards, left, right, print, block and cursive. He was a horrible speller when it came to certain words and double consonants. Just like the Zodiac.

20) Neal cracked the ciphers naming Ed as the Zodiac

21) Last but not least, the composites match.

The Zodiac case had been fraught with misinformation since it started. The media hyped up the lies and the story grew and grew as the decades went on. Once the internet came about in the 90's, people exploited the case.

After Ed's death in 2011, I contacted Tom Voigt, from Portland, Oregon. He was the owner of the web site Zodiackiller.com, said to be one of the most knowledgeable people regarding the Zodiac investigation. Phil Stanford also lived in Portland and had written a book that named Ed as a suspect in a double murder in 1960. They agreed to meet in May of 2011.

Phil Stanford was an editor for the Portland Oregonian and had written extensively about a 1960 lover's lane murder he felt Edwards was responsible for. In that case a young man and woman were killed while parked on a lover's lane on Thanksgiving. Three innocent men were tried for that murder in 1968-70. Edwards was living in Portland at the time of the murder and had written about being there in his book.

I shared my information on Edwards and showed Phil his extensive notebooks of findings. After watching the "To Tell the Truth" episode, Stanford said, "I'm most interested in Edwards' exploits in Portland. I've always been convinced he killed the couple here in 1960 and they convicted the wrongs guys."

Ralph Edward Jorgenson and Robert Brom were both convicted of the 1960 lover's lane murders of Larry Peyton and Beverly Allan. The murder occurred Thanksgiving weekend, 1960. Edwards had been caught at the scene shortly after it happened and escaped the Portland jail. He made the FBI Most Wanted list and went to Leavenworth in 1962. They couldn't prove he did the murder.

Phil Stanford began sharing some fascinating information. First, he provided transcripts of two telephone conversations he had with an unidentified male caller in 2007. The calls were made from a local Fred Meyers grocery store. The caller apparently knew that Stanford was writing about the Peyton-Allan murders and appeared to have intimate knowledge of the case. The first call came in June.

> Phone msg 6/29/7 7:26 p.m.
> Fred Meyer phone booth
>
> Ask not what Larry Peyton did in Portland State. Ask what he did in high school to earn the enemies.
>
> Ask about the sailor who walked south on Highway 26 and blew himself up with dynamite. Larry access to dynamite.
>
> Ask -- because there's no statue of limitation on murder — how the sailor got there without a car. He had a partner.

(June 29, 2007 Phil Stanford Anonymous Call)

> Recd phone message 7/13/7
>
> Mr Stanford, return with us now to the days of yesteryear. I'm surprised that you quoted me directly. I've got another quote. Life is like chess. The threat is always stronger than the execution. I'm anonymous, sir. You should have waited till you got all the facts. Though (something) on the side.
>
> So Mr Peyton may have been in on the dynamite theft, maybe not. It came from a quarry, stashed up in an abandoned house on Cooper Mtn, long time gone now.
>
> The police didn't hook up the connection with the dead sailor bec they didn't know about the dynamite. Mr. Peyton you said was getting nervous. It was probably because he found out someone was putting out a contract on him because of the dead sea scout. It happened on a New Years Day. Larry was in charge, the young sea scout died.
>
> The end of the story essentially is: Who drove the sailor out there. The sailor was supposed to be strong on bushido, a Japanese honor (something) philosophy.
>
> Did he wake up? Was he participating in the rape and murder? Did he take the dynamite and walk south — several miles west? I don't know exactly where she was found. Was he going to Tongue (?) Point with another sailor? Who was driving him? That's your murderer. If it was a contract (voice: end of msge)

(Phil Stanford Phone Message, July 17, 2007)

"That is Edwards talking!" I exclaimed. "Phil, I don't know if you are aware of this but a Navy man named Wayne Budde was blown up with a bomb on the morning of the 1960 lover's lane murder. His ID was deliberately placed at the scene to be found, but there was nothing left of his body. They claimed he committed suicide. I am convinced Edwards did it and stole the man's identity."

Phil thought the call was very suspicious and wanted to know more about Wayne Budde and his connection to Ed Edwards.

I opened my briefcase and pulled out an article, handing it to Phil.

Allan Case Spotlight Switches

Navy Deserter, Jail Fugitive Sought By Police

By HERMAN EDWARDS
Staff Writer, The Oregonian

A deserter from the Tongue Point Naval Station at Astoria and a paroled convict who obtained his release from the Portland City Jail in December on a ruse are sought for questioning in the Nov. 27, 1960, murder of Larry Ralph Peyton and Beverly Ann Allan.

Navy Man Said Dead

Body Blasted By TNT Charge Near Knappa

Picture on Page 9

The blasted body of a man, tentatively identified as that of sailor Wayne A. Budde, 26, of the Tongue Point Naval Station was discovered Monday night in the Knappa-Svensen area near Astoria.

(Portland Oregonian, January 1960 Portland, Oregon)

I explained, "Wayne Budde had been picked up hitchhiking that morning and told his ride he was meeting someone in the area to go hunting. He didn't have a gun and wasn't dressed properly. Residents heard a loud explosion the morning after the murder. His ID was found a month later near a large crater. He had been placed in a pre-dug hole, a large log placed over the top of him, and he was blown to bits by a bomb. Police only found his I.D. conveniently placed near the site. The bomb was made of material that left no trace of what it was. Officials labeled Budde's death a suicide but were insistent at first that there was a connection between his death and the Peyton-Allan murder."

  I pointed out to Phil, "As the Zodiac killer, Edwards wrote the bomb letter 9 years later that described the bomb that blew up Wayne Budde."

  "Take one gallon of Coleman fuel, bag of gravel and ammonium nitrate, set that shit off and it would obliterate everything."* (Zodiac Killer Bomb Threat, 1969)

  "He also sent a letter about 'shooting a man with a .38' while he was sitting in the car, teasing police about 'I hope you have fun figuring out who I blew up.' Wayne Budde was most likely that man, Phil. Edwards had placed Wayne in the book, calling him Johnny."

  "One evening, in November 1960, in a lover's lane on the west side of town, a boy was shot to death, and his companion was abducted. The crime received extensive news publicity. Many sightseers visited the scene of the crime. Since I had an appointment for a demonstration the following day in that part of town, I asked Johnny if he wanted to check out the area with me. Like everyone else, I too was curious."* MOAC

  I furthered, "Don't you have a report of Edwards being questioned that day?"

  Phil provided it.

  Multnomah County Sheriff's Office Police Report
  Officer Baumgartner Subject: Peyton Allan Case

SUBJECT # 1: Edward Wayne Edwards, 27 WMA
6730 South East Woodstock
Phone: 5-8536
60 Chevy-White
SUBJECT # 2: Wayne Everett Berggren, 22 WMA
4805 South East 71st St.
Phone 4-0937
AUTOS:
59 Prix-Yellow
60 Olds-White
60 Chevy-White
TIME & LOCATION
Forest Park at the location of murder.
11:00am to 12:30 pm 11-27-60
Writer contacted above listed subjects who were at the scene of the crime on the above listed date. Subject # 1, Edwards at this time listed the three autos as those he owned or operated at that time. Writer and Officer Bergstrom talked with both subjects at this time & then directed them to leave the scene. Subjects checked 10-4 at the time.
END REPORT

"Did you notice Edwards' age of 27 is within one year of Wayne Budde's age of 26?", I asked. "They were even similar in stature. Edwards stole his identity and fled Portland shortly after. What's even more incredible is that during the Zodiac killings, Portland was trying the 3 innocent men that were arrested in 1968 for the murder Edwards had done."

I whipped out an article from the New Castle, Pennsylvania, newspaper dated April 6, 1971, recovered in my investigation. Edwards is quoted as saying he recalled two men who were serving time for a crime that he alone committed.

(New Castle Pennsylvania Newspaper, April 6, 1971 Former Fugitive Tells YDC Audience. Prison Breeding Grounds)

Paragraph 7: "The pleasant-speaking Edwards said he committed just about all crimes 'except those of violence (murder) and sex.' Ironically he made the FBI's '10 most wanted' list for suspicion of murder."

Paragraph 8: "This happened in Portland, Oregon, where Edwards said he was a suspect of a double murder. Working through his mind was the awful realization that he could very well be executed for something he said he did not do, and he recalled two men who were serving time for crimes that he alone had committed."

Stanford noticeably paled when he heard Edwards confess to setting the two men up in Portland. I pulled out one more article from 1972 where Edwards admitted to being arrested for a double murder and admitting again of people serving time for his crimes.

> Later he was arrested as a suspect in a double murder. Knowing people who have served time for his crimes, he didn't want to get time for a murder he did not commit. So he escaped. Edwards has a record of 37 escapes from various institutions.

> WHERE TO CONTACT EDWARDS!
> Anyone wishing to contact Ed Edwards about personal problems or interested in arranging a speaking engagement for him should write to him at

(Photo - Ed Edwards 1972 interview with Reporter Regina Costigan, Ohio)

    That confirmed Stanford's premise of the wrongful convictions in Portland during the Zodiac killings.

    After meeting with Stanford, I drove to Washington State to meet Michael Kelleher and his wife, Cindy. Mike had written a book about the Zodiac killer titled, "This is the Zodiac Speaking." I wanted to present some of my information to him.

    Several hours out of Portland, I arrived at their wonderful countryside home. Kelleher proved to be a tough, no-nonsense investigator, full of suspicion and skepticism. Kelleher confronted me with a barrage of questions and oaths of confidentiality before any more conversation would ensue.

    After passing the initial exam, I was invited inside and joined the couple for coffee. I began to share my wealth of information on Edwards. Kelleher remained a staunch skeptic, probing and questioning at every turn. At length, he made his only concession. "You have really done your homework." He explained that Zodiac wackos from around the world would hound him with wild tales and "proof" that their father or uncle was the Zodiac. By now, he was unwilling to even discuss anything, especially with strangers.

I pulled out my laptop and retrieved the episode of 'To Tell the Truth.' As Kelleher and his wife viewed the episode, I found the file containing Neal's translation of the Zodiac cryptograms. I handed Kelleher Neal's work and described Neal as a friend with an extremely high I.Q. Kelleher studied the pages for several minutes. He finally set the file down, pondered, and then spoke: "This is the most incredible interpretation I have ever seen. It is so far in first place, I don't even know what second place is. It is so Zodiac-like, so out-of-the-box thinking that I am speechless. I am blown away. This stuff is incredible! I don't know if it's right or what it says, but it's just how I envision the Zodiac talking."

After reading the solved cryptograms, Kelleher took a break. He paced in the front yard, cryptograms in one hand, cigarette in the other. Obviously, the solved Zodiac cryptograms disturbed him. The message the Zodiac was portraying was a Biblical message. Edwards was Satan.

The Kellehers were able to reach Tom Voigt and set up a meeting with me for later that evening. I met Voigt at Club 21 in Portland. The fears of walking into a strip joint were unfounded—the club was originally built about 100 years ago as a Russian church. In the 1940's, it became a steak house, and a few years later, a bar. It is a tiny, quaint structure resembling a hobbit house. Inside were some gaming machines, a few old Gottlieb pinballs, and a small home crowd cheering for the Trailblazers in the first round of the playoffs. The place quieted as the cop-looking newcomer found a spot and prepared the laptop, notebooks, and information for Tom. A couple soon arrived with a hat proclaiming, "I am the Zodiac." Voigt introduced his significant other Angie and they joined me at the table. Voigt and Angie had their own favorite Zodiac suspect and were not really interested in Ed Edwards. I decided this was the time to tell about a case I encountered during the investigation. A victim had contacted me and told her story.

"In 1974, I was 15 and a runaway. I had been hitchhiking on the 101 freeway near the Golden Gate Bridge at 2-3 in the afternoon. On July 4, 1974 a man picked me up driving a newer white Cadillac. When I got in, the passenger door handle was missing. The driver was a white male, in his late 30s' to early 40s', a shaved head with a mole on his face, glasses, and well dressed. I think that he was either a cop or in the military. The man said he was a psychiatrist and that he was on his way to Ohio. He stated he was married and had children and showed me a picture of a dark haired girl. He added he had a good wife that took care of his kids. He mentioned studying Egyptian literature and then gave me a card that represented himself as a San Francisco police officer. He wrote his name on the back of the card. I no longer have it and I don't remember the name.

"As we were driving towards the mountains near Marin County, he tried to convince me to go to a motel so he could tie me up. He then told me that he had to kill me. He made me reach in the back seat and grab a box. I was told to open it and inside was a square handled automatic handgun with bullets and a clip. He made me hold the gun for a while which only made me fear him more. I asked him if he had ever killed anyone and he said he had killed his wife and baby in Idaho. He said he had to kill me and then drove into a mountainous area near Santa Rosa, California. We encountered some hikers and I ran away. He never caught me."

I explained to the Voigts, "She contacted me after watching a You-Tube video of Ed Edwards on the show "To Tell The Truth." She wanted me to know that Edwards was the man that picked her up in 1974. He had a shaved head at the time and a mole on his face."

Voigt was familiar with the now 51-year-old woman who had contacted me. Voigt knew every detail of her story and even furthered that the victim had submitted to hypnosis which seemed to back it up. He was a wealth of information and had incredible recall of facts and events surrounding the Zodiac. Angie also proved to be extremely well informed and seemed to be the more interested of the two in my findings. Polite thanks were shared all the way around, a final toast was made, and I headed back to the hotel to research the Highway 101 murders.

The Highway 101 coastal highway had a string of killings which occurred from 1972-73 in Sonoma County, just north of San Francisco. Investigators felt the Zodiac was responsible for killing countless young girls in this area. Egyptian symbolism had been left at the scene of one of the dump sites. The meaning of the symbolism was, "To carry the souls into the afterlife."

The 101 Highway victims totaled 8 known. They were all young, teen hitchhikers, strangled, bashed and left for dead. Edwards sent the Zodiac Albany New York letter August 1 and then traveled to California August 4th to promote his book.

YOU were WRONG I AM NOT DEAD OR IN THE HOSPITAL I AM ALIVE AND WELL AND IM GOING TO START KILLING AGAIN.
Below is the NAME AND LOCATION OF MY NEXT VICTIM But you had Better hurry because I'm going to kill Her August 10th at 5:00 P.M. when the shift change. ALBANY IS A Nice Town.

(Zodiac Letter Albany NY, August 1, 1973 Edwards California Tour, August 4, 1973)

The significance of the Zodiac Albany letter was that it was a puzzle. Edwards made everyone think he was going to kill in New York but he was referring to Albany, California, right across the bay from San Francisco; Vallejo is just north, right where he is doing his book promotion. This is the same time he is committing the Highway 101 murders. He is doing it on the anniversary of his mother's death and funeral. The 10th is the weekend and the 11th is the anniversary of his mother's funeral. Killing on the weekend is a Zodiac trademark.

I was able to place Edwards in New York in 1973, where the Albany letter was sent from, promoting his book on "Dialing for Dollars" on WTEN. He recovered a picture with the host, Lee Leonard.

LEE LEONARD, host of the television show "Dialing for Dollars" in New York City and ED EDWARDS.

(Edward Edwards, "Dialing For Dollars," New York, 1973)

Edwards didn't say he was going to kill in Albany, New York in the letter. He said: 'I'm going to kill her August 10th at 5.00 P.M. when the shifts change. Albany is a nice town.' He meant Albany, California, the heart of the Zodiac and Highway 101 killings.

As the investigation wrapped up in Oregon I reminded Neal, "When you get the right guy, the pieces just fall into place. Everything starts to fit and it snowballs. Edwards is sending letters from the East Coast and traveling to the West Coast to kill. Every letter he sends is a puzzle about who he is. You can see the symbols in the Albany letter. It all connects to Egyptian history, and Satanism. Everything Edwards did was against Christian beliefs. Neal, your solutions proved that Edwards was acting out as a mythological Satan."

Neal's theories on the ciphers were correct and having Mike Kelleher so highly praise them was nice to hear. People have fought over the Zodiac ciphers for decades, speculating as to what they meant. Edwards sent puzzles, letters and killed repeatedly in August of every decade. His daughter, April Edwards, had told me that her father acted out in August more than any other month during their childhood. The reason Edwards killed in August was the anniversary of his mother's death by gunshot August 1938.

A friend of mine, Deb Laveson, had recovered the original death certificate of Edward's mother, Lillian Cecelia Myers, born April 1st, 1911 and died August 8th, 1938. She was born April Fool's Day and Edwards will kill on that day, and in August, throughout his life. Ed was 5 when she was shot and his real name was Chuckie. Charles Edward Myers. He was named after his grandfather who is the informant on the death certificate.

Edwards' 2010 confessions were lover's lane killings in 1977 and 1980 on the anniversary of his mother's death. As the Zodiac killer he sent his debut letter on the anniversary of his mother's death. In the Zodiac debut letter, he claimed that when you crack his codes you will have him. Neal cracked his codes in 2010 and it named Edward Edwards as the Zodiac killer.

(Death Certificate Lillian Cecelia Myers, Edwards' Mother)

Chapter 17
Dropping the Bomb
April 2011

After visiting with Tom Voigt in Oregon, I headed to Boulder, Colorado. The investigation of Edwards had taken me from Montana to Ohio, Pennsylvania, Oregon, California and now Colorado. In my interviews with members of Edwards family; they had mentioned staying in campgrounds there, hiding out as dad went around doing whatever he was doing. They had to change friends, and sometimes their names, as they moved from state to state.

Edwards had close ties to Colorado as early as 1954 and mentioned it 19 times in his book. He had been staying near Boulder in 1996. His family said he was hiding out in Brighton, Colorado, waiting to collect the insurance money after he killed and beheaded Dannie Law Gloeckner. Edwards planted his body in a cemetery in Troy, Ohio, hoping someone would find it and he would get rich.

It was Christmas 1996, the year of one of the biggest unsolved murders in the USA. JonBenet Ramsey.

Shortly after tying Edwards to the Zodiac killings, Neal and I connected Edwards to the 1996 kidnapping and killing of JonBenet Ramsey in Boulder. In April of 2011, I traveled to Boulder to meet up with the Boulder County Sheriff's Office. I had tried contacting the Boulder Police in 2010 but they were not interested.

I explained my evidence to Detective Steve Ainsworth of the Boulder County Sheriff's Office, a well-respected cold case detective.

"First off, Steve, you have to remember that Ed did his crimes for the recognition. Perhaps sensationalism would be a better word. He loved to commit murders that would create terror throughout a community and then stir the police to go after innocent people. And he would do it on holidays. In Great Falls and Portland both, he killed young couples in safe communities on New Year's and Thanksgiving. As the Zodiac he killed teen couples on 4th of July. JonBenet was killed on Christmas. Edwards geared everything against religion. He created terror by killing her on the holiest day of the year. That's his motive, he thrives off it. He represents Satan in his crimes and JonBenet was ritualistically laid out, covered in white blanket. Using this as his motive and looking back over the last 50 years of the biggest unsolved crimes, what comes to mind? What crime was so bazaar that it made no sense?"

"JonBenet Ramsey." Steve said.

"Exactly. The main evidence was the three-part ransom note written on yellow legal pad and it was a puzzle. The first Zodiac puzzle was also in three parts, sent to three different newspapers, written on separate pages. The famous FBI profiler John Douglas claims the ransom note in the Ramsey case is a puzzle and the only piece of evidence that could eventually identify the killer. He also claimed that the Zodiac killer has a close connection to Deer Lodge Prison. Games? Puzzles? Deer Lodge? Sound familiar?

"Initially, I didn't want to think about the possibility that Edwards killed JonBenet; he was 63 in 1996. It didn't fit what I thought was a normal serial killer's M.O., to kill adults and kids. But Edwards is not normal. He is every serial killer wrapped up in one. It seemed too far-fetched that he would also kill children, but in August of 2010, I spoke with two former employees that had worked with Edwards at a trucking company in Ohio. They claimed Edwards tried to stage the kidnap and ransom of their 5-year-old daughter in 1970. I dismissed that information because the Zodiac case seemed enough to deal with. When I went to Ohio and met his family, they said he was in Colorado on Christmas Day, 1996, just 30 miles from Boulder. Five months prior to the JonBenet Ramsey ransom note, Edwards executed Dannie Gloeckner in Ohio, beheading him and denying his remains. That's almost a quote from the JBR note."

"Any deviation from my instructions will result in the immediate execution of your daughter. You will also be denied her remains. Speaking to anyone about your situation, such as police, FBI etc... will result in her being beheaded."

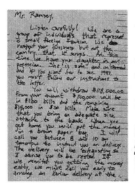 

(photo - JonBenet Ramsey Ransom Note)

"Edwards writes parables to the police, press and victims in many of his crimes and they contain personal information on the victim's family. This steers the investigation to focus on someone within the family. What police didn't know is that Edwards made his crimes to look like that, knowing they would focus on the family. He wants to make a point with each killing that he is smarter than the police and this note is full of him telling you how smart he is. The note was never intended to be a ransom—it was a puzzle as to the identity of the killer."

In his book Edwards said he was going to stick to federal crimes such as kidnapping, insurance fraud, forgery and bank fraud. This type brings in the FBI, and they were his favorite target to taunt. He mentioned the scam a dozen times in his book. Once it's labeled a kidnapping the FBI is called. The thing is, his kidnappings were always false and the victims already dead. But the killer knew personal facts that he placed in the note to help identify him, just like the Zodiac puzzles.

"The three-part ransom note was printed in block style lettering from Patsy Ramsey's note pad to make it personal. The handwriting was obviously disguised but in block lettering, like the Zodiac writings. As the Zodiac, Edwards disguised his writing by using felt tip markers. He used felt tip in the ransoms note. I would like to point out some specific items.

"First: The experts determined several quotes from the note are from movies; 'Now listen. Listen very carefully. If we catch you talking to a stray dog, she dies.' This quote is from the movie Dirty Harry. The movie was based on the Zodiac killer. The plot was a young girl kidnapped and, in the end, she was dead all along. This is what happened to JonBenet. Everyone thought it was a kidnapping, but she was dead in the basement for 6 hours before they found her.

"There was another movie quote in the note, 'Don't try to grow a brain. You're not the only fat cat around.' The movie was Speed and it was about a bus bomb terrorizing a California city.

That's exactly what Ed as the Zodiac threatened to do in his bus bomb letter.

The Zodiac letters had misspellings and problems with double consonants. The ransom note has the same problem with 'Bussiness' spelled wrong."

I pointed out the terminology, use an Attaché case, in the note. "That is a term used by an older person. Edwards used an attaché as a ruse when he portrayed himself as a Dr. of Psychiatry, and he is carrying one on the front cover of his book."

(1972 Book Cover Depiction of Ed Edwards and Attaché)

"He mentions, 'Now he is a writer.' He was a writer, Steve, his entire life. The ransom note stated, 'The two gentleman watching over her.' Both are mirrored on the cover of Edwards' book. Edwards was always two people. He was the family man and the killer. There was never two people involved in that crime. If there had been it would be solved.

"The ransom note states, 'We are a group of individuals that represent a small foreign faction.' Edwards' 'group' is his secret society of sick Satanists. He impersonated police officers his entire life and claimed to be a criminal investigator for the United States Government, the CIA. He was the foreign faction. He worked for the FBI as an informant in the early 50's. What most agents didn't know is that Edwards had badges, guns, false credentials and portrayed himself as an investigator with a degree in psychology. The ransom note says, 'We are familiar with police tactics and counter measures.' Edwards was one of them."

I continued, "John Ramsey owned Access Graphics, was a pilot and owned two planes. Access Graphics was part of Sun Corporation and Lockheed Martin. Edwards' son works for Lockheed in Alabama. His son was also in the Army and worked in Bosnia just before JonBenet was killed. John Ramsey was in the Navy and Ed was a former Marine. John Ramsey's company dealt in defense contracts and Ed targeted military people to kill his entire life. He wanted to prove that he was the best killer ever, not criminal ever. This is why he wrote 'We respect your bussiness but not the country that it serves.' Edwards' son was hired by the 'bussiness' and Ed was against the USA since he was caught at age 17 enlisting in the Marines and thrown out in 1950.

(Edward Wayne Edwards Marine Photo, September 19th, 1950)

"Edwards went AWOL from the Marines just after this photo and started killing people everywhere. He was mad that he couldn't go to KOREA and kill communists. The war started in June of 1950 and Korea was horrible. Steve, what was the only word on the paint brush handle used to garrote JonBenet?"

"KOREA, John. Patsy's paint brush handle was made in KOREA, and he broke it into pieces only leaving the word Korea on the portion used to strangle her."

"Personalization, that's also why he knew of John Ramsey's Navy service, and bonus of 118,000 dollars in 1996. Ed was the foreign faction he mentioned in the note, killing military people and their loved ones his entire life."

"How about the writing, John? Are there any similarities?"

"Oh yes."

I had confronted Edwards in 2010 as the killer of JonBenet Ramsey after Neal solved the Zodiac ciphers. I felt the ransom note was written by Edwards and was a puzzle. Edwards wrote puzzles against authority his entire life. The letters I got back from Edwards after confronting him had striking syntax consistencies to the ransom note text.

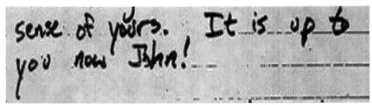

(Quote in JonBenet Ransom Note)

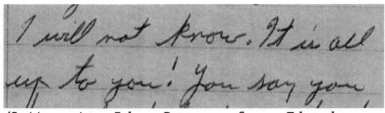
(Letter to John Cameron from Edward Edwards)

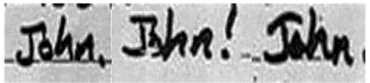
(JonBenet Ransom Note "John")

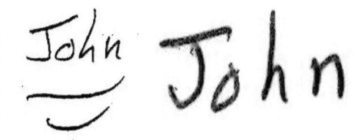
(John Cameron Letter from Edwards "John")

I pointed out to Steve the J's. "The handwriting was identical. Edwards' letters were puzzles like the ransom note. He was a writer. He wanted to be challenged and would never just give it away. He gave slight hints in every correspondence with police.
"The signature on the ransom note:
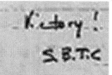
It was the most important part of

the connection to Edwards." I explained. "Victory is a Christian phrase and SBTC meant: Signed By The Cross- SBTC, the Zodiac cross and circle. I used this signature in a letter I sent to Edwards, confronting him as the killer of JonBenet Ramsey. I told him I won the game."

Dear Ed:

Got your letter today, Nov 22, 2010. Am I a liar? Oh yes! I have lied, cheated, stole a lot in my life. They always said Booze, Broads & Bucks in the Police Academy. I got hooked on all during parts of my life. But I live life! Always have.

But do I lie about things of importance when it comes to changing the lives of many forever? NEVER. "TO TELL THE TRUTH." That has been my motto in Law Enforcement for 30 years. And I've told it when it hurts! That damn Catholic guilt trip they put on me from 61-79 really messed me up. 😊

Of course I lied to members of your family and told them I wouldn't tell you I talked to them. I had no choice but "To tell The truth." I know they love their father regardless, if not more now. They are hurting and want it to end and "To tell the truth".

The small "Dawn Bellor" defense is useless at this point. This has been the best investigative ride any Montanan could ask for.

> Just when I thought it would end JonBenet Ramsey comes along. By the time you read this it will probably be international knowlege.
>
> I also lied when I said I put money on your account. I knew you wouldn't write me. Your family would have come first.
>
> So I am placing a $100 money order in here. Merry Christmas Ed. And I mean that. I will have a blue Christmas, but it's what I do best.
>
> Victory! I won
>
> S.B.T.C.
>
> John Cameron
>
> P.S. I have a hard line phone number and will accept any call. Best time to reach me is after 4:00 p.m.

(Photo - Letter from John Cameron to Edward Edwards, November 2010)

"Steve, Edwards frantically tried to call me for two months after he got this letter. He was trying to get executed in Ohio and I was making things messy. He was giving me just enough to keep me at bay until he got his execution date. He sent me this letter, pissed off that I wouldn't answer the phone."

Edward Edwards 584893
P.O. Box 209-FHC
Orient, Ohio 43146

John Cameran
820 5th Ave North
Great Falls, MT.
59401

Hi Friend, 12-1-10

I wrote you a note last night & told you I got your letter, but no money. I just wanted to let you know. I hope you are not putting me on. I tryed to find out today but I was unable to. I guess I'll just wait and see. Thank you! I tryed calling last night & tonight but could not get through. I called at 6 PM your time. I'll try again tomorrow. I sent a note to Neal & gave him a note for you. I don't like for things to go like this as it keeps me down! I just like to stay on top of things. I do enjoy your

(Edwards' letter to John Cameron 12-1-10)

"'Only Girls! SMILE.' Edwards writes in parables with half-truths, Steve. The word SMILE after girls is a clue that it's all a lie. He was only killing GIRLS at that time is what he

is saying. Here's another letter. He makes fun
of the police in it for thinking he's a nut.

Hi John,   12-13-10

I received verification today that there was $100.00 in a M.O. put into my account on 11-27-10. Thank you very much. It will help me out. Merry Christmas!
I received a letter the day after yours from Neal. He wrote me a P.S. & said you mailed me an extra $100.00. I tell you this because I have not heard anything yet. He also told me, as you did, to call, 406-454-0663. You said after 4 PM & he said after 6 PM M. Time. I have called that number 34 times! In the AM & PM up to 8 PM M. Time & am told the call won't go through. You know it is collect?

2.

I keep trying! I told Neal he could call the Customer Service at 1-800-231-0193, and the Direct Bill account set-up, 1-877-873-8567. All they would need is my name, Inmate No. 584893, my address & they might need my Pin Number which is 2708. An automated message will be sent asking if you will accept or deny calls from me. I cannot complete calls until you respond to those, or Neal. Let me know what you want done on this subject please! I also told him about a Xmas box we could have & told him to go on line www.ohiopackages.com. It tells you everything, or you can call

3

1-800-546-6283. The last letter I got from Neal & he said he has not been getting my mail. Why, I don't know! If I could have got through on the phone I could have clear this all up. Anyway I enjoy the letters from both of you & the fact you both have been real nice. You should see some of the letters I am getting from people who want to write a book. You know I will be going back to court next month and maybe this month for a day or 2. But the big part of it will be next month. My atty's might be here to see me tomorrow. I guess you know the police

> 4-
>
> back he think you are a nut! Smile! they think I am also, but the competency evaluation was submitted to the court on Dec. 3rd. Guess what? I am not a nut! Well, I'll wait for your letter to get some answers. Thanks again! Tell Neal to write to me. I have been writing both of you.
>
> Your Friend,
>
> El Edwards

(Edwards' letter to John Cameron 12-13-10)

"This man has been playing these word games for 6 decades, Steve. The JonBenet case was staged to look as if someone in the family had done it and the ransom note was a parable of Ed's life. This was a signature M.O. of Edwards'. He spent his life setting others up for his murders, steering the evidence toward the innocent with false letters and ransom notes. He got John and Patsy indicted but the prosecutor didn't charge them, thank God."

"Well he certainly seems to be playing games in these letters to you and Neal. 'Killing was not on my mind then, only girls!' He is telling you to reverse what he is saying. Look at the K's in the word killing. That's the Zodiac K."

"The Zodiac's K's always stood out because it was a clue to his identity—KAY Edwards, his wife. And one final point. JonBenet was born in Atlanta and buried in Marietta, Georgia right alongside Patsy. Patsy lived alone in Atlanta while John lived in Boulder during the late 80's and early 90's. She didn't move to Boulder until 1991, but they were married. Edwards was released from prison in Pennsylvania in 1986 and had been living in Atlanta and Colorado. He was arrested in 1982 in Marietta, a suburb of Atlanta, and he had a Marietta, Georgia police uniform. Here's his NCIC record."

```
Arrest Date            1982-04-29
Arrest Case Number     53080
Arresting Agency       GA0330000 COBB COUNTY SHERIFFS OFFICE
Subject's Name         EDWARDS, WAYNE EDWARD
Arrest Type            Adult
Charge                 1
Agency                 COBB COUNTY SHERIFFS OFFICE; GA0330000
                       SHERIFF
Address
                       185 ROSWELL STREET
                       MARIETTA, GA 300909650
```

(Edwards' NCIC Record)

"He had been using the uniform to kill, Steve. He mentions Atlanta 39 times in his book. In fact, one of the chapter titles is 'Love in Atlanta.' I spoke with his relatives who live in Marietta and he was there 1979- 1982, during the period of the unsolved Atlanta Child Killings.

Remember those? Twenty-four little black kids murdered, some laid out in church and police parking lots in ritualistic killings?"

"Wow, John, if there's a tie to those killings—that might explain killing JonBenet."

"Look at this 1982 Zodiac letter Edwards sent just before he was caught in Marietta."

> Hello its me. Havent you people figured out who is killing these little people yet I'll give you a hint, I used to be in San Fransisco. I used to stalk women, but I like to kill children now. At all my victims bodies I have left certain clues, but I guess it's too much for you Rebels to handle. So I guess I'll have to tell you. I'll kill children because they are so easy to "pick off". By the way, if you still have letters from the other murders, I am not writing in the same hand writing.
>
> Zodiac

(March 1982 Zodiac Killer Letter Sent During Atlanta Child Murders)

"This letter was never released in 1982 for fear of causing terror. The Atlanta police had arrested Wayne Williams and publicly stated he was the Atlanta child killer. Edwards was telling the police that 'HE, The Zodiac, It's ME' was the killer and has been planting evidence, changing up his writing and killing kids since 1980. The Atlanta child murders brought in the largest FBI task force in USA history and Edwards conned his way into it. That's why I found that picture of him with the Atlanta police captain. He was standing right in front of them."

"I had no idea of the amount of research you have done, John. These letters do have similarities in the ransom note and clearly Edwards has been everywhere. I will let the Boulder PD know about this. But I have one question. How did he get in the house?"

"It's nothing like it's been portrayed. There is no doubt that John Ramsey brought JonBenet in from the car asleep at 9 p.m. She was placed in bed and John, Patsy, and Burke went to sleep. They were all leaving at 5 am on the 26th for a plane trip to Michigan.

Sometime after midnight JonBenet awoke and joined someone in the kitchen for a bowl of pineapple. It was discovered on the counter near the fridge the next morning. When John and Patsy were questioned they adamantly denied she was fed anything, yet it was on the counter and in her small intestine during the autopsy."

"That has always bothered me, John. Someone fed her before she was killed and it was shortly before her death."

"It occurred on Christmas, Steve. Every kid feeds Santa Claus on Christmas Eve night but JonBenet had told people she was getting a special visit on the 25th. It was Santa Claus that killed her. Someone she trusted had entered the home and felt comfortable enough to feed her just before killing her. In the days before her death, a neighbor overheard JonBenet telling her daughter 'I'm getting a special visit from Santa Claus Christmas night.' The neighbor corrected her by stating that Santa was coming the night before—Christmas Eve. But JonBenet insisted, 'No, no, my Santa Claus told me yesterday

(12/24/96) he would pay me a secret visit after Christmas.' Edwards had groomed his way into their life and he was the secret Santa, Steve.

"The Ramseys hosted a party, three days before JonBenet was killed, and there were a lot of people. It included journalism professor Bill McReynolds playing Santa Claus. Police actually questioned him as a suspect because there were questions regarding a suspicious man claiming to be Santa approaching JonBenet just before her death. During the party, someone dialed 911 from inside the house. The caller hung up without saying anything. Officers arrived and everything was okay, yet nobody admitted calling 911."

"Edwards checking police response times?" Steve mused.

"Exactly. Edwards would have attended the party. He would have been under assumed name and false appearance, most likely bragging about his degree in psychology and former Marine service. He stated in his book how he would plan each crime."

"I would plan every crime patiently, deliberately and cold bloodedly. The world must be made to realize how smart I was." (Ed Edwards, 1950, MOAC)

"There was also a police flashlight left on the counter near the pineapple bowl. It was left as a clue as to who the real killer was. Edwards had used flashlights throughout his life and had bragged about it in his Zodiac Debut letter dated August 1969.

"What I did was tape a small pencil flashlight to the barrel of my gun. If you notice in the center of the beam of light, if you aim it you will see a black dot with a circle, approx. 3 to 6 inches across. The bullet will strike exactly in the center." (Ed Edwards, August 4th Zodiac Debut Letter)"

Edwards had used a flashlight in 1956 when he was housed in Deer Lodge Prison to communicate with his wife.

"I made a deal with a guard to sell me his flashlight. I set up a code with Jeanette through the letter, and we were able to communicate. At nights when the lights went out, I'd talked to her by blinking my light, and she'd answer by flipping the outside trailer light on and off."

"The experts never figured out how entry was made into the Ramseys' house. What nobody has ever considered is that JonBenet let her killer in by following Ed's flashlight code. Edwards was highly intelligent and smooth. He got his victims to come to him. He was a master at establishing trust. He targeted the Ramseys because of Patsy being a beauty queen and traipsing JonBenet around at such a young age. John Ramsey owned a computer software company attached to Lockheed Martin and defense contracts. He had just received mass recognition for his billion dollars in sales in 1996. Edwards would have met them at a public gathering. JonBenet was the star of the Christmas parade in Boulder just before her death. She had been to Michigan and Atlanta and so had Edwards. The grandmother claimed that a man had approached the motorcade at the parade that made her feel uncomfortable. The family had no idea who it was. JonBenet had told her friend that she was getting a special visit from Santa Christmas night. Look at him in 1993. He's wearing a fake beard."

(Edward Wayne Edwards, December 19th, 1993, West Memphis, Arkansas)

"Steve, Edwards had groomed his way into the family and was let in by JonBenet. He fed her pineapple and immediately garroted her with such force it almost beheaded her. He wanted that pineapple in the stomach, so the autopsy would show that whoever killed her was a close family member. He would have been right in front of them, only he wasn't Edward Edwards. He would be portraying himself as a former Marine hero with a degree in psychology and he had the gift of gab. Picture him standing behind JonBenet as she's eating her pineapple with Santa. She's happy, quiet because this is a secret that she can't tell her parents. The alarm system was shut off and there was no chance of getting caught. If John had awoken Edwards would have killed them all."

"This is making more sense than any other theory. What about the luggage underneath the basement window." Steve admitted. "Why did he do that?"

"To confuse the police as to the point of entry, and as a clue as to who the real killer was. Edwards plants evidence at the scene that will leave clues to his identity. He mentions luggage and suitcases 17 times in his book, making one reference to stuffing a body in it."

"One convict was caught at a bus station with the dismembered body of his wife stuffed in the suitcase"

"Steve, I'm almost positive this is your guy. This ransom note is a complete version of Edwards' life. He targeted that family to destroy. Picture how it went down. Just as she is eating, he suddenly garrotes her with such force that it practically decapitates her. He then carries her to the basement; places strange blood patterns on her body, draws a red heart on her hand and stamps strange looking triangles on her cheeks. He rubs DNA on her inside thigh, scratches her vaginal wall to make it appear as a sexual assault, and plants someone else's DNA. He says he plants evidence in that letter. He had access to Dannie Boy's remains, Christmas of 96. He then takes the 'police' flashlight that he signaled her with, bashes her head in, covers her with a white blanket, and lays her out as a ritualistic killing. He makes it look like an inside job and leaves the flashlight on the counter next to the pineapple. The parents become the suspects and the press frenzy begins."

"What about letters?" Steve said. "You said he likes to send letters to steer the investigation to someone else."

"He did in this case, too. It was sent January 27th, 1997 from Shreveport, Louisiana during a Miss America Pageant. That date is Burke

Ramsey's 10th birthday, and the letter was intended to target him as sexually assaulting JonBenet. Remember, Patsy was a beauty queen also and that's why Edwards sent it from Shreveport during the pageant. Everything this man does is planned years in advance."

"I remember Boulder Police asking the public for help in locating the author of that letter," Steve said.

"I haven't been able to get a copy of it but read news reports," I said. "Everything I have read suggests Edwards is the author. The letter purported to be from a mother claiming that JonBenet was molested within the family."

Report on JonBenet letter
'Speculation,' Official Says
Associated Press
BOULDER — Reports on the contents of an anonymous letter sent from Shreveport, La., to Boulder police concerning the JonBenet Ramsey case are "pure speculation," a city spokesman said Saturday. The letter was mailed last week and contained information that might be important to the case, said police officials, who have made a public appeal to the author of the letter to come forward.

"I can't get you that letter, John. Boulder PD holds this case tight to their chest."

"I didn't figure you could, Steve, but thought I would try. This letter is the answer to it all, and if I could just get a copy. They were begging for help in 1997, and now they don't even want to hear it."

Steve Ainsworth listened politely and took in all of my information, stating he would pass it on to Boulder Police. I tried to obtain the Shreveport letter through the Freedom of Information Act. As of September 2013, the Boulder Police refused to release the letter. I presented my evidence to them in 2011 and moved on to the next Edwards murder. But I would be back.

Chapter 18

The Atlanta Child Murders

By now I had spent the better part of a year investigating Edwards and connecting him to murders all over the country. I had traveled to Napa, Vallejo and met with law enforcement giving them everything I had uncovered on Edwards. Many in law enforcement could not wrap their minds around a serial killer such as Edwards. The Atlanta Child Murders changed that.

I called Neal and asked him, "Did you watch TV last night?"

"No," he replied. "I was studying up on the Egyptian Book of the Dead. Why?"

"Edwards would have loved this. They aired it right on the anniversary of his mother's 'suicide.' It was a special on a convicted killer named Wayne Williams out of Atlanta. I remembered Wayne and the Atlanta Child Murders because they all happened while I was in the police academy in Alexandria, Minnesota, 1979-1981. We followed them as a class project. It was the biggest FBI manhunt at the time. Someone was killing black teens and dumping their bodies in church parking lots, police parking lots, etc... It was causing a race war in Atlanta. Ed repeats Atlanta 39 times in his book and one of the chapters is titled, 'Love in Atlanta.'"

"Tell me more, I'm intrigued." Neal replied

"I always expected Edwards was doing something brutal in that city. Remember when April, Ed's daughter, told me Ed killed two little black kids with a baseball bat? Well, I started snooping and here's what I came up with. In 1979, Edwards, his wife, and 5 kids were hiding in campgrounds traveling between Florida, Arizona and Colorado. They had lived in Pennsylvania, but their dad burned down their house. April told me this story when I interviewed her in 2010."

"It was during the time my great aunt Lucille was visiting us. And one wet night, my dad came home all muddy. The next day was when we heard kids were missing. My aunt questioned my dad on this. She suspected him of something. So much so, she talked about it with some of us kids. We befriended two boys, they were African American brothers. One day they just stopped coming over. We heard rumors that something happened to them. I remember thinking it wasn't good and we never saw those boys again. We left Florida after selling almost everything. It didn't make sense to me because we had just bought everything. It was also odd that one day when we came home from school a police car was pulling out of the drive and dad wouldn't tell us what it was about. We moved shortly after that—into a campground. We suspected dad of killing a little African American boy, 5-7. The boy was giving Jeff a hard time. One day the boy wasn't in school. Dad said someone hit him in the head with a baseball bat and he died.'

From the investigation we have done, Edwards was in and out of Atlanta his entire life. He was captured there in 1962.

KINGSPORT TIMES NEWS, January 22, 1962
POLICE CAPTURE EDWARD EDWARDS

Atlanta Georgia (AP) Police today arrested suspected bank robber Edward Wayne Edwards, 28, one of the Nation's 10 most wanted criminals. Edwards and his wife Marlene were captured by Detective L.N. Bradley, and other officers who surprised the couple in an Atlanta apartment they rented yesterday.

After his capture, imprisonment and release in 1967, Edwards went back to Atlanta in the 70's to get himself photographed with the cop that caught him in 1962, Captain Bradley.

Capt. Larry Bradley, Atlanta, Georgia Police Dept. and Ed. While Capt. Bradley and Ed are the best of friends today, it was Capt. Bradley who led the raid and arrested Ed in Atlanta in 1962.

(Capt.Bradley abd Ed in Atlanta, 1962)

The Atlanta Child Killings occurred from 1979 until 1981. During this period someone was kidnapping and killing young black boys and taunting the police with anonymous calls and letters. Over 24 young boys were brutalized and left dead, many left on 'Memorial Drive,' near churches. Edwards' daughter April provided more information regarding their stay in Atlanta.

"1979-82 'My dad was arrested for shoplifting. I didn't know this at the time, my mom told me later. She had to bail him out of jail. Dad set fire to the house we were renting. Authorities suspected him of arson. We left town quickly. When we moved, dad wouldn't allow us to write or call friends. We had to break all connections. I do not think he left forwarding addresses. We stayed with a police officer's family in Atlanta and authorities from Pennsylvania found a Marietta Georgia police uniform in the burned out remains and came to Atlanta and arrested Dad for arson, March 1982.'"

In 1981 many in Atlanta thought that a white police officer was killing black teens and trying to start a race war. The killer started taunting preachers and the press with anonymous calls.

Associated Press, March 9, 1981
Atlanta Letter-Writer Claims Killings
ATLANTA (AP) —-Someone claiming to be the Atlanta child killer has written taunting letters sprinkled with police jargon, and a man making the same claim has been telephoning the minister of a church near the site where the 20th body was found.

The latest developments have fueled some existing theories about the case that has baffled investigators and terrorized the black community for 20 months. The police jargon written in the letter, written to reporters at the Atlanta Constitution, could spur speculation that the killer poses as a police officer to gain the trust of victims.

The minister said the body was found near the church soon after, and a man who said he was the killer, contacted him on the church's 24-hour help line. There has been evidence the murderer responds to publicity, and the minister had issued a well-publicized plea for the killer to contact him.

The letters purportedly written by the killer were disclosed Sunday by the Atlanta Constitution and the Atlanta Journal. The newspapers said they decided to publish only part of one letter because it contained a veiled threat that another child may be killed Tuesday during a benefit concert for the investigation.

Television station WAGA, however, reported Sunday that one of the letters was signed "Ghost Killer" and included a phrase suggesting the writer was responsible for more deaths than have been contributed to him. The letter contained police jargon and phrases taunting police.

The CBS affiliate said the letter referred by initials to three Constitution reporters who have written about the cases, and that the newspapers responded by placing a classified ad in the personals section, addressed to "GK" for ghost killer. The ad read:

ATTENTION GK: Received your message, your information informed and challenged us. Send us another verse and chapter.

(Atlanta Journal and Constitution, March 9, 1981 Classifieds

Neal replied, "Three reporters contacted? In every case, the circumstances are identical. He writes the press, makes demands; they comply and then hear nothing. It's the same M.O."

"He wrote in his book about being in Atlanta in 1955, long before he killed in 1980."

"While in Atlanta, I met a seventeen-year-old girl whose father was a police officer. She lived about two blocks away from a drug store I frequented. Several times I'd been over to her home when her parents weren't there. When the policeman and his wife left for work the next morning, his daughter and I put all of her clothes in the trunk of my car. Her father had a huge gun collection, and I helped myself to some choice pieces. Then we went downtown and wrote 400 dollars' worth of checks against her father's account. After we rode around for a while, I dropped her off at the house, picked up Jeanette, my wife, and took off for New York City with all the girl's' clothes, the stuff she'd bought, her father's guns, and all the cash."(Ed Edwards MOAC 1955-56, Atlanta)

I wanted to clarify something. "Even though he's killing in the 80's and his book was written in 1972, he follows the same ritualistic patterns. He replicates and mimics his crimes over and over in the same cities, returning throughout the decades to taunt them and repeat them. If a city convicts an innocent man he returns to kill. He's always inside the police, knowing the details of the investigation. He's essentially a police officer."

In Atlanta, the FBI brought in a task force bigger than any other in history. Edwards had started a race war in 1980; a white police officer, killing black kids, and setting innocent people up. This was one of Edwards' biggest crimes of recognition. There is no doubt about the religious connotation. The boys were left on Memorial Drive near churches and he called and taunted a minister.

"Tell me about the letters to the press." Neal demanded.

"They will make you sick. Here is a poem he sent to the press and police in 1981."

Well you're all afraid, you're all upset.
Cause none of those cops have caught me yet.
I struck again and didn't leave a clue.
Now the whole city doesn't know what to do.
You finally found Lubie, he's been there all the while.
Keep looking you might find another child.
You think that number starts at nineteen?

(Original March 1981 Atlanta Letter)

Man, there are some things you haven't seen.
One night some kids got killed in a fire.
I struck the match so the death toll is higher.
But you can't seem to catch me, I wonder why.
Thousands of you see me every day when I pass by.
It's pathetic to know that I can get away.
With first degree murder on any chosen day.
Politicians are worried as the plot thickens.
Leaders running around like headless chickens.
All different cops can't cooperate with the others.
You'll never catch me you bumbling mothers.
Go back from the ridiculous to the sublime.
And you'll find that I've been with you every time.
You'd better start looking before it's too late.
Or there'll be another "50-48".
So as I leave you with this piece of evidence.
Don't do something stupid like dust it for prints.
      Signed, the Ghost Killer

(March 1981 Atlanta Child Killer Letter)

The handwriting on the Atlanta letter matched letters Edwards sent to me. I furthered that a "50-48" in Atlanta police terms represents the 28 police officers killed in the line of duty. I continued with another incredible letter written by Edwards in March of 1981.

> PLEASE STOP FORCED BUSSING OR I WILL KILL 3 MORE BLACK BOYS IN ATLANTA IN MARCH !

(Zodiac Letter Atlanta, 1981)

"He sent this letter with a threat containing the misspelled word 'bussing' just like the Zodiac did."

Neal responded, "How could anyone deny that the Zodiac was the Atlanta Child Killer? It's the Zodiac talking. 'I used to be in San Francisco. I used to stalk women, but I like to kill children now. At all my victims' bodies, I have left clues.'

"He's the killer of JonBenet, Neal. There is no doubt. Compare this letter I got from him to the Ghost Killer Letter.

(Edwards letter to John 12-14-10)

The Atlanta letters confirmed that Edwards had been changing up his handwriting his entire life, confusing experts. He could write cursive, block, left hand, right hand and he always played games within the letters, speaking half-truths and giving leads to be followed. It was the letter that Ed sent to Neal in 2010, and the way it started, 'It's Me!' that led to tying Ed to the Atlanta Child Killings.

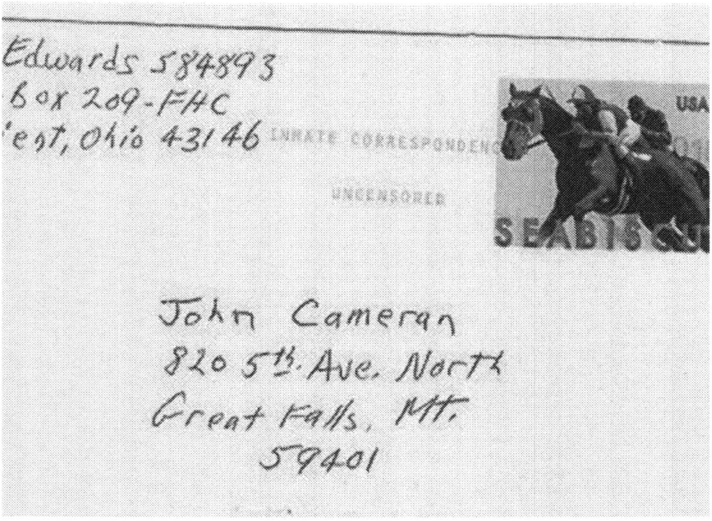

Edwards 584893
Box 209-FHC
'est, Ohio 43146
INMATE CORRESPONDENC
UNCENSORED
USA
SEABISCU
John Cameran
820 5th. Ave. North
Great Falls, Mt.
59401

Hi John,   12-14-10

Thank you very much for the letter & $25.00 I received today. I got a letter from Neal & he sent me some much needed envelopes! You asked about coming to see me. I would have to have them send you some papers which you would fill out & send back. Then they would give me a visiting day. Not a date, but just a day in the week. I'll see about getting it done & let you know. I think you know I'll be going back to court next month. I'll fill you in on days & times but don't let the police know. Like you said, your a nut & a pain in the ass!

2.

they even told my atty. about you. ☹. You said you were born in 1961 when I was a "Nut Dr." in Minn. I was a good one also. That would make you 49. How could you be 49 & a retired cop with 30 years? I thought you retired 10 years ago. By the way, how old is Neal? I take him to be about 50. So tell me which of my kids you had a visit with. Now I'm being a cop! You know my health is bad don't you? Did they tell you every thing that is wrong with me. By the way, you know Det. Johnston thinks your a nut, smile! We are aloud to have a Xmas box & I told Neal but I think he don't

3.

want me to get sick! Smile
He is a good man! Thank
you for everything and I
do hope you have a Merry
Xmas — or a Blue one — which
ever one you want! What do
you really want for Xmas?
I have not got a Xmas
card from any of my
family, but then that is
all up to them — I have
hurt them but it started
long before they came
along, or even my wife!

Thanks for everything
& write soon. Don't
wait so long.

Your Friend
Pat Edwards

(Ed Edwards Letter to Neal Best November 2010)

Edwards had been killing children and staging horrific murders his entire life. After his 1982 capture in Atlanta, he started informing to officials. He contacted investigators in Erie, Pennsylvania, looking for a deal and a way out of prison. He had information on an arson that he had committed but wanted to set someone else up for it. The arson resulted in the death of two children. He confessed to doing the crime in the above poem. "One night two kids got killed in a fire. I struck the match so the death toll is higher." In typical Edwards' fashion, he pinned the whole deal on someone else. Edwards convinced investigators to go after Louis DiNicola for the August 30th, 1979 arson at Deborah Sweet's home, which killed two children and an adult man. Edwards testified that DiNicola had made admissions to him while in prison, in 1983, resulting in DiNicola's arrest. After testifying and serving only 3 years of a 12-year sentence, Edwards was released after filing an appeal and walked out the doors in June of 1986. Prosecutors claimed in later filings that Edwards had received "no benefit" for his testimony. Edwards NCIC records showed his long history of custody in other states, yet he was always released early when caught.

```
Charge                      02
    Charge Literal          THEFT BY UNLAWFUL TAKING
    Agency                  PAPSP0900 STATE POLICE BUTLER
    Severity                Unknown
Court Disposition           (Cycle 015)
Court Disposition Date      1982-09-25
Court Agency                Unknown
Charge                      01
    Charge Literal          ARSON & RELATED OFFENSES
    Severity                Unknown
    Disposition             (Convicted 1982-09-25; CONVICTED- 4Y-10Y
                            CONFINEMENT, FOUND GUILTY AT WESTERN, PGH PA)
Charge                      02
    Charge Literal          THEFT BY UNLAWFUL TAKING
    Severity                Unknown
    Disposition             (Convicted 1982-09-25; CONVICTED- 1Y-2Y
                            CONFINEMENT, PG TO RUN CONSE W/TT 5 TO 12YR AT
                            WESTERN)
****************** INDEX OF AGENCIES ******************
Agency                      FBI-CJIS DIV-CLRKSBG CLARKSBURG; NWEBINF00;
Address
                            1000 CUSTER HOLLOW RD
                            CLARKSBURG, WV 26306
Agency                      POLICE DEPARTMENT DAYTONA BEACH; FL0640100;
Address
                            ATTN PERSONNEL DEPT 129 VALOR BLVD
                            DAYTONA BEACH, FL 321148169
Agency                      SHERIFF'S OFFICE JACKSONVILLE; FL0160000;
Address
                            RM 207 501 E BAY ST
                            JACKSONVILLE, FL 32202
Agency                      PD-RECORDS AND IDENT PHILADELPHIA; PAPEP0000;
Address
                            RM 212 8TH & RACE ST
                            PHILADELPHIA, PA 19106
Agency                      USM PHILADELPHIA; PAUSM0200;
Address
                            601 MARKET STREET
                            PHILADELPHIA, PA 19106
Agency                      SHERIFF'S OFFICE BILLINGS; MT0560000;
Address
                            219 N 26TH ST
                            BILLINGS, MT 59101
Agency                      POLICE DEPARTMENT BILLINGS; MT0560100;
Address
                            220 N 2TH ST PO BOX 1554
                            BILLINGS, MT 591011554
Agency                      STATE PRISON DEER LODGE; MT039015C;
Address
                            RECORDS DEPARTMENT 400 CONLEY LAKE RD
                            DEER LODGE, MT 597229765
Agency                      SHERIFF'S OFFICE PORTLAND; OR0260000;
Address
                            12240 NE GLISAN
                            PORTLAND, OR 97230
Agency                      POLICE DEPARTMENT PORTLAND; OR0260200;
Address
                            RM 1250 1111 SW 2ND AVE
                            PORTLAND, OR 972012724
Agency                      USM CLEVELAND; OHUSM0200;
Address
                            STE 1200 801 W SUPERIOR AVE
                            CLEVELAND, OH 44113
Agency                      US PEN LEAVENWORTH; KS052017C;
Address
                            1300 METROPOLITAN ST PO BOX 1000
                            LEAVENWORTH, KS 660481254
```

(Edwards NCIC Records Listing Other Agencies with Arrest Records)

Chapter 19

A Big Piece of the Puzzle

The Zodiac case always had a close connection to Deer Lodge prison from the beginning. Surviving witness Bryan Hartnell stated the killer said: *"I'm on the way to Mexico; I escaped from Deer Lodge Prison in Montana. I killed a couple guards getting out of prison and I'm not afraid to kill again."*

There was also a Zodiac connection to the famous Deer Lodge Prison riot of 1959. Prisoners had killed a guard and threatened to kill hostages by rope, knife, gun and fire. That is how the Zodiac claimed to have killed.

Edwards was in Deer Lodge from 1956 until 1959, doing time. He was picked up in Billings on March 8, 1956 for auto theft and robbery. In exchange for copping pleas to robberies around the country, they dropped the auto theft charges. 1959 was the year the famous Deer Lodge Prison riots made the cover of Life Magazine. Edwards was actually working on an escape at the time, but his plans were thwarted when the National Guard stormed the prison April 18th, 1959.

"I decided to escape so I could seek my revenge. I began to tunnel my way out of my cell.

I worked my way into the heating pipe system. I can't recall any sensible demand by the rioters and they knew they hadn't a chance. They killed the deputy warden."

In his book, he claimed to have helped carry the bodies of the two main instigators, Lee Smart and Jerry Miles, out of the prison.

"Turning to Miles, Smart shot him in the head and killed him instantly. Then Smart turned the gun on himself and pulled the trigger. This ended the riot. The toll was enormous. The deputy warden was dead, three guards had been cut. Many inmates had been beaten up. Countless others had been forcibly raped or otherwise molested. During that week the only men allowed out of their cells were the three orderlies. I was one of them. Our job was to carry out the bodies of Smart and Miles. A month before the big riot broke out I had made parole." *MOAC

Edwards curried favor with the parole board for his help in the riot and he was released in June of 1959 to Portland Oregon.

Edwards had mentioned in a letter to me that he survived the riot with a guy named Frank Dryman. "I read in the paper that Frank Dryman is still there. He is a real nut when he wants to be. I knew every person in that place. That was my job!" (Ed Edwards, 2010)

I had met Frank Dryman in March of 2010, while working for the parole board. Dryman was a killer that had spent time in Deer Lodge Prison back in the 50's and 60's. He was paroled by the Montana Board of Pardons in 1968 to Vallejo, California, and disappeared in 1971. He remained as a missing parole violator for 40 years until his capture in Arizona in 2010.

The connections to Frank Dryman, the Deer Lodge Prison riot and the Zodiac killer are undeniable. Dryman was born and raised in Vallejo. He was a cryptologist in the Navy but discharged due to mental problems in 1949. In 1950, he was hitchhiking north of Great Falls, Montana when he thanked his ride by shooting him 5 times in the back and stealing his car. That landed him on death row in Deer Lodge where they planned on hanging him. The records show him covered in tattoos; some of them linked directly to Egyptian mythology and the Zodiac cryptograms. He also has images of a revolver (gun) a hangman's noose (rope) and the sun (fire) tattooed on his body. When arrested in 2010 he was portraying himself as a preacher in a wedding chapel, calling himself Frank Valentine.

(Photo of Frank Dryman's Hands, March 2010, Deer Lodge Prison)

Dryman was caught in 2010 after 40 years on the lam. The reason he had run from parole is that Edwards was trying to set him up as the Zodiac killer. Edwards hated Dryman when he was in Deer Lodge because Dryman got all the recognition. Dryman had shot his victim in the back 5 times in 1949 and Edwards as the Zodiac killer shot his first victim, Betty Lou Jenson of Vallejo, in the back 5 times, using a flashlight taped to the barrel. He was steering the evidence towards Dryman who had just been paroled to Vallejo. What Edwards didn't know was that Dryman was granted parole in November of 1968 but didn't walk out the door of Deer Lodge Prison until January 8, 1969. The first Zodiac killing was December 20th, 1968. Cameron traveled to Deer Lodge Prison in 2011 and spoke with Frank Dryman.

(photo - **Deer Lodge Territorial Prison**)

Deer Lodge was actually built before Montana had even been admitted into the union. Construction began shortly after the civil war. It was full of sick demented people and had no running water or electricity. Edwards and Dryman were cellmates from 1956-59.

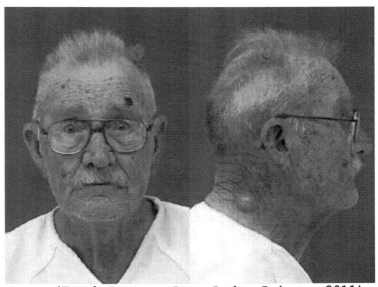
(Frank Dryman, Deer Lodge Prison, 2011)

Dryman spoke freely about his exploits in Deer Lodge back in the 1950's. "I had obtained a guard's gun and I was out searching for this big nigger that had given me trouble. I was going to kill him, but I couldn't find him. One of those big magazines snapped a picture of the riot and in the background, was a big sign hanging out a window with a list of demands. That was me holding the sign," he proudly announced. "You see, I was a sign painter and a calligrapher, and they picked me to do all the lettering." A huge smile crossed his face as he said it.

Dryman continued, "The riot was national news. The National Guard had to be called in and they used a bazooka to blow a hole in the prison wall. I think every Montana resident within 100 miles was waiting outside to see what happened. They all brought their own gun with them. Reporters flocked from every big city, you couldn't get a room. Just about every inmate was involved, but only two got tagged with the killing of the guard. Both of them ended up dead in a murder-suicide. I tried to talk them out of it, but they were set on going out with a bang."

Dryman spoke of stories of prison life, conditions, and painted a first- hand picture of how horrible Deer Lodge was during the late 50's. He wanted to make sure Cameron understood what the Zodiac and Edwards was all about. "It's all about history, John, history, world history, and ancient history." He concluded the four-hour interview with a few details about his life of 40 years on the lam, never reporting back to his parole officer. "I had no intention of straightening out after my parole in 1969."

Edwards became very jealous of Frank Dryman while sitting in Deer Lodge. Dryman is a well-known killer and Edwards is a well-known escape artist. They both gained enormous amount of recognition while they were in Deer Lodge in the 50's. Dryman was all over the papers about his pending execution by hanging; Edwards all over the papers as the most dangerous criminal and escape artist ever caught in Montana. They both end up in competition in Deer Lodge in 1956 and lived through the 1959 riot. They are not friends. They are enemies. Edwards is actually the best killer ever by this point, but nobody knows it and he can't tell them. He's doing 10 years for armed robbery, not murder. He can't stand the respect Dryman is getting, so he targets him when he gets parole in 1968. They both get parole the same year but Dryman doesn't walk out the doors until January 1969.

Dryman was parading around Deer Lodge acting as the high priest. He wore a black Catholic Cossack with the Zodiac cross and circle on the front. That's why Edwards wore the black hooded getup with the cross and circle at Lake Berryessa. It was a cross between the Catholic Cossack and the Executioners hood.

The Zodiac case had a religious connotation to it from the beginning and most experts agreed he would be an ex-Catholic if discovered. Edwards and Dryman had both been abused by the Catholics. They both mocked the

Catholic Church. Dryman traipsed around in that Cossack at Deer Lodge Prison as a satanic priest. Dryman was a Satanist and Edwards could relate. They both studied Egyptian history and science fiction. This was not about finding Jesus. They both were members of a secret society that worships and acts out Satan.

Dryman and Edwards were very sick inmates who competed with each other in Deer Lodge for the respect of the other inmates in a miserable environment back in 1959. They were both mentally ill, ex-Catholics who took religion to the dark side at a very young age. Dryman was walking around waiting to be hung, wearing his Catholic robe, pretending to be the high priest. Edwards was planning his next escape, killing and setup as the judge, jury and executioner.

Edwards' book detailed his hatred for the Catholics and the reasons he sought revenge, mocking them.

"Failing to say, 'Yes, Ma'am,' 'No, Ma'am,' or 'Yes, Sister,' 'No, Sister,' invoked punishment. I learned right away that if you were unfortunate enough to be a bed-wetter, you were in serious trouble. Every morning I was forced to stand under a cold shower, holding my linen for approximately an hour, but to no avail. When they saw that this didn't work, they took me downstairs in the cottage and I was beaten on the backside some 15 or 20 times.

"Sister Agnes Marie then made me walk over to a little tree, stand against it, and put my arms around it to hug the tree. She instructed the children to form a line: and each, in turn, would kick me on the backside. She placed the first kick on my rear herself. She was going to break me of my bed-wetting, she warned, or kill me in the process. I hated Sister Agnes Marie with all my heart, and I hated everyone else in that gruesome place.' (Ed Edwards, age 7.) *

Edwards took his beatings from the orphanage and acted them out on his victims his entire life. His book was a puzzle and contained stories and parables of his own miserable life.

He profiled himself in the book but made the reader think it was someone else like Frank Dryman.

"This demented individual showed an overwhelming interest in science fiction and Egyptian literature. He believed that anyone he killed would be his slave in his next life. Unfortunately, this inmate idolized me, for the simple reason that I had earned the respect of the population— something deep down he wanted desperately to do." (Metamorphosis of a Criminal)

Edwards had more respect around the inmates then Dryman. Everyone considered Frank a nut. Dryman was a murderer, paroled to Vallejo in 1968. He shot his victim five times in the back in 1950 just like the Zodiac did in 1968. The tattoos on his arms look like Zodiac cryptos and Edwards points the cops in his direction. Dryman would have been the first person the cops looked at and they did. And he ran away from parole in 1971 for 40 years after Edwards went to the Ohio press and pointed the finger directly at him in a newspaper interview.

As the Zodiac killer Edwards wrote the 'citizen card' mailed to the S.F. Chronicle May 8, 1974. It quotes a blurb from a movie, "In 1959, most people were killing time." Edwards wanted people to look back to 1959 and find the guy that was doing time. It's ME!

He shared a similar blurb to Neal and myself in 2011.

be it. It's not like it was when I was doing time there in Mt. back in 1956-59.

(Ed Edwards Letter, November 2011)

Poetry, parables, games and puzzles. That was Edwards' M.O. throughout his life. Everything he wrote had a double meaning. Everything was for recognition. The Zodiac killer has been killing for 50 years and nobody has followed his life. The investigation of Ed Edwards would never end.

Chapter 20

Edwards' Recognition

Neal started out, "John, I'm totally on board with you on how Edwards tried to set up Dryman, but I'm confused on a big issue and I'm not alone here. Edwards says everywhere that everything he did was for recognition. It's repeated in his book; he said it on 'To Tell the Truth,' and it's in his interviews before his death. Most people feel that with the Zodiac's affinity for the press and recognition that he would have bragged about it to the world. At the least, he would have left the story somewhere to be discovered upon or before his death. He would have told everybody how smart he was."

"I've analyzed that," I responded. "He did."

"He did what?" Neal asked.

"He left the story. He has been confessing for 60 years and nobody would listen! He wrote a book, he cut an album, he was on 'To Tell the Truth'; he did radio shows and gave lectures everywhere. We have pictures of him with the highest officials in government. What was he telling us? Nobody listened! Look at this brochure he was handing out during the Zodiac."

He looked at Neal, "This is what Ed meant by recognition. He loved to stand in front of everyone. It fits the whole deal: The Zodiac letters, the press, the mystique—all Edwards stoking his fires. Down to pulling the fire alarms in Great Falls and in Portland. Calling the police in the Zodiac cases. He didn't want to be recognized—he wanted his deeds recognized, thrown all over the front pages, as he sat back and listened to everyone. He was reverting back to childhood. He kept his mouth shut, never told anyone anything, and never got caught. He said exactly that in a January 2011, letter to me."

Jan 25, 2011

Dear John,

Got your letter you wrote 18, I want to thank you for the candy and the money. I ate all the candy and putting the money to good use. You made a comment about "nice try". You also said you did not like the "Dumb Cop" comment. Are you saying I called you a dumb cop? I don't remember doing so, but if I did I'm sorry and it was all in fun. You said you became a cop for the recognition. You are wrong if you think I killed people for the recognition. I did not let anyone know when I killed someone, so therefore I wasn't doing it for the recognition. Most everything that I did in life was for recognition. Let me tell you right now, that if there is anything you want to know, you don't have to pay me to get the answers. You have been good and nice to me and I plan on returning the favor. As for what you might say in your book, do as you said and let the chips fall as they may. There's not much that can hurt me anymore. As for hurting my family, I've already done a good job of that.
As I read thru your letter here,

I get the Ideal that you are upset with me, and resent me. Why I don't know. I have never really ask for anything and I won't. If I ever do, it's to make our freindship better. You were telling me about Neal, and how good of a man he was. I feel he is one of the most sincere people I have ever meet and I like him very ~~much~~ much. I will try to never hurt his feeling.

You said I was the best criminal you knew of. And I should give up tring to stir the shit. I gave up that a long time ago. As me ~~writing~~ writing ~~games~~, you can forget it because it's to much work. Anyway if I am doing something wrong or if I said something on the phone to upset you, please let me know. Remember you wrote to me first. And I have enjoyed all of your letters. I hope everthing is okay.

As for my glasses, I have went since September of 09' without them and I guess I can go longer.

> There not that important. When I was talking to Neal, I'm not sure if he said you're leaving in a few days or a week to go to Hawaii to see your son. I do hope you have a good time and everything goes well for him. When you publish your book, I wish you all the luck in the world and become a millionaire. I have had two or three people write to me and ask if I would be interested in writing a book with them. I even had a movie suggested. You know there are a lot of things that I could talk to you about that no one knows, but if you publish your book now you won't have that information to put in it. Anyway it's getting late and this down and out killer is not only broke but I'm getting tired. Don't wait so long to write your next letter and tell Neal I said Hello.
>
> Your friend
> Ed

(Letter to Cameron from Edwards, January 2011)

"Everything I did in life was for recognition"

At this time, Neal and I had it exactly right. But we had no idea of the magnitude. The Zodiac, JonBenet and Atlanta cases were only the tip of the iceberg. The answers were just beginning.

237

Chapter 21

A Living Victim Speaks

The local police had warned me in 2010 to stay out of their cases. I was no longer a licensed police officer and they threatened me with arrest if I contacted anyone. After waiting a year and finding out they never contacted ANY witnesses, I decided to go on my own and take my chances. I said to Neal. "I think I'm going to look up Jeanette White, Ed's 1956 wife. The cops certainly aren't doing anything. Throw me in jail. I don't care."

"They've had over a year to look into this, John. We're going to have to do something on our own. If she's alive it could bust this thing wide open."

I started to get caught up in Neal's enthusiasm. Jeanette White had traveled with Ed Edwards during 1955, and they both ended up in Great Falls, Montana on New Year's Day, 1956. I had been ordered by the Cascade County Sheriff's Department to stay out of their case and not contact any witnesses. It had been nearly 18 months and they never contacted her so I called her up: And called back Neal.

"I can't believe it! I found her and I 've already talked to her. She's agreed to a meeting. I've decided to risk it and interview her. We're going to Idaho Falls!"

"What!? She's still alive? She must be into her 70's. When are we leaving? What'd she say? How'd you find her?"

"Whoa, slow down. Last question first. I did lengthy research, I accessed the FBI computers and I got 3 P.I.'s on board, and wham! I got her!"

"John, it's only been 15 minutes since I left," Neal pointed out.

"She was in the phone book," I confessed.

"The cops have had over a year to find her and she's in the phone book?"

"Yep, and my fine detective skills, years of experience and police genius took me right to her," I responded.

"Yeah, genius, all right; keystone cops."

On January 11th we booked a room, grabbed a rental, and left Great Falls. We were going to meet Jeanette White, Ed Edwards' ex-wife.

The night before the meeting, we decided to go over our strategy. Sitting in our motel room, I began, "In police interviews, it's best to let the suspect do most of the talking, and it's important not to influence them or direct them with what you already know or think. Now, Jeanette's not a 'suspect,' but I'd like to give her the ball and let her run with it. I'd want her to just tell us everything she can remember about Ed."

"Does she know Edwards wrote a book and that she's in it?" asked Neal.

"No, I didn't tell her. On the phone she told me; 'I learned right away not to cross him. He let me call home every once and awhile to talk to my mother. But he would always make the call, speak for a moment, and then hand me the phone. By then, my mother would be crying. She told me years later that every time, Ed would tell her,

240

"if you speak to ANYONE about this call, or tell ANYONE where we are, I'll kill your daughter." Then he'd hand me the phone.'"

"Oh, my God," gasped Neal. "Can you imagine the terror she was in?"

"I could hear her fear on the phone," I answered. "One thing I learned is Edwards was a killer clear back in 1955. He wasn't bluffing about killing her. He would have, he killed others. He killed Patty and Duane 2 months after they were married."

"O.K. So what next?" asked Neal.

I answered, "Might depend on what she tells us. If she provides any concrete testimony about knowledge of any homicides, I'm obligated to inform the locals. After she's done talking, we'll dig out the book."

The next day we arrived at Jeanette's house, looked at each other nervously and I said, "Here we go," We went to the door.

Jeanette warmly welcomed them into her upper middle class, well- kept home. I pulled out my laptop while chatting casually about some background information. I asked her if we could record the conversation and move to the kitchen table. Jeanette froze up, but reluctantly agreed. I instantly knew this conversation was not leaving the couch nor would it be recorded.

Jeanette started the interview.

"I almost called you and canceled. This is too painful."

I saw how sensitive she was, so I gently approached her with, "Did you know he wrote a book?"

It took a few seconds before she spoke. "He raped me." Jeanette was trembling as she continued. "I almost called you and asked you not to come, but I didn't have your phone number."

I patiently consoled her, "I understand. This must be very difficult for you. I hope we can help a lot of other people that were hurt by this man."

"He was the devil. He was Satan," stated Jeanette.

I was taken aback by the statement. Neal and I had theorized that Edwards considered himself Osiris, an ancient Egyptian god. Jeanette just confirmed this and he wasn't quite prepared for it. She also confirmed the book was a lie. Edwards had detailed his first encounter with Jeanette in his book, but he didn't describe a rape.

"I turned to Jeanette with the most intense feeling of love I had ever in memory had. This was it. This was real love. Bells and cymbals were clanging around in my head: I was almost dizzy. I leaned over and kissed her, patiently."
*MOAC

"I don't know why he never killed me," Jeanette said. "Maybe it's because I had his son, Wayne. I never told Wayne about his father. I didn't want him to ever find out. I thought he might worry about himself, coming from a man like that, so I never told him. Then one day my sister- in-law told him. I have never spoken to her since. I almost called you and asked you not to come, but I didn't have your phone number."

I continued by asking, "Do you remember any cities that you and Ed might have visited after you were married?"

"New York. Atlanta. We were everywhere."

"He mentioned that you went there, in the book. "We went to Atlanta, found an apartment and I became a milkman for a dairy."* MOACA

"Do you remember when Ed first showed up in Idaho Falls? Did he have another woman with him? Her name might have been 'Verna.'"

"I remember that," responded Jeanette. "She was pregnant and he said it was his sister. I don't know why he never killed me. Maybe it's because I had his son."

"Maybe," I answered. "You are very lucky to still be alive."

"Ed liked killing people. He enjoyed it," said Jeanette. "I drove the getaway car and partook in some of his things. There's nothing I could've done. We were always traveling and changing."

"Jeanette," I asked, "Do you remember a girl named Theresa?"

"Oh, yes," she answered. "She was my friend in high school."

"Can you tell us her last name?"

"I can't remember but she is still around."

"Ed said in his book that Theresa came over to your house with Verna and a detective."

"I was eating supper at Jeanette's. There was a knock on the door. When Jeanette answered the knock, she found that a detective had come to talk to me. Out in front of the house, standing close together, in the dusk, and both very angry, were Theresa and Verna, Verna's belly forming a distinctive silhouette against the grey sky." *MOAC

Jeanette responded, "That was so long ago. I don't know what happened to Verna and Theresa. Verna was pregnant."

I recognized the behavior. Many victims of violent crimes or tragic situations block out entire events or times in order to deal with them. Sometimes it's the only way a person can move forward with their life and cope. Plus, I was taking her back over 55 years. She had commented in my first phone call to her that no one had ever asked her about those times.

I asked, "Jeannette, did you ever speak to anyone, particularly law enforcement, about Ed?"

She answered, "One time, two FBI men came to my home and warned me Ed had escaped from jail in 1960. They wanted to know if I had heard from him. I remember going to the grocery store with Ed. I think it was in Atlanta. He told me to wait in the car and he'd be back in a bit. He returned an hour later with four girls. They all pointed at me and then they laughed. He directed them to make fun of me."

Jeanette had been raped, kidnapped and taken all over the country, and Ed was having other women tease her to keep him in control of her. She described the crimes they partook in.

Nobody would suspect a Marine with a pregnant wife committing crimes. She admitted to doing most of the driving while they were on the road. They would seldom pay for a hotel; they would just pull over and sleep in the car a lot of times. They stole a different car every other week.

Jeanette continued with her story. She said she moved to Deer Lodge after the birth of their son in August 1956. She got a job waitressing and remained faithful for about a year and half, visiting Ed at the Deer Lodge Prison regularly. The Mormon bishop was terrified for her. He insisted she take the boy and leave Ed forever. She finally relented and told Ed of her decision. He lost it.

"When I returned to my room I found I couldn't sleep. Jeanette had obtained a divorce from me while I was still in Montana. I broke into a sweat, 'Do I still want to kill her?'" *MOAC

Jeanette described him screaming he was going to kill her. He violently thrashed around the cell, unable to restrain himself, and vowed to get even. She concluded, "We left Deer Lodge right after that."

I ended the interview and started packing up. I glanced at Jeanette and she was beaming. She looked like she had been relieved of a tremendous burden.

The travels she and Ed had done were accurate and in his book. The names were real and the places he killed accurate. Ed's book was a puzzle and all the murders he did in 1955 and 56 with her, were written as parables in his autobiography.

The Zodiac had started killing long before 1968.

Chapter 22

Hollywood!

As we pulled away from the curb, I ordered Neal to find the chapter when Ed's in Deer Lodge. "He talks about when he was released on parole to Portland."

Neal said, "I found it. Edwards says, 'The reality of the moment hit me. I was a free man. I was still consumed with bitterness because she had walked out on me. I broke into a sweat thinking: "Do I still want to get even with my ex-wife? Do I still want to kill her?" Once again resentment surged to the fore. Impulsively I gave into my feelings and took off for Idaho. I would seek out Jeanette and make her pay for what she had done to me. I'd convinced myself that I wanted to kill Jeanette, a thought I just couldn't turn off.'''* MOAC

"Jeanette documents it." I said. "This is the same period the FBI agents came and warned her. Edwards was a bonafide killer in 1956. He was killing his whole life. He was wearing a uniform, pretending to be a doctor and traipsing Jeanette all over the country as part of his ruse. Listen to how he described he and Jeanette's doctor ruse in the book."

"We became Dr. and Mrs. Jerry Love. Joyce and Jerry. It had a nice ring to it. I represented myself as a psychiatrist. I had several reasons for posing as a psychiatrist. Mostly, I liked the prestige. Then, of course, doctors weren't bad check risks. 'Doctor' Love could cash a check immediately just on his title. 'Mister' Love would have to wait until his credit was established. Then, too, I hated psychiatrists. I'd been tested by many of them when I was a child, and had been able to fool them with great ease. I delighted in the thought that I could impersonate them so easily, but might even do somebody some good. My patients would like me." *MOAC

"By 1956 he had the ruse down to a tee. Portraying himself as a doctor and getting his victims to come to him. He had been doing this long before then! We need to do a timeline of his life starting from when his mother was shot in 1938."

Neal agreed.

I looked things over and suggested we try a couple of things before leaving Idaho Falls. First, I wanted to go to the courthouse and search for a copy of their wedding license. Second, I wanted to find out who was Theresa.

Neal said, "We need to find Jeanette's year book, class of '55."

We called Idaho Falls High School and connected with the librarian. After a moment, she returned and announced, "Yes, I have a copy of the '55 yearbook in hand." I gave her Jeanette's information and the librarian found her right away, "Here it is! I'm looking at her picture."

I informed her we were on their way, "We are also looking for her friend, Theresa. She might be in the same class. I don't know how big the school was back then, but we'd like to look through the book for her. I hope there aren't a lot of Theresa's."

It turned out the high school was only ten minutes away, so we checked in at the office, and then found the library. A charming lady escorted us to a back room and opened the annual.

"There's Jeanette," she proudly announced. "And guess what? The girl right next to her is Theresa!"

I immediately said, "That's gotta be her; too coincidental. Back then you were seated together by the spelling of your last name. This has to be Jeanette's bud." We headed out of the school now armed with Theresa's last name. The librarian had even been so gracious to insist we take the annual with us and return it later.

I decided to risk another call to Jeanette. She answered the phone and he provided Theresa's last name. She confirmed it was her schoolmate. We called her and an elderly sounding woman answered the phone.

"My goodness," she began. "Jeanette. I haven't thought of her in years. We weren't close, but we were in the same class. She disappeared one day and the police came to our farm and questioned us about her being kidnapped. Whatever happened to her?"

"She's still alive and living in Idaho Falls," I said. "We talked to her yesterday. We were hoping you might be able to fill us in on a few details from 1955. That's why we called you."

"How did you find me?" she asked incredulously. "That was so long ago."

"Actually," I began, "we are investigating a serial killer named Edward Wayne Edwards. He wrote a book and you're in it."

"What! I'm in a book?!" she replied in disbelief.

"Yes," I answered. "Edwards wrote about you and Jeanette both in his book. You wouldn't have known him as Ed Edwards. At that time, he was going by the name Jim Langley."

"Langley?" she exploded. "If you find him, he owes me 57 dollars! I cashed my paycheck and loaned him the entire amount. I never got a nickel back."

Theresa continued, "What'd you mean, I'm in a book? You're not going to write about me, are you? I don't want to be in any book."

"You already are," I explained. "We will not write anything about you without your permission, but you are already in a book.'"

"I had no idea," she miffed. "Someone should have told me. What is it you want to know?"

I reassured her that we were just doing background research and wanted to know more about Langley. I continued by asking her to describe the first meeting.

"Oh, do I remember!" she exclaimed. "It was September 1955. I was working my first job out of high school, carhopping at the drive- in. He drove up in a 1955 blue and white Ford convertible and started hitting on all the girls. He thought he was hot stuff from Hollywood. He had a girl with him that was pregnant. They both looked destitute and tired. Langley kept referring to the girl as his sister. My dad hired them on the potato farm, but Langley wasn't interested in working. He was always sneaking around the house, scoping it out trying to steal things. My mother didn't trust him."

"Your mother had good instincts," I said. "Do you remember the girl's name and what she looked like?"

"That was a strange deal," she answered. "She was pretty, young, and pregnant and he was really rough with her. It was as if he wanted her to abort the baby. I'm not positive, but I think her name was Verna. She had dark hair and was about 17."

"That's her," I confirmed. "He put her name in the book, too. Do you remember what happened to her?"

"No," answered Theresa. "They all disappeared. The police came out to the farm looking for Jeanette. Her mother said that she had been abducted. I heard years later that Jeanette had a baby with him. I don't remember who told me that, though."

"When did the cops come out to your farm, Theresa?"

"It was around December 1955."

"Wow," I thought. "The cops were looking for Edwards and Jeanette at the same time they were hiding out in Great Falls." Another close call for Edwards.

I thanked Theresa for her time. She asked if she could get a copy of Edwards' book, but those were quite pricey. Later, I copied the appropriate pages and sent them to her.

Neal said, "A flash to the past. That was pretty cool. I'm amazed that Edwards used their real names in the book. I can't get over it; it was like being there, 57 years ago. Ed was only 22!"

"He was accomplished by that age. So where do you think he dumped Verna's body? Everyone saw her and talked to her, and then she mysteriously disappears? Listen to what he says in the book about her. It all ends in ritualistic phrasing from the Bible."

"'Now, you listen, sister, and let me tell you something. You and I are going into Jeanette's house and you're going to tell Jeanette with a perfectly straight face that you are my sister—but definitely! And the reason you did what you did was because you don't like Theresa, and you wanted to hurt her. Now, is that clear? Can you just open your dumb trap long enough to pull this off and wait until tomorrow night!'

"'All right,' she sniffled. 'But I won't go along with this one more minute after tomorrow night.'

"'You won't have to, Verna, not one more minute!' When we got home, I said to Verna, 'Start packing everything. That detective as sure as hell is going to check out the car's license number, and he's also going to check me out. You can bet your ass on that. As soon as I get that 2000 dollars from Jeanette, we are going to clear out fast.'

"Verna had everything packed. Because of her condition, I controlled my urge to hurt her physically. I contented myself with brusquely yelling at her for causing me so much trouble; that was the extent of it.

"'Now here is what the setup is. She (Jeanette) wants me to marry her. She suggested going to a friend's house, and stay there for three days.' After dropping (Jeanette) off at home, I returned to the farm, where Verna and I remained for three days. Verna of course was blissfully oblivious. On the third day, Jeanette and her brother picked me up at the farm. We stopped for the results of our blood tests, got a marriage license, and were married by a judge."
* (Metamorphosis of a Criminal.)

"Neal, did you catch that line, 'Verna was blissfully oblivious'? Webster's dictionary describes bliss as, 'The ecstatic joy of heaven.' And then he says, 'On the third day'."

"He is ritualistic, John, and kills repeatedly in similar manner representing biblical passages and mythology. This all goes back to ancient history and the Zodiac."

"Let's go to the courthouse and get their wedding certificate. That will give us specifics as to where he was in October 1955."

We headed to the courthouse with our newest information, went to the archives and found the original wedding application for James Garfield Langley and Jeanette White.

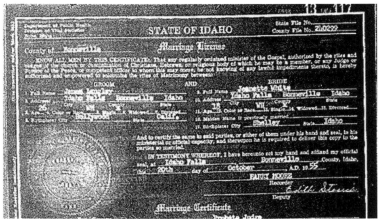

(James Langley (Edward Edwards) and Jeanette White's October 20, 1955 Wedding License)

I pointed out to Neal some of the important info contained in it. "He says he's James Langley, age 26 from Hollywood, California. And they were married October 20th, 1955. That's the date we should use to look for the next murder. Remember Jeanette said they headed towards Chicago."

Neal pointed out, "The book says he got a fake social security card in Jacksonville, Florida under the name James Garfield Langley. There's a reason he lied about Hollywood in the book."

"Well if Ed's lying there's a murder to be found. The Zodiac bragged about Hollywood and having movies made about him. I'm sure there's a reason Ed put Hollywood on that fake ID. He had to have been there before."

"Let's keep following his life back to 1933," Neal said.

Chapter 23
Profile of a Ritualistic Killer

Two years into the investigation and I realized Edwards was a killer far beyond what I had first suspected. Jeanette had confirmed the worst. "He liked killing people. He enjoyed it." She traveled with him from October 1955 until March 1956. Edwards was 22 years old in 1955 but was portraying himself as a 26-year-old doctor from Hollywood, California. He had Jeanette as his wife and had perfected executing couples on lover's lanes in Great Falls, January 2, 1956. He had been killing a long time.

The ruse was incredibly thought out and planned. He would portray himself as a Dr. of Psychiatry, Criminal Investigator for the U.S. Armed Services Division and a preacher. He would create a kidnapping which would bring in the FBI so he could taunt them. He was always under false identity. He mentioned kidnapping 8 times in his book. He said he was a criminal investigator or detective over 10 times, and alluded to be a doctor 24 times. He was describing his M.O.

Using criminal and court records, psych profiles, and the thousands of documents that Cameron had uncovered on Edwards, a detailed timeline came together revealing the horrific crimes of recognition Edwards had been bragging about his entire life.

There was no need for another psych evaluation of Ed Edwards. The Yellowstone County, March 17th, 1956 court-ordered evaluation I recovered in Deer Lodge proved Edwards was a highly intelligent psychopath that married women and used them for his sick criminal activities. Jeanette confirmed it all. He had two other wives later in life that went through the same thing.

Edwards was arrested April 28, 1952 in Jacksonville Florida for burglary, auto theft and suspicion of kidnapping with force. He copped a deal and served a two-year suspended sentence for illegally wearing a uniform.

```
Arrest Date            1952-04-28
Arrest Case Number     11588
Arresting Agency       PAUSM0200 USM PHILADELPHIA
Subject's Name         EDWARDS, EDWARD WAYNE
Charge                 01
Charge                 02
       Charge Literal  ILLEG WEAR UNIFORM
```
(Edward Edwards NCIC Records)

A suspended sentence means he served no time. He cooperated with law enforcement and was given favorable consideration. He continued to travel all over the country using his Marine uniform to kill and get away with it. He got caught again in March of 1955 but escaped April 6th, 1955 from an Akron, Ohio courtroom. He ran free again until he was caught in Montana March 7th, 1956.

```
Arrest Date            1956-03-07
Arrest Case Number     8074
Arresting Agency       MT0560000 SHERIFF'S OFFICE BILLINGS
Subject's Name         EDWARDS, WAYNE
Charge                 01
       Charge Literal  ARMED ROBBERY
```

(Edward Edwards NCIC Records)

That gave him 11 months on the run; everywhere, portraying himself as a married family man with Jeanette and Verna. He killed Verna in Idaho around October 12-17th, 1955. Both women became pregnant with Ed's child but Verna's was killed and he wrote about it in his book.

"Another fellow had been going with a girl and gotten her pregnant. When they both decided they didn't want the child, he attempted to abort it by stabbing her in her swollen abdomen with an ice pick. He was successful in getting rid of the baby and his girlfriend as well." *MOAC

What made Edwards a serial killer like no other is that he used the real names of some of his victims in an autobiography he wrote 13 years after killing some of them.

"John," Neal began, "you're the criminal profiler and much more knowledgeable in this area. We need to start at the beginning to understand Edwards. So far, the Great Falls murder and the Portland murder were both in the book, disguised. So was Verna's. There must be more murders in the book that we don't know about. He liked killing people, and the more sensational he could make it, the more it 'stoked his fires of desire for attention.'"

"Neal, most serial killers have an insatiable appetite for sex and that gets them caught. Ed didn't have that compulsion. His addiction was the kill and the sensationalism. If he thought he might get caught he changed it up. Ed loved the game. He required that whoever was going to catch him was going to have to do the work. He gave it out the last 77 years, but you had to be an out-of-the-box thinker to catch him. He would get his rocks off standing in front of everyone, watching the bungled police investigation. That's why he contacted the press and the police in the Zodiac case—or every case, for that matter. Remember, Edwards made phone calls and sent letters to the press in 2010 to announce his 5 killings in Ohio and Wisconsin.

He wanted the headlines but wasn't going to just stand up and say, 'I'm the Zodiac!' He respected anyone that challenged him. That's why he wrote you back, Neal."

"He and I did connect, that's for sure." Neal admitted. "Here's the next thing, and I think it's huge. Edwards would get his victims to come to him. He was a cop, a doctor, and a preacher. You can't get any more trusting than that. He got access to thousands of victims."

"He would send anonymous letters, giving details of the murder and steering the police toward the obvious. He would have murder cases going on in every corner of the country at the same time. His ability to compartmentalize each crime was incredible. We already know about the setup he accomplished in Portland during the Zodiac killings. It wasn't a coincidence that Edwards got out of Leavenworth in 1967 and in August of 1968 three innocent men are arrested on anonymous tips, letters and false testimony. Those convictions were deemed wrongful in 1977 and they were released. Edwards thrived off being in the middle of courtrooms and funerals, standing in front of everyone. That was his addiction. That is what he meant by recognition." I explained.

The final thing we needed to look for was the religious connection to his murders. Edwards was a ritualistic killer. He made that clear in his book. Quoting, 'And on the Third Day' repeatedly and killing on Sundays, Christmas, Easter etc... This is all satanic worship. Dryman confirmed it all. Jesus rose again on the third day after he was crucified. Edwards rose again on the third day after he has killed someone. The Zodiac was killing slaves for his afterlife. He would rise again through satanic spirituality. We need to start looking for killings that have the following three characteristics:

1) Sensationalism, anonymous letters and phone calls.

2) Wrongful convictions. People serving time and screaming that they are innocent.

3) Religious symbolism taken to the dark side.

"These are the traits we should be looking for," I said. "They will stand out because when something looks satanic, the press goes crazy."

Now on the right path with the profile, we summarized who Edwards had killed so far:

1) Judith Straub and Billy Lavacco in Ohio, 1977

2) Timothy Hack and Kelly Drew in Wisconsin, 1980

3) Dannie Law Gloeckner, Ohio, 1996

4) Verna in Idaho Falls, Idaho, October 1955

5) Patty Kalitske and Duane Bogle in Great Falls, Montana 1956

6) Larry Peyton, Beverly Allan and Wayne Budde in Portland, Oregon, 1960

Edwards had killed 11 people spanning a period of 41 years. This would be just the beginning. He had traveled with Jeanette from October of 1955 until March of 56, killing people. He mentioned her 119 times in his book, detailing everything they had done together, but not using the word murder. They had traveled to Chicago, New York, Atlanta, San Francisco, Portland, and Great Falls, then finally to Billings where Edwards was arrested and went to Deer Lodge. Their entire travels formed a Zodiac cross and circle around the USA creating crimes of recognition.

Chapter 24
Chicago

(Chicago Illinois, October 16, 1955)

Days later, I ran over to Neal's house. "Guess what I found—the murder he did three days before he married Jeanette and you aren't going to believe it. It's the same type murder as the West

Memphis Three triple murder in 1993. Only this one happened in 55."

"What? Those three innocent teens from '93 were just released after serving 16 years."

"I know. Edwards did a murder exactly like the West Memphis Three back in 1955!"

Edwards' book, NCIC records and documented travels led me to one of Chicago's most horrific murders ever. The crucifixion of three Catholic school boys on a Sunday night, and it occurred "three days" before Edwards married Jeanette. Edwards' rise through satanic spirituality and killing before getting married is a rebirth. On the third day he rises again. The crime was horrible. The families were devastated.

Two brothers, John and Anton Schuessler and their thirteen-year-old friend, Bobby Peterson, left home on October 16, 1955. All three were good Catholic boys. Bobby had received a phone call from an unknown male just before leaving. The boys were supposed to be headed to a nearby bowling alley, but ended up going to the Monte Cristo in downtown Chicago. They had never done anything like it before. They had gone to the Garland Building, a downtown doctor's plaza where Bobby Peterson signed the register and went to the 8th floor. The plaza was known to house doctors of psychiatry and was closed for the day, but the doorman remembered the boys coming in, asking to use the 8th floor bathroom. Only Bobby, the oldest, went up. When he returned, he and the other two boys left. They were spotted throughout the day in various bowling alleys and they had enough money to get something to eat. They didn't when they left home and did when they left the doctor's. Whoever Bobby met on the 8th floor must have given them some extra cash.

The last time the boys were seen was around 9:00 pm. One of them was standing on the curb, hitching a ride. The other two were huddled out of the rain. A truck pulled up and one of the boys was heard saying, "Hey Ed."

Three days later their bodies would be found laid out in the sign of the cross, beaten and naked near a ditch bank in Robinson Woods Park. The astrological sign Ursa Major had been carved in the thigh of one boy and the word Bear engraved. Some of the flesh had been removed meticulously with a scalpel.

This is the way the bodies were positioned when they were first discovered.
Photo courtesy of Dr. Richard Ritt

(Photo of Crime Scene, Robinson Woods Park, Chicago, 1955)

As for the crime fitting Edwards? First, the profile was three for three. There was sensationalism, anonymous letters and phone calls. Secondly, forty years after the murder, a man named Kenneth Hansen was convicted and died in prison screaming he was innocent and set up. His conviction was controversial and based on information provided by anonymous informants and letters to the press and police in 1993.

Finally, the Satanic religious connection to the crime. The boys had been beaten just as Sister Agnes Marie beat Ed in the orphanage. *"Sister Agnes Marie then made me walk over to a*

little tree, stand against it, and put my arms around it to hug the tree. She instructed the children to form a line: and each, in turn, would kick me on the backside, and then return to the end of the line. To demonstrate how this was done, she placed the first kick on my rear herself. She was going to break me of my bedwetting, she warned, or kill me in the process."
(MOAC)

    I considered the astrological connection. The killer carved "Ursa Major" the "Big Dipper" into Bobby Peterson's thigh. This astrological sign is considered the Lost Zodiac and spans the dates of August 8th through August 15th. The big dipper never sets below the northern horizon. It has eternity, exactly what the Zodiac sought. Edwards was born June 14th which made him a Gemini, the twins, good and evil. But on August 8th, his mother died, and his name was changed. This new date, August 8th, made him The Great Bear, Ursa Major, The Lost Zodiac. The connection to the Zodiac case was undeniable.

    I felt that the pieces all fit. Now, I had to prove that Edwards bragged about getting away with things in Chicago. A 1975 Chicago Tribune interview of Ed Edwards proved me right.

    "The thinking criminal could get away with it for a life time. It was in Chicago at the Greyhound Bus Station that I first found out I was on the most wanted list. I was waiting for the bus to Norfolk, Virginia, and I went to the newsstand, and there was my picture in True Detective magazine—wanted for double murder. The thinking criminal could go a lifetime without being apprehended if he played it the right way. I spent a year on the most wanted list, something I'm not proud of, but at the time considered it a game. The FBI concentrated its efforts on me because I did things to aggravate them. Because I found out later I was in crime only for the recognition. I wouldn't let the FBI know where I was going, but I wanted them to know I'd been there. I changed cities often and completely reversed habits to throw off what they had on my previous modus-operandi. I found cab drivers to be the most observant people, and many times was confronted by citizens who knew they knew me, but couldn't make the final association of the top ten list."

(Edward Wayne Edwards, Chicago Tribune interview, August 5, 1975)

I got another verification to place Edwards in Chicago in 1955 when I traveled to Oklahoma in 2012 to interview convicted cop-killer Bill Rose, who did time with Edwards and Dryman in Deer Lodge. Rose reminisced in the interview about Edwards being so enraptured with people's gullibility in believing he was a doctor and a psychiatrist. He said Edwards had portrayed himself as a doctor in Chicago before his arrest in Montana in 1956. He had befriended him and was impressed with his intelligence. Rose stated, "I 'd forgotten about this. After Jeanette left Edwards, he was in the infirmary and asked me to get him a knife, so he could commit suicide. I told him he was on his own."

Edwards had used the doctor ruse for many years and at one time had paying clients in Minneapolis.

Now that I could place Edwards in Chicago in 1955, I checked the exact dates. The boys were killed October 16th, on a Sunday night. Edwards married Jeanette Thursday, October 20th in Idaho Falls. Those two dates were indisputable. Edwards had detailed these three days in his book. In "Metamorphosis of a Criminal," Edwards claims to get rid of Verna and after "three days" returns to marry Jeanette. The wedding certificate proves this took place with a justice of the peace on Thursday, October 20th, 1955. The three days that Edwards writes about in his book, claiming to be hiding out on a farm waiting for blood tests, are the days Verna disappeared and the boys were killed in Chicago. Jeanette said he had left with Verna and came back without her.

The Idaho Falls newspaper dated October 21st stated that the wedding reception for James Langley (Ed Edwards' alias) and Jeanette White, for Saturday, October 22nd had been canceled. The reason this was in the paper is that Edwards had grabbed Jeanette a few days earlier, forced her to marry through a justice of the peace, and was heading back toward Chicago to attend the funeral of the three boys he had killed three days earlier.

The Schuessler boys' funeral took place Saturday, October 22. Life Magazine snapped this shot, showing the grieving family weeping before the casket.

(Life Magazine, October 22, 1955)

There is a young man standing near the cropped right-hand side of the picture with his tie pulled down, shirt unbuttoned and collar turned up. It appears his left cheek is swollen. The man has many characteristics of Edward Edwards. The police reports stated that one of the victims had gotten a few good hits on the suspect. Whether or not this is Edwards will be left for someone else to answer.

(Ed Edwards, 1955 - Unknown Male October 22, 1955)

I had always proclaimed from the beginning that Edwards' book was a puzzle of murder, and it was proving to be true.

Chapter 25

Stephanie Bryan

Berkeley, 1955

After reviewing the Chicago case the entire investigation had shifted. Edwards was the killer of Patty and Duane in Great Falls, Verna in Idaho Falls and the poor little boys in Chicago, all in less than three months. Edwards was a serial killer beyond anything we had imagined. Who had he killed before October of 1955?

Neal asked, "Where do you want to go next?"

"Well, let's get back to Jeanette," I said. "The stuff she gave us is incredible. Edwards was running around with her, killing people. They had been to California prior to December of 55. Maybe we can find something else."

"How old was Ed then?" asked Neal.

"Let's see," I answered. "He was born in 1933, so he would have been 22. He claims to be 26-year-old James Langley from Hollywood. Here's another thing I have always felt strongly about. The answer to the Zodiac puzzle would be intertwined with the question 'why.' I understand why Edwards would pick Vallejo, because he was setting Dryman up. But why the score keeping against the SFPD? The taunts, letters and puzzles to the papers all fit Edwards' profile. But why San Francisco? There's that speed bump in the book—that Edwards doesn't want to return to Frisco in 55. Why?"

"We packed our suitcases, nestling the money among our clothes, and headed for Portland, Oregon, by way of San Francisco. When we reached Frisco, Jeanette said, 'Ed, let's stop here for a while. Let's just go out for the evening.'

"'I'd rather not, Jeanette. We've already pulled two robberies in California, and I think we'd better get the hell out. I think if we stay here we'd be pushing our luck. If something happened in San Francisco, they would have us cornered. All the law has to do is block off the bridges.'" *(MOAC)

I reminded Neal, "Don't forget the court detainers for Edwards in Oakland and Sacramento after he went to Deer Lodge in 56. He had been there in 55 before Jeanette, but he doesn't want to go back."

"Why did he think it was too dangerous?" asked Neal. "He must have killed someone. There's no other reason."

"Well, I can certainly check it out," I said. "I've never gone back that far. I've searched San Francisco around the time of the Zodiac, 1968 and after. If Edwards killed somebody in 55, we know it would be spectacular and receive massive 'recognition.'"

I got out my laptop and started plucking away. Neal went to the counter and ordered another round of coffee. He returned about 5 minutes later and looked at me. He had learned to recognize my "bird-dog-on-a-hot-scent look."

"What?" he asked. "You've found something already?"

"There's something big here, really big!" I answered. "This goes beyond case of the month. This looks like case of the century!"

("Body of 14-year-old Stephanie Bryan" Burton Abbott held after body found at cabin)

The investigation took on an entirely new direction in March of 2012, after connecting Edwards to California in 1955. Edwards' ability to set up others and taunt the press was mastered in San Francisco, 13 years before the start of the Zodiac.

On Thursday, April 28, 1955, three weeks after Edwards had escaped in Ohio, 14-year-old Stephanie Bryan was abducted in Berkeley, California at 3:30 pm. She had left Willard Junior High School on her usual walk home. She was the daughter of a well-known radiologist, Dr. Charles S. Bryan Jr. Over a dozen witnesses observed the abduction and subsequent fight with her abductor on Mt. Diablo Boulevard. Three witnesses saw the suspect beating her with a flashlight. That's the last time she was seen alive.

On Sunday, May 1st Stephanie's French text book was found on the side of Franklin Canyon Road in Contra Costa County, north of the Bay area. Then, on May 2nd, a ransom note arrived at the Bryan home.

> "Bryan:
> Don't be Idiotic. This is not a hoax. Don't contact any law enforces if you expect to see your ~~daughter~~ Girl in the near future.
> Your instructions are on Tuesday, May 3 have 8000 to 10,000 no less than 10000 in 5-10-20. Wrap it in a small box then wrap the box in brown paper. 9:30 p.m. Go to the T and D Theatre be in the last row of the television lounge at 9.
> There you will be contacted. Give the box to your contact. He will give you instruction. Follow them and you will reach your child.
> Don't Contact anyone it will take the package a while to reach me but your child will be okay if you follow Instruction. If the man that contact you in the Theatre is followed the Instructions won't do you any good. Wear Brown HAT. Put Pipe in mouth don't drive your car I have my reasons for waiting before Contacting you. Things HAVE BEEN CAREFULLY Planned So Don't be Foolish"

(May 2, 1955 Ransom note mailed to Dr. Charles Bryan (Recreated))

The police followed the instructions of the note and nobody appeared to pick up the ransom. The family prayed Stephanie was still alive and pleaded for her safe return. The ransom note was followed by several mysterious anonymous calls. Three days later a second note arrived.

> 5-5-1955   2nd Note Received
> "You tipped law wise up They can't help you only I can. You will get instructions."

(May 5, 1955 Ransom Note (Recreated))

During the month of May, the Bryan family begged desperately for the release of their daughter and offered a reward. With the advent of television, the paper press learned quickly that gore sells. The newspapers had to compete. The Bryan case was all over the front pages of the San Francisco Examiner, Chronicle, the Vallejo Times and other Bay area newspapers. Reporters from opposing papers competed for the scoop. For two months they had nothing new to report, but the crime was still selling papers.

Then, on July 15, 1955, they had to print extra copies. Burton Abbott and his wife, Georgia, phoned the police with a remarkable discovery. Abbott's wife had gone to the basement and discovered a red purse containing the I.D. of Stephanie Bryan, a red wallet and other possessions. When she brought it to her husband, they called the police to inform them of their find. Arriving in minutes, the obvious question was asked, "How did this get in your basement?"

Burton Abbott became the prime suspect in the kidnapping and abduction of 14-year-old Stephanie Bryan. The press surrounded him.

It had been two and a half months since Stephanie was last seen alive. Abbott was of similar stature as the kidnapper seen fighting on Mt. Diablo Boulevard. He also had a similar car, a 1949 Chevy. There was one big problem. Abbott was a disabled veteran attending the University of California Berkeley, studying to be an accountant. He had no violence in his past and had recently had surgery. Evidence was found buried in his basement. He was subjected to brutal interrogation and press scrutiny after the discovery of Stephanie's items in his house. Then, on July 17th, Abbott issued the following statement to the press and it was printed word for word in the Oakland Tribune and San Francisco Chronicle.

"I have not the slightest idea how these things got down there. I never buried the things; never saw the purse and I haven't seen the other things yet. I do not know who could have put them there. I know I don't have to submit to a lie detector today but I want it gotten over with. My conscience is clear."

He submitted to a lie detector and passed. He then released the following statement as to his alibi on the day Stephanie Bryan was kidnapped. It was airtight.

Burton Abbott Typed Statement to the Press, July 18, 1955

"On last April 28, a school spring vacation. I decided to go up to our family cabin in Trinity County. I left my home in Alameda, driving my old Chevrolet sedan, at about 11 a.m. I drove across the Carquinez Bridge and up highway 40 to Sacramento, thinking to stop at the State Land Office there to find out something about our cabin property for my brother, Mark.

It was about 2 p.m. and I could not find the office, so I drove back to the Davis junction and turned north on highway 99W. I stopped near Dunnigan to have lunch at Bill and Kathy's Place, a roadside restaurant next to a service station. I was there about a half an hour and then drove to Corning where I stopped for gas at a Shell station and went in the restroom. Then I drove on and stopped at about 5:45 p.m. at a place south of Red Bluff and ate dinner at a roadside restaurant.

Later, I continued the drive and at the nearby Beegum junction I turned into the dirt road leading to the cabin. A sign there said the bridge was out but indicated that it would be in use after working hours. So, I continued on, crossed the bridge on planks. A flagman was there watching it.

I went through Beegum and Platina and stopped at a tavern in Wildwood. I stayed there 20 minutes talking to a man at the bar named Cox. Then I went on to our Cabin which is situated right on the road. I had not been there all winter and so I checked over the outside to see its condition. Snow was still on the back porch six inches deep. I went to bed the following morning, April 29, 1955."

All the details checked out. Stephanie had been taken at 3:30 and by that time, he was 200 miles north near Red Bluff.

Stephanie had a nursing book with her when she was taken. Edwards detailed meeting Stephanie Bryan, a junior high student, in his book and placed the time around May 1955. He called Stephanie Laura.

"I met Laura, a student nurse. Nurses were always more than attractive to me. She still had a year and a half of nursing school. She was auburn- haired, freckled and pleasingly feminine. She'd been a virgin when we met, and felt particularly close and loyal to me, since I was the first man who'd ever made love to her.

(Stephanie Bryan, age 14)

"Two days later, I followed her and took a large apartment across the street from the hospital. My new job was driving a truck for a soda pop company. Laura and I had sex at every opportunity. The next day at work, I had a violent argument with my boss, and was fired. By this time, I was tired of Laura and had found a new girlfriend. Verna was seventeen, small, dark-haired, and good-looking. We took off traveling to various cities. Did some scams and stopped in Idaho Falls, Idaho. Verna was two months pregnant by this time." *(MOAC)

One of the books Stephanie was carrying when kidnapped was a student nursing book. Her dad was a radiologist at the hospital. Edwards was portraying himself as a doctor, grooming his way into the lives of his victims. He had made himself known around the university. His alias was Dr. Jim Langley.

After Edwards kidnapped Stephanie, he teased the family with hopes of her safe return by mailing several ransom notes. Even though Stephanie was already dead, he claimed to be holding her for ransom which is what he did in the JonBenet Ramsey case. After the police searched for three months, letters started to arrive.

The first on July 16th, 1955 was a post card to the Berkeley police from the killer. It depicted the San Francisco Golden Gate Bridge. Cameron recovered it from the Berkeley Library archives in 2012.

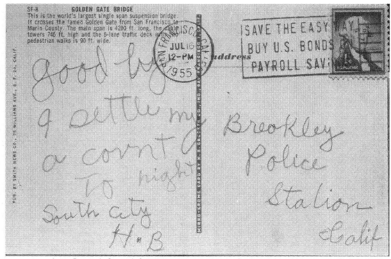

(July 16, 1955 Post Card Sent to Berkeley Police Department)

The post card was sent three days before Edwards planted the body of Stephanie Bryan at Burton Abbott's cabin. This card would tie Edwards to the Zodiac killings just by its very content. The handwriting matched. It was the Zodiac killer's first "Count" he was so famously known for.

Zodiac 13 SFPD 0

On the day after the card was sent, Edwards contacted the San Francisco Examiner and lead the paper to the body of Stephanie Bryan. He had planted it on a hillside across from Burton Abbott's cabin in Trinity County, California, at Dead Man's Cabin (named for a prior murder there). He planted it the day after the police had searched it to make them look like fools. It worked, and Abbott was arrested.

Next, Edwards sent an anonymous letter to the press detailing how the ruse worked.

"According to the astrological horoscopes of Stephanie Bryan and Burton Abbott, she had been under surveillance by her abductor for some time. He lay in wait for her at various times until she became familiar with his being there.

In her chart it shows that she was destined to die at the hands of someone whom she trusted and had become infatuated with, only in a platonic way...This secret love not only caused her sorrow but also her life... (Nurse Letter, Burton Abbott Trial, 1955) Edwards continued to taunt police with letters. He sent another letter that was termed, The Melody Letter. It described the last few moments before Stephanie's abduction.

"I am writing this letter as I have thought about this since Burton Abbott was accused of the murder of Stephanie Bryan. I have fought with my conscience against my home. I have twin daughters and...my husband works at night. I met a man some time ago who was a friend of my husband in the Army. On April 28th I met my friend in Oakland, near Berkeley at the Claremont Hotel. We were to meet at 4:15 for a cocktail and then go to dinner and then home. I was early so I strolled around. I walked up some steps and a path with bushes at the side. Then I came near the end of this path but stopped. I saw a young girl with saddle shoes on talking to a young man about 25 or so I guess, and they walked up toward a car—he behind her. I turned and walked back to my hotel." (The Melody Letter, October 1955)

Like the Shreveport, Louisiana, Letter Edwards sent in the JonBenet Ramsey case, police begged for Melody to contact them, but she never did. It was a hoax. It detailed how Stephanie walked with her kidnapper to the car and got in. She went willingly.

More letters arrived; this one was called the Domestic Worker Letter. It also is purportedly from another anonymous woman.

"April 28 was my daughter's birthday. I work near the Bryan home and was on the way to take a cake and a present and ice cream from where I work to get the bus to my home for a surprise party for my girl when I meet the little Bryan girl coming out of the path I was returning in. We stoped and talk like we did when we always meet and I showed her the cake. I saw your name in the paper and that you were the FBI man." (Domestic Worker's Letter, Berkeley 1955)

This letter was Edwards giving the details as to how he groomed Stephanie. The day of her abduction, she had removed 10 dollars from her piggy bank so she could purchase something for her father's birthday. She was killed on his birthday. In the letter, there was one word misspelled—stoped. It meant Stop Ed. Edwards bragged repeatedly for decades that the first crime he ever committed involved the taking of a birthday cake in the orphanage. He was beaten severely for it and it was the beginning of his sadomasochist behavior.

One Sunday afternoon, one of the boys had a birthday. His mother had brought him a round chocolate layer birthday cake. I wanted some of the cake, but he wouldn't give me any. I made up my mind that that evening I would get the cake and eat it all. How sweet was my revenge!

"Ed, did you take that cake?"

"No, Sister, I didn't take it."

"You're standing there lying to me. You'll go to hell for that!" She grabbed hold of me and proceeded to beat me on my back, my head, my arms, my legs—anywhere she could land her stick. When I broke down and admitted I stole the cake, she stopped beating me, and turned to the other boys and said: "Boys, I'm going to my room for five minutes. If you think this lad should be punished for breaking the Seventh Commandment, that's your business."

As she walked out of the room, several of the boys jumped on me. They beat me wildly, kicked me, and called me a thief. I wasn't strong enough to fight back; in desperation, I determined then and there to run as far away from that 'prison' as I could. And if I were caught I'd run away again—and again—and again. I would continue to run away until I escaped. I was determined to throw off this horrible life. Nothing would stop me. *(MOAC Ed Edwards age 7)

Stephanie had become infatuated with Jim Langley, the good looking, 22-year-old college student, from Hollywood. Edwards groomed her into trusting him and hung around the university at Berkeley, where Stephanie's father was a doctor and her mother a nurse. He had promised to meet Stephanie at 3:30 to deliver the birthday cake for her father. Stephanie had brought the 10 dollars and Edwards had lured his victim once again to come to him. As he got her inside the car, she realized something was wrong. Witnesses saw her fighting in a 1950 Chevy speeding off on Mt. Diablo Boulevard with a guy matching Edwards' description.

Another anonymous letter arrived from Cleveland, Ohio, August 15th, 1955. By this date Edwards had set up Burton Abbott, fled California and was headed to Idaho Falls with Verna.

"Just read paper short account of murder Stephanie, asked help on some info re Delbert Cox. You see, twenty five years ago, my father, Archibald Delbert Cox, disappeared. At that time he worked here in Cleveland for Ohio Bell Telephone Co. Now since the name Delbert isn't very common, I thot per chance it may be my dad. Look up Cox's background. You would make a very old lady, who still awaits word of her son, very happy, even tho this man may not be him. My grandmother has spent money and time for 25 years looking for him. This may sound very unkind, too, sir, but if this man is my dad you can be assured his word is not worth a dime in court of law." (August 15, 1955 handwritten letter from Cleveland, Ohio, to District Attorney Coakley.)

This letter was mailed from Edwards' hometown of Cleveland, where Parmadale Catholic Orphanage is located. It was a parable on Edwards' life of being raised by his grandmother, Annabelle Meyers and not having a father. It was another clue to look towards Ohio for the answers to Stephanie's abduction.

Burton Abbott was convicted of killing Stephanie Bryan in January of 1956. Edwards was hiding out in Great Falls at the time. He left Great Falls with Jeanette and went to San Francisco where he mailed a letter to the judge in the Burton Abbott case. The letter was post marked San Francisco, February 7, 1956. It threatened if Burton Abbott was executed, the Bay area would pay the price.

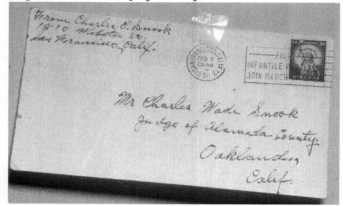

SAN FRANCISCO
FEBUARY 4th 1956

Judge of Alameda County
Charles Wade Snook

Dear Sir

Mr Snook you had better give Burton Abbott more time than one week. As you an the Twelve Juors are standing or sitting close to a Bomb. In fact if Burton Abbott is to Death row at San Quintin. You an the twelve Jury men will not be here to convict another not guilty man. Why in Hell dont you get the guilty? You Damn Fear you know that Burton is not guilty. You had better get more aquinted with Feromon. I can get Twenty Thousand peapels that will swear that your going to have the wrong man sent to the gas chamber.

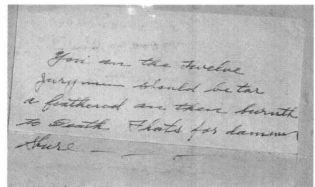

(Judge Snook Letter and Envelope, February 6, 1956)

The letter and envelope matched the many dozens of styles of handwriting that Edwards provided law enforcement for 60 years. It also matched letters sent to Neal and myself in 2010. The bomb threat in the letter was written 13 years before Edwards later threatened that he had a bomb and sent in a map of Mount Diablo in the Zodiac case.

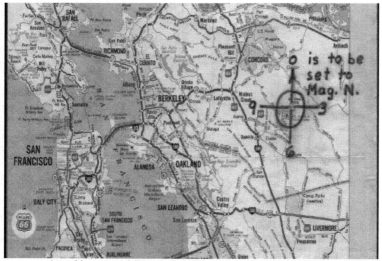

(Zodiac Killer's 1969 Mount Diablo Map)

The last place Stephanie Bryan was seen fighting with her abductor was in a 1950 Chevy on Mount Diablo Boulevard. Edwards owned a Chevy as did Burton Abbott. After killing Stephanie and setting up Burton Abbott, Edwards got rid of his 1950 Chevy and wrote about it in the book.

"In Minneapolis I took the '50 Chevy to the car dealer and traded it in for a new 1956 Pontiac convertible." *(Ed Edwards MOAC)

This writing was positive proof of the Zodiac connection to Stephanie Bryan's case, and the Zodiac was Edward Wayne Edwards. Edwards traveled from Great Falls, Montana in February of 1956 to San Francisco with his wife Jeanette. He mailed the letter, returned to Montana and got caught March 8 for robbery. Nobody knew who he was in California. Nobody really knew who he was in Montana. He went to Deer Lodge Prison, and on March 15, 1957, Burton Abbott was executed.

Keith Walker is a well-known writer from Santa Rosa, California, who wrote a book called, "A Trail of Corn." The book detailed the setup and execution of Burton Abbott. It was written with the cooperation of Burton's Abbott's mother, Elsie Abbott, who fought until her death in 2004 to prove her son's innocence. The 1957 picture of her after her son's conviction tells it all.

Keith Walker was contacted by me in 2012 and provided all my case material. It was Keith's tenacious 40-year investigation that proved Edwards killed Stephanie Bryan and Burton Abbott was innocent.

Edwards became the judge, jury and executioner in 1955 and continued to set up innocent people until his death. Burton Abbott's appellate lawyer wrote a very telling letter to Keith Walker about the case and Burton's innocence.

LAW OFFICES OF
GEORGE T. DAVIS

**POST OFFICE BOX 2411
KAMUELA, HAWAII 96743-2411
TELEPHONE (808) 885-3500
FAX (808) 885-3836**

SAN FRANCISCO OFFICE 415/928-5960

April 24, 1995

Keith Walker
4969 Hoen
Santa Rosa, CA 95405

Dear Keith:

Thanks for sending me the manuscript of your forthcoming book on the Burton Abbott case.

My immediate reaction is that your book is very accurate and is the result of extensive research and careful cross-checking.

As set forth in your book I was not the trial attorney for Burton Abbott but because of my serious doubt as to his guilt I made a rather unusual effort to contact the Governor on television on the day Abbott was scheduled to die and to request a stay of execution, which of course was denied.

Your detailed description of what happened on that day between myself and Governor Knight is so graphic and well-written that when I read it, it made my hair stand on end.

Now that I've read your entire book I'm convinced more than ever before that Burton Abbott did not commit the crime for which he was executed by the State of California in the gas chamber at San Quentin.

I believe your book is a valuable contribution to the law in many ways and the fact that it is written in the style and form of a murder mystery adds to its appeal.

I hope this letter will be of some use to you and if there is anything else I can do to be of help, please let me hear from you.

Sincerely yours,

GEORGE T. DAVIS

GTD:jb

Keith Walker's book on the execution of Burton Abbott was released in 1995, and one year later, Edwards killed JonBenet Ramsey in a similar fashion as he had done to Stephanie Bryan.

Burton Abbott and Ed Edwards were of similar stature, age and had similar cars. A 1950 Chevy Edwards sold after killing Stephanie Bryan.

(Photos - Burton Abbott   Edward Wayne Edwards)

There was way more to the book, "Metamorphosis of a Criminal," than I had ever suspected. Edwards was telling of murders he did, but he made it a puzzle. I asked Edwards in a phone conversation how much of the book was accurate. He replied:

"The book itself, a good....oh, 95% of it is correct. There's a lot of things not in there....for example, when I was on the FBI 10 Most Wanted List, some of my very very best friends every Friday and Saturday night, were cops."

From his escape in April of 1955 until his capture in March of 1956, Edwards created crimes of recognition THAT HE PLACED IN THE BOOK, covering California, Illinois, Montana, Nebraska, Idaho and Oregon. He killed 8 people in those 10 months.

Chapter 26
Marilyn Sheppard, 1954

By mid-2012 I made the decision to tell the story of Ed Edwards in a different manner. Writing a book was not something I was known for. Writing police reports and affidavits was something I knew inside and out. Edwards had killed in every decade of his life since he was a teen and the story would only get convoluted if every murder were talked about. The decision was made to stick to the murders he placed as a puzzle in his book for now.

I proceeded backwards, to before April of 1955. Edwards was free to kill from October of 1953 until his capture in April 1955. The next murder of recognition he committed was in the book and fell right into place.

On July 4, 1954, Marilyn Sheppard, the wife of Dr. Sam Sheppard, was brutally murdered in the bedroom of their home in Bay Village, Ohio, on the shores of Lake Erie. Dr. Sheppard, a prominent Cleveland doctor, was asleep in another room at the time. Marilyn was 4 months pregnant. The two had spent the night entertaining friends. Around 3:30 a.m., an intruder snuck into the house and savagely beat

Marilyn to death while Sam slept on the couch. Sam heard his wife scream and ran to help, only to be knocked unconscious. When he awoke, he saw a male running through the yard. He gave chase but was attacked by the suspect. Three hours later he came to on the shores of Lake Erie. He returned to his house and found Marilyn lying in bed, face mauled and her legs spread open. Sam Jr. was still asleep in his own bed.

Sam Sheppard became the prime suspect. He denied any involvement in the murder, describing the killer as a man with puffy hair on top, as if it stuck up in front.

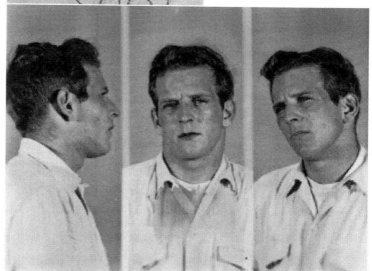

(Composite of suspect, Edward Edwards, 1955)

The similarities in this case to Edwards and the Zodiac were undeniable. Marilyn had curved wounds on her mauled face. Months later, an anonymous tip led police to a mysterious flashlight found in Lake Erie near the Sheppard home. The flashlight was thought to be the murder weapon. A flashlight was used by the Zodiac, a flashlight was left at JonBenet's, and a flashlight was suggested as a murder weapon in the Chicago triple slaying. The July 4th date is the anniversary day of the Zodiac killing in Vallejo in 1969. Flamboyant young defense attorney, F. Lee Bailey, represented Sam Sheppard in his appeal in 1966, after his conviction for killing his wife. The Zodiac demanded in a phone call to talk to F. Lee Bailey in 1969.

"This is the Zodiac speaking. I want you to get in touch with F. Lee Bailey. If you can't come up with Bailey, I'll settle for Mel Belli. I want one or the other to appear on the Channel Seven talk show. I'll make contact by telephone." (Ed Edwards,1969.)

The Sheppard murder had become a national obsession and was particularly exploited in the Cleveland newspapers. As in the Zodiac, the editor of the paper played a large role in Sheppard's conviction, claiming him guilty even before his arrest. Edwards had just been released from Chillicothe Prison 9 months before he killed Marilyn Sheppard. He detailed his release date in this letter he sent to the FBI in 1993.

The arrest record I have at this time is as follows.

```
5-30-51  Daytona Beach, Fla.  B&B-GL  Suspended Sentence
4-24-52  Phila., Pa.  ITSMV-Illegal Wearing  2 years, Fed. Referal,
                      of Uniform.           Chillicothe Rel.10-4-
                                            53.
```

Edwards was released from Chillicothe on October 4th, 1953 and moved to Medina, just a few miles from Cleveland just before the killing. He wrote about meeting Marilyn Sheppard, placing it at the right time of the murder. "Barbara" is Marilyn Sheppard.

"Although I never really understood what love was, I was engaged many times in my life, especially after my release from Chillicothe. I found engagement rings opened doors to bedrooms. I purchased several engagement rings on time, and repeatedly presented them as tokens of my love, only to demand them back when I tired of the girl. One ring had been worn by four different girls. I enjoyed playing Casanova. Lying was easy for me. At a cafeteria two doors away from the store, I met a girl named Barbara. She was a well-built, auburn-haired girl, with a lovely personality. I truly liked her. She was the mother of an eight-month-old girl. She was a challenge. I set my sights on persuading her to leave town with me, something a girl in her position shouldn't have even considered. One night, I awakened from a sound sleep to find her missing. 'Barbara, where are you? Barbara! Are you in the bathroom?' No answer. I waited anxiously with the lights out, until about 3:30 in the morning when a taxi drove up. Barbara tiptoed silently into the house and slipped smoothly into bed. I waited silently for 30 seconds. Then I said:' Why are you being so careful?'"

Barbara: "Oh, my God, you certainly scared me!"

Ed: "While I was worrying over how to get rid of Barbara, she had provided the perfect excuse. I pulled her over to me and put my hand between her legs. She was damp."

(Marilyn Sheppard, July 4th, 1954)

"I'll tell you something right now, Barbara. In the morning, when you get up, you can pack your things and the child's. I was talking loudly and roughing her up, but I really didn't want to hurt her. We'd been close, and I had enjoyed her baby. I was mad but in control. The next morning, I wasted no time in putting her on the bus to Denver."

Every detail of her murder was put in the book, but he changed it to make it appear she was the one sneaking in. Marilyn Sheppard had been killed at 3:30 in the morning on a Sunday. She had been pulled by her legs, just like Edwards had described in his book. Edwards went on to describe the day of the week he had his last conversation with Barbara after he "put her on the bus."

Ed: "Around 11 the following evening, I received a long-distance call from Denver."
Barb: "Ed, what are you doing?"
Ed: "I'm just sitting here, Barb."
Barbara: "Ed, are you really mad at me?"
Ed: "Yes, I am. I think you did me wrong."

Barbara: "Why don't you come to Denver, and let's start all over again?"

Ed: "I tell you what, Barb. Let me think about it for a couple of days. Give me a call Sunday afternoon."

Barbara: "Will you think about it, Ed?"

Ed: "Yes, I promise. You call me back Sunday afternoon and I'll give you my answer."

Barbara: "Okay, I'll call Sunday. I love you, darling."

Ed: "I put Barbara out of my mind and went about the business at hand."

M.O.A.C.

Edwards had detailed the killing of Marilyn Sheppard in his book. He placed the correct day and time of death as a clue. By repeating the word Sunday three times, it was a hint. He had done the same type of hint in the chapter titled, "Juggling Women," when he repeated the phrase, "on the third day." Everything in the book is a puzzle of murder.

Neal stated, "John, it's amazing you found all of this in the book. Did you get the doctor connection? Dr. Sheppard's medical bag was discovered in the hallway ransacked and scalpels missing."

"Neal, a scalpel was used on the three boys in Chicago to remove the skin from the inner thigh. That happened a year after Marilyn! Ed would have had the scalpel."

I contacted Sam Sheppard Jr. to inform him of my findings. He was 4 years old when his mother was killed; he is 66 today. He remembers it like yesterday. His father was destroyed by it and died shortly after his release. Dr. Sheppard had served 10 years by the time F. Lee Bailey got him out of jail. It was one of the biggest miscarriages of justice in U.S. history."

"John," Neal said, "you got it! This is incredible. We have to go back in his book and research every one of the women. It looks like Ed started killing long before 1954! Aren't the cops interested in this? Shouldn't they be forming a task force or something? He has killed dozens over a 50-year-period and nobody seems to care!"

"Neal," I said with frustration, "they haven't cared since we began. I think we now know why. I know cops and I know when they 'circle the wagons.' Edwards pulled it over their eyes repeatedly, in every jurisdiction. There is no way a cop is going to come forward and say, 'Yup, we were wrong.' It doesn't happen. They don't want to open up Pandora's Box."

"Maybe we can be like Woodward and Bernstein with Watergate, and the press will force the issue," projected Neal.

"Don't count on the press," I said. "He pulled it over their eyes, too. We are going to have to break it. Like I said, it will take years to decipher what he has done. No pun intended. Psychiatrists will be studying Edwards for decades. There's never been anyone like him. I swear he is the 2013 revelation of Satan. What's crazy is how we've been led. We could have stopped last year when we knew he was the Zodiac. He is so much more than that. No one yet has had even a glimpse of the entire picture."

"Ed kept telling you in the letters 'Don't write your book, John. You don't know the whole story. I have lots more to say. Just hold off.'"

"Every letter was a puzzle, Neal. I am sick of this. How many more murders do we have to delve into?"

"We should take one more look at Ed's beginning," Neal said. "It looks like I might have been right about him shooting his own mother at age 5."

"I never wanted to go there, but you were right. We need to go back to his birth and track every year in his book. I was looking at unsolved murders in the 40's, and found a peculiar one in Chicago, 1945."

"Let me know what you find out," muttered Neal.

I knew how to find the bodies, but the stories were heart- wrenching. I wasn't sure if

Neal could take another. I decided we needed a break. "Neal, I gotta take care of some stuff, let's meet again tomorrow."

Chapter 27
The Early 50's

"Neal," I said. "I think we now both realize that 'Metamorphosis of a Criminal' is a complete confession to murder. Everyone said the Zodiac wouldn't leave this earth without revealing how clever he was. He was revealing something much more primal than murder. He wanted to be challenged to reveal the deeper meaning of it all. That's what the book is; a challenge, a puzzle. Figure out the clues, look at the dates, and look at 'Where I was.' It's all there. Stephanie Bryan, the three boys in Chicago, Verna, Marilyn Sheppard, Great Falls. They all fit exactly as in the book. One murder in the book would be considered a coincidence, not eight. Edwards was smart and exclaimed loudly that he committed all crimes except murder. He left the reader thinking he wasn't such a bad guy. I figure there are a lot more murders that we haven't found."

"Page 127 begins the chapter on Barbara," I stated. "No doubt, she was Marilyn Sheppard. Edwards concludes the prior chapter by heading to Denver. He is just released from Chillicothe Prison, and states he is 21, but this is another spot that falls under the 5 percent rule that's not quite true. We both know when Edwards lies, someone was murdered. NCIC has Edwards leaving Chillicothe, October 4, 1953, at the age of 20. He relays of being 'chopped by a sleazy pin-curled blonde' and being taken for 32 bucks. He is quite affronted to be, 'beat at his own game.' He was in Denver when this happened and I think I found the murder."

On April 6th, 1954 the unidentified nude body of a beautiful blonde girl, who was strangled and beaten, was found near a creek dumped on the side of the road in Boulder, Colorado. The community rallied around her and erected a memorial to the unknown victim. The stone memorial stands today. In 2006, her remains were finally identified. Her name was Dorothy Gay Howard.

(Dorothy Gay Howard Memorial, Boulder Colorado)

I continued, "From the timing, the book, and her picture and manner of death, I think Edwards is the killer. He was there when it happened and fled to Cleveland to kill Marilyn Sheppard 3 months later. This is also an early link to Boulder and JonBenet. I informed the Boulder Sheriff's Office. Working backwards from Dorothy Gay Howard, Edwards was in Chillicothe from April 25th, 1952 until October 4, 1953. I recently researched the time period just prior. From June of 1950 until he went to Chillicothe in 52, he was free to roam. Ed joined the Marines June 20, 1950, one week after his seventeenth birthday. The Korean War broke out 5 days later. Ed wanted to kill. After completing 6 weeks basic training he is informed he can't see combat until he's 18, so he goes AWOL August 4. This date coincides with his mother's death anniversary. It was the height of McCarthyism and the papers were full of people being arrested, interrogated or accused of being a Communist.

After going AWOL, Edwards ran around the country for 8 months, finally getting caught in Jacksonville, Florida May 31st, 1951. He was charged with burglary, auto theft and illegally wearing a uniform. He fessed to being AWOL, admitted his real name and informed them of being only 17. Officials are shocked! He is turned over to the military police and on August 22nd, given a dishonorable discharge.

I commented, "This is really suspicious right here. He's been AWOL for eight months, he gets caught for three felonies and they let him off. That doesn't make sense. It stinks. Between August 1951 and April 1952 Edwards is free to run and kill again."

Neal asked, "What do you think was going on?"

"He's a rat." I responded, "Edwards was portraying himself as an agent for the Criminal Investigation Bureau of the U.S. Government. He was arrested in the uniform. He was committing serious felonies while using assumed names and false credentials. Using his military uniform, he was his own foreign faction like he said in the JonBenet Ramsey note. So, from 1950 until 1954 there was only about 18 months he was locked up. The rest of the time he was killing."

"All right," Neal concluded. "That gives me a good picture of that period. It's clear that Edwards was a highly intelligent psychopath at age 17."

"It probably started earlier. We need to go over the timeline of his entire life."

We decided next to take a look at Edwards when he came out of Leavenworth in 1967. This was the time frame of the Zodiac. Once on parole, he was free to kill again.

I told Neal, "There's a part in the book that caught my attention. Edwards complained of being pent up while in Leavenworth. He's nervous about getting out and I don't think he waited until the Zodiac to start killing again. I want to look into this thread and see what I can find."

Neal said, "Call me when you find something."

A few weeks later, his phone rang.

Chapter 28
Edwards Gets Out 1967

When Neal answered, I instructed him to grab his copy of the book and come on over. Neal greeted me with his usual barrage and it took a few moments to get him calmed down before any conversation could ensue.

"It's his book, Neal. It's got all the answers. It goes miles beyond what we originally suspected. Let me lay it out. To start, the copy you bought was inscribed:

'To Patrolman Ken Carver, Please read this book with an open mind and remember that it is written as I lived my life. I do hope that this book will help you in some way with your work.'

Obviously, Edwards handed this book to Officer Carver as a taunt. He meant it literally—writing to a cop that the book is of some help to police work. We know that was true now. I found something in the book that proves that point beyond anything else we have discovered."

"Early in the book, Edwards introduces a Catholic Service League worker named Mr. Robinson. Edwards chides this man for lying to him. The man succeeded in convincing Edwards to walk into the Catholic reformatory in 1948 without a court order, and trapped Edwards when he was 16 into a two-year sentence into a horrible reformatory at Valley Forge, Pennsylvania. It was Edwards' first reformatory lockup. The name change in the book was deliberate. He was leading the reader to look at the name Robison and the time frame of 1968, just before the Zodiac started."

(The Robison Family 1968)

On July 22nd, 1968 near Cross Village, Michigan, a family of six was found executed in their summer cabin. Through the Freedom of Information Act, I had obtained the entire police investigation of a case known as The Good Hart Murders. The crime was the worst in Michigan's history. I spent weeks pouring over police reports, photographs and news articles, interviewing surviving relatives. The case was unimaginable.

The Robisons were headed on a planned vacation to Kentucky and Florida on the day they were murdered, June 25th. Almost a month passed before the crime was even discovered. The mother and father had been killed with two shots to the head. The 7-year-old daughter Suzie had been brutalized with a claw hammer. The victims were ritualistically laid out throughout the house and the cabin door was locked from the inside. A note was left by their killer on a window near the entrance.

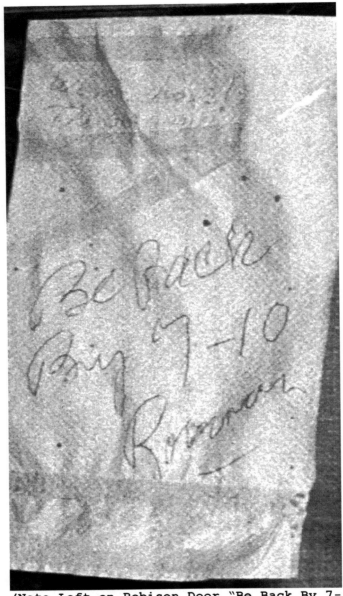

(Note Left on Robison Door "Be Back By 7-10, Robison")

Mr. Robison was the owner and editor of Impressio Magazine, a popular monthly movie and entertainment publication. The family was Lutheran and Richard was a member of the Masons. The Robisons were well off and raised their 4 children in a loving, healthy environment. They lived in Detroit, but spent summers on Lake Michigan near Good Hart and Crossover.

The original investigation meticulously documented that sometime in April of 1968; Mr. Robison began dealing with a mysterious man only known as Mr. Roebert. He was described as a prominent, wealthy tycoon from Canada, who claimed to be the head of the Superior Table, an international organization working toward world peace. No one besides Richard Robison had ever actually met Roebert. An exhaustive police investigation was conducted, and the Superior Table's existence never verified. Police found Superior Table documents in Mr. Robison's property after his death, describing the structure of the organization.

> **Superior Table**
>
> Mr. Roebert
> Sylvia***
>
> Mr. Richard
> Joyce - Joe
>
> Mr. Joseph
> Betty
>
> Mr. Martin
> Gail
>
> Mr. Thomas
> staff
>
> Mr. Peters
> Pam
>
> The above shows the chain of power as decided by Mr. Roebert, Chairman and Director of the Superior Table...the govern power of this world wide organization which is souly set on complete peace and unity among all countries of this Earth.
>
> Each of the above mentioned directors will receive a complete organizational break-down from Computer Headquarters.
>
> If you have any questions, please direct them through the proper channels.
>
> Thank you,
> Sylvia–Secretary to Mr. Roebert ***
>
> cc: Mr. Richard ✓
> Mr. Joseph
> Mr. Martin
> Mr. Thomas
> Mr. Peters

(Document Recovered by Police from RobisonFamily Murder, Good Hart, Michigan)

The documents listed Mr. Roebert as the Chairman and Director. The names of the other organization members were listed as Mr. Joseph, Mr. Martin, Mr. Thomas and Mr. Peters. These names were all connected to Catholic saints. Edwards was Mr. Roebert and he left a letter at the scene implicating that Mr. Robison had written it to Mr. Roebert. Under the EBE in Roebert are three strange dots. These dots also appeared in the above Superior Table document. The highlight was the initials EBE.

IMPRESARIO ... Richard A. Robbins 6/17/03 1:00 PM

Dear Robert (my father)

I'm most honored and pleased with the message given me by "Steamboat Joe" this morning. I have it where we decided and have instructed for not to allow me to "drop my wallet". Also - if something (how?) almost happens to me to take the entire wallet and pass it "up" to where the proper people would know what to do with it.

Please forgive me for writing so many words to you. I should not take

---

IMPRESARIO ... Richard A. Robbins 2.

your precious time over anything but important matters. In the future when Joyce arrives I'll be sending far better, more easily-read messages.

Ted Surveyor, Jr. (Exec. Editor) and Ernest Halbert (the educated idiot) (and Managing Editor) drive cars. Ted - the Mustang and Ernie - the Thunderbird.

Ernie - with his increase, was told his own allowance was included - so he could make his choice as to ease at his own expense... or buy. In one day he bought a '65 Thunderbird. Ted, when told, also, that his new wage included his auto,

---

IMPRESARIO ... Richard A. Robbins 3.

quickly stated his "Mustang" was still very good... and he was happy.

Now... a favorite story of mine was the one where a fellow arrived at work excited about the "tremendous" collision that must have taken place on the company's corner earlier. No one was aware of it... but he insisted a Mustang and Thunderbird had to have hit, head on 'cause there were feathers and hairs (manure) all over the place.

Now... It should prove, in the future, most interesting to see whether we have

---

IMPRESARIO ... Richard A. Robbins 4.

a similar mess strewn about the halls of ole Impresario' over Ted, the Mustang and Ernie, the Thunderbird. It will be interesting to see if wonderful "Steamboat" has a keen sense of smell.

Now, I promise, I'll stop writing selfishly and stick to more and cleaner facts in the future. Anyway, by the sound of your voice, you sketch is to the point where you no longer require "trivial humor."

I thank God for you, father,

Your son, always,
Richard

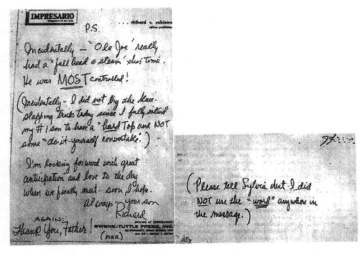

(Letters to Robert from "Richard")

The entire writing was a parable written by Edwards as to what happened to the Robison family and eventually Mr. Robison's partner, Joe Scolaro, who became the prime suspect in the case and killed himself in 1975 as the police were hounding him for years.

Edwards got out of Leavenworth prison just months before the killings. He detailed the Robisons picking him up at the airport.

"I was met at the airport by my friends, the Winthrows. After treating me to a delicious steak dinner, they took me home with them. I was still having sporadic attacks of the shakes and still had to fight the recurrent, terrifying feeling that I'd wake up at some point to find out that I had dreamed up the whole release episode."

The investigation showed the Robisons were supposed to pick up Mr. Roeberts at the airport on the day of their demise, June 21, 1968. Mr. Robison had met Roebert in San Francisco June 14th, 1968, which is Ed Edwards' birthday. Mr. Robison handed the phone to Roebert when they were in San Francisco and Mrs. Robison spoke to Roebert. Nobody had ever met Roebert except Mr.

Robison. Edwards went home with the Robisons using the name Mr. Roebert. He sat down to dinner with them, played cards and then jumped up and killed every one of them. He speaks of a confrontation with one of the younger Robison boys in the book.

"I was positive the plane was going to crash. Overcome by my neurosis I requested a seat change so I could get as close to the emergency exit as possible. Just as I started to relax, a kid about 13 years old was fiddling with fate. I was paralyzed with fear. I swear that kid almost had the door open. Wasn't that something? Locked up all those years, finally freed and then some stupid kid almost destroys my life trying to be smart." (*MOAC)

Randy Robison, the young teen, almost got away. Randy was found down the hallway and he wasn't shot. He died from multiple traumas to the face and head. He was beaten to death. The killer did the two youngest last, after shooting Mom, Dad, Richard Jr., and Michael. All the biggest threats were executed first, with two shots to the head. Just like Patty and Duane were shot in Great Falls. The two youngest were most likely asleep when the shots were heard and awoke to the massacre, only to be chased down and brutalized with a claw hammer.

I continued, "Edwards had conned his way into the Robison family within months of his release from Leavenworth. This is where all the ties start coming into JonBenet Ramsey. Remember in the Ramsey ransom note when Ed wrote, *'We are a foreign faction. We respect your bussiness but not the country it serves.'* Well, he wrote that the Superior Table was a worldwide organization devoted to world peace when in fact it was just Edwards conning a rich editor of an arts and entertainment magazine. JonBenet was actually garroted with a paint brush and then smashed in the head. Seven-year-old Suzie Robison was also smashed in the head with a claw hammer."

Mr. Robison believed he was about to be rich. Mr. Roebert had promised millions in an international computer headquarters located out of an airport in Michigan. The con had been so carefully planned that Mr. Robison even kept it secret from his closest business partner, Joe Scolaro. Police never could find Mr. Roeberts or any other viable suspect, so they tried to pin the whole deal on Scolaro. After all, "Who else could have possibly done it?" they maintained. Scolaro committed suicide a few years later leaving a note proclaiming innocence of any involvement in the murders. My years on the force prove that such final notes are almost always truthful. Why lie on your way out?

"Mr. Robison had promised everyone in the company they would soon be filthy rich, giving them all raises just before he was killed. Roebert would be flying into Good Hart on June 25th to take them to Kentucky and Florida. Mr. Robison was going to buy a condo on the beach and look at some race horses."

I told Neal, "In the book, he calls the Robisons the Winthrows and describes being picked up at the airport that day. The murders occurred that night after supper, around 9:00 pm. That is when 5 to 8 shots were heard by neighbors. A deck of playing cards was found scattered on the floor of the cabin. The Robison family had been playing cards before their execution. A Saint Christopher medal was found. Crudely engraved on the back of the medal was the following:

"Richard — To my chosen son and heir — God bless you — Roebert."

The medal was not Richard's and the killer had placed it around his neck. Underneath the letters ebe in Roebert, the killer placed three dots, highlighting those letters. The killer also left a 5-page letter purported to be written by Richard Robison praising Mr. Roebert, using the term My Father when greeting him as if Roebert was God-like. Police have always tried to identify the author of this letter. Some experts said it was written by Mr. Robison, but the letter was written by the killer—Edward

Edwards. Dots again were placed under the letters EBE.

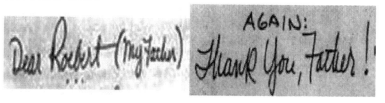

(Letters Greeting and Ending)

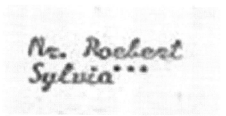

(Superior Table Memo)

"EBE," mused Neal. "Here's something. Did you know that in the first Zodiac crypto there were eighteen unexplained characters, EBEORIETEMETHHPITI. Interesting that they start out EBE. Anyway, we have anonymous letters, taunting cryptic messages and an editor of a magazine being targeted and killed 6 months before the Zodiac, and Ed put it all in the book!" Neal excitedly concluded.

"Exactly," I said. "That takes me to my next point. Some investigators have maintained there was a Zodiac connection to this case even back then, but most dismissed the theory as too far-fetched. You are going to love this!

"The Detroit Free Press put up a reward fund and tip line to help solve the crime. An informant wrote them saying he had information, but in order to get it they had to place a classified ad. They ran it in September of 1968 and again in January 1969, but there was never a response. Here's the ad."

DR GUIDINI: Your prescription

good. However, need additional.
-Zodius
Detroit News, September 1968

"John, this is incredible!" exclaimed Neal. "He signed it Zodius. The first Zodiac killing was in December 1968, just 4 months later and he wrote the press demanding they print his Zodiac cryptos or else."

"Once again," I said, "it all points to Edwards and the Zodiac and it's all in the book. He describes having dinner with the Robisons, playing cards. He described how the 13-year-old almost got away. He mentions being picked up at the airport for their planned trip to Florida and Kentucky. Edwards had strong connections to both Florida and Kentucky. The bodies hadn't even been discovered and Edwards is running to Kentucky and Florida with his new wife Kay. That is exactly where the Robisons were headed."

I commented here, "Did you notice the similarities to all of Ed's murders? A suicide, the religious connections, the deliberate placement of the bodies, stacked like the Chicago boys. Mrs. Robison was laid out like Marilyn Sheppard and she was covered with a blanket like JonBenet. The letter he left was intended as a clue. There's a lot more connections, Neal; this all happened in Northern Michigan. Guess who has a summer home in the same area 20 miles away? The Ramseys! They were headed there the day JonBenet was found dead in their basement in 1996. Suzanne Robison was the same age as JonBenet. She had been laid out like JonBenet, only stacked on top of her brother and her other brother on top of her father. Even little Suzie's head was smashed like JonBenet's."

"Everything fits like a glove, John. Sensationalism doesn't even begin to describe the killings. Letters to the press, phone calls, and a 6-page rambling letter left as a clue, ties to Christianity. This matches every point on our profile of Ed."

"The final point is—the killer took a couple of items. He took Robison's watch and his wife's expensive wedding ring. I obtained pictures of the watch and I have a picture of Ed wearing a watch similar in 1970."

(Edward Edwards Left Hand, Omega Watch, 1970)

Edwards' ability to con people was unsurpassed by any criminal Cameron had ever dealt with. The Superior table and Mr. Roeberts was just another con, manipulating the editor and publisher of Impressio Magazine months before starting the Zodiac killings.

Police spent most of their time trying to identify Roebert. Nobody knew his first name and nobody had ever heard of the Superior Table. Police concentrated on a group based in San Jose, California, that used similar symbols as were left on the notes and at the scene of the Robison murder. The group is known as The Supreme Temple, an ancient order that follows a philosophy against Christianity. They are a secret society. Some investigators were convinced that whoever wrote the Roeberts letter had been involved in such an order. The order was founded in late medieval Germany. Its logo symbol was called the Rosy Cross. Some of the symbols associated in the cross are found in the Zodiac ciphers.

(Rosicrucian Rose Cross)

Neal interrupted. "John, that contains some of the Zodiac cryptogram symbols. Do you realize what a Superior Table is? A magician's prop. It's the table he uses to pull the rabbit out and deflect the audience's attention."

I responded, "I had no idea, but that is exactly what Edwards did his whole life. This order was into magic, allusions and the occult."

Neal noted, "Four months after killing the Robisons, Edwards began killing in the Zodiac case. In between, police arrested three innocent men in Portland, Oregon for Edwards' 1960 Peyton-Allan lover's lane murders. A month after killing the Robisons, Edwards roared into action. He had crimes of recognition going on in Michigan, California, and Oregon — all at once — between 1968 and 1970. The Robison family murder has remained one of the most controversial unsolved crimes of modern times in the Midwest. I find it interesting that there was a Zodiac link to the Robisons and you discovered it, once again by following Edwards' life. Just like the Stephanie

Bryan case, we didn't try and figure out who killed the Robisons. His book led us there."

Chapter 29

The 70's

August 7, 2012

They decided to follow Edwards after the Robison killings and the Zodiac, which put them into the early 70's. By then, Edwards was 37 years old with 3 kids and a wife, running all over the country claiming to be a rehabilitated criminal. Kay stayed at home in Akron taking care of the family, while Ed had conned his way into the University of Ohio and was teaching with faculty. He traveled the entire length of the country preaching that he was an authority on crime. Many college professors, high schools, junior highs and police academy officials were fooled. During this time, he was preparing to release his book. His autobiography was written and handed out to people that heard him speak. Neal had a copy and in it were testimonials.

COMMENTS

As a criminologist on the faculty of the University of Akron, I have often utilized Ed Edwards' services. I have had Ed talk to many of my criminology classes concerning his experiences and feelings, both as a criminal and now as a conventional member of this community.

He, consistently, has done an excellent job and is very well received by my classes and equally well by other groups he has spoken to on this campus.

Carl A. Bersani, Ph.D.
Associate Professor
of Sociology
* * * * *

You are doing a wonderful and important job, and you have a way of communicating with young people.

Henry P. Briggs, Jr.
Western Reserve Academy,
Headmaster
* * * * *

We were quite impressed with your philosophy of life and needless to say, feel you have a real message for the young people of today.

Duane Bachman, Principal
Bath Local Schools
* * * * *

The Student Executive Board at Canton South High School would like to convey the thanks of the entire student body to you for your presentation at our assembly.

The applause was tremendous and you are most deserving of it.

Martha J. Cook, Advisor
Student Executive Board
* * * * *

Your talk to our group was really thought provoking and timely. The message that you can give to those of us who are parents is especially important because you have the facts.

Rollin S. Reiter
Canton, Ohio
* * * * *

We really like your honesty and great manner of speaking to us. I learned a lot from it and I am sure lots of others did too. You really cleared up a lot of misconceptions we had about the law and life in prison.

Diane Pergl
Bedford Heights, Ohio
* * * * *

I had the privilege of hearing your remarks on TV and was impressed by your desire to influence young people against crime and drugs.

Allen K. Smythe
Cincinnati, Ohio
* * * * *

It is my pleasure to thank you on behalf of WKYC-TV for your invaluable help on our community affairs programming. We are grateful for your assistance in the public service program entitled SCENE ON SUNDAY.

Neal A. Van Ells
Vice President and Gen. Mgr.
* * * * *

I have heard several comments on your program, and they have all been very good. The students at the high school were very impressed with you and several of them have asked if you would be back in the Logan area soon.

Marv Smart
Logan, Ohio Police Dept.
* * * * *

(Testimonials on Edward Wayne Edwards, 1970-71)

The next set of horrific murders that I located was the 101 Santa Rosa Hitchhiker Murders, from 1971 to 1974. Someone was killing teen girls and dumping their bodies. Edwards had been in California talking to junior high schools. The testimonials proved it. One was from 12-year-old Jennifer Kanis from Pleasant Hill,

California. She was the same age as many of the victims.

> I truly admire someone who could rehabilitate from such a life of crime. I thought that the way in which you told your story was very interesting and I enjoyed it very much.
>
> Jennifer Kanis
> Age 12
> Pleasant Hill, California

* * * * *

(Testimonial Documenting Edwards' Timeline in California)

I had been contacted by a surviving victim of Ed Edwards. She provided her account of a terrifying ride with Edwards in 1974 when she was 12. Edwards matched the description of every detail she had provided.

During the 70's, law enforcement and the press were confused as to whether or not the Zodiac was still alive. There were still a lot of killings of young women going on along the 101 Highway and the Zodiac was sending letters claiming responsibility for some. The Los Angeles Times received a letter on March 13, 1971 which was the same time Edwards contacted the San Francisco Police trying to put the Zodiac on Frank Dryman.

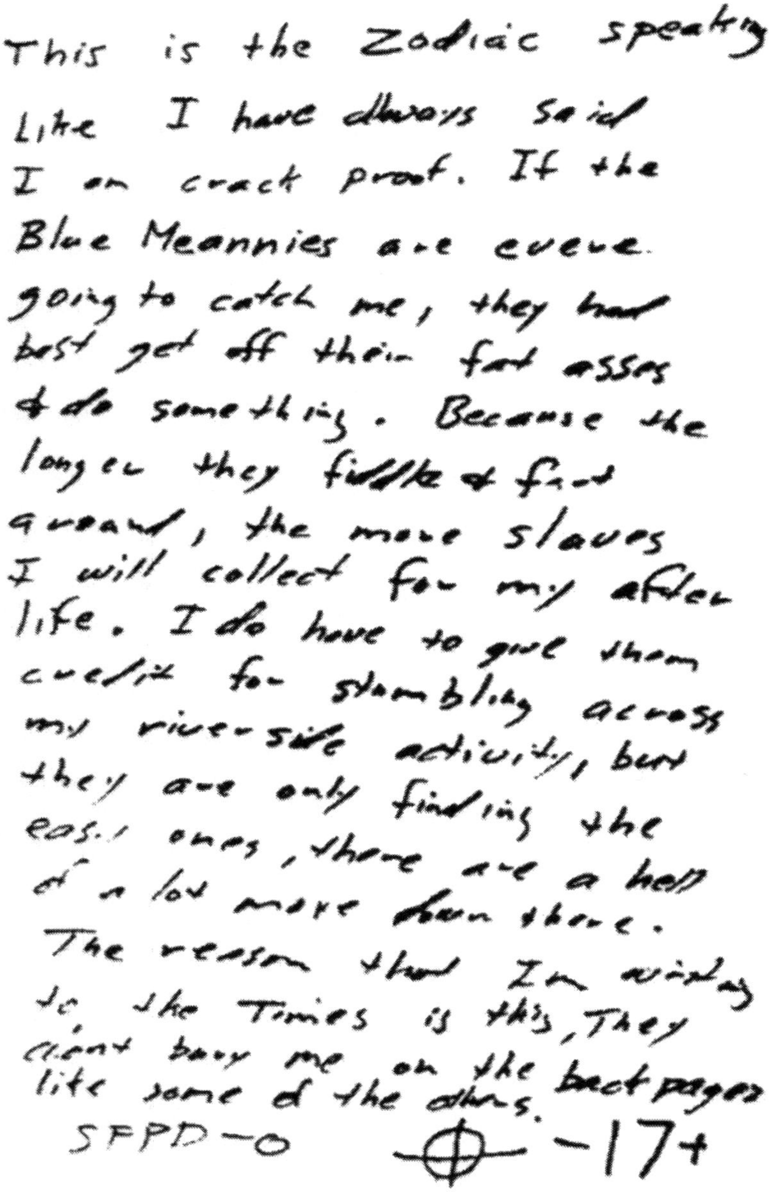

This is the Zodiac speaking
Like I have always said
I am crack proof. If the
Blue Meannies are evere
going to catch me, they had
best get off their fat asses
& do something. Because the
longer they fiddle & fart
around, the more slaves
I will collect for my after
life. I do have to give them
credit for stumbling across
my river-side activity, but
they are only finding the
easy ones, there are a hell
of a lot more down there.
The reason that I'm writing
to the Times is this, They
don't bury me on the back pages
like some of the others.
SFPD—0   ⊕—17+

(Edwards sent the "Exorcist" letter on January 29, 1974.)

> I saw + think "The Exorcist" was the best saterical comidy that I have ever seen.
>
> Signed, yours truley:
>
> He plunged himself into the billowy weve and an echo arose from the sucides grove
>   tit willo   tit willo
>   tit willo
>
>
> Ps. if I do not see this note in your paper, I will do something nasty, which you know I'm capable of doing
>
> Me - 37
> SFPD - 0

(March 17, 1971 Zodiac Killer Exorcist Letter)

Edward's daughter, April, had told me that he had forced his kids to watch the Exorcist when it came out. Edwards kept the public guessing by changing up his writing and adding to his count. In 1971 he was claiming 17 kills, by 1974 it was 37. Our investigation so far had uncovered 11.

> YOU Were WRONG I AM NOT DEAD OR IN THE HOSPITAL I AM ALIVE AND WELL AND IM GOING TO START KILLING AGAIN
>
> Below is the NAME AND LOCATION OF MY NEXT VICTIM But you had Better hurry be cause I'm going to kill Her August 10th at 5:00 P.M. when the shift change. ALBANY is Nice Too!!.

(August 1, 1973 Albany New York Zodiac Letter)

Neal pointed out, "In 1973 It was concluded the Zodiac was either dead, incarcerated or in a mental institution, because no one had heard from him. No one believed he had just stopped killing. That's what the first part of this letter refers to."

I interrupted excitedly, "This also fits with Edwards! Kay told me he broke his back during this time and he was in the hospital, laid up for 6 months. That letter is no hoax. It was Edwards. After Ed appeared on 'To Tell the Truth', he went to Albany to promote his book and do a radio program, 'Dialing for Dollars.'"

LEE LEONARD, host of the television show "Dialing for Dollars" in New York City and ED EDWARDS.

(Ed Edwards, New York, 1973)

Neal continued, "August 4th is the anniversary of the troubled times during his mother's death. People had trouble accepting the Albany letter as being authentic, because it was mailed from Albany, New York. Now, we can put Ed there at that time."

Cameron interjected, "You know what else? There is an Albany, California in the Bay area—the heart of the Zodiac killings. This is just more smoke and mirrors by Edwards with truth intertwined. Albany is right between the Stephanie Bryan case and the Highway 101 murders. Just days after mailing the Albany letter, Edwards was back in California promoting his book. That reminds me of another article I got from Edwards' stuff. It definitely places him in Redwood City in the summer of 1973."

Peninsula Living

Post Office Box 5188
REDWOOD CITY, CALIFORNIA 94063
Teleph

AUG 4 1973

Crime

than mere nostalgia would suggest.
—John A. White

* * *

"METAMORPHOSIS OF A CRIMINAL," by Ed Edwards (Hart, 449 pages, $5.95).

Here's the autobiography of a fast-moving, smooth-talking thief, check forger, holdup man, God's gift to females and bank robber who — after two jail terms — has reformed.

His childhood was most unhappy; he says lack of love developed in him a rebellion toward authority along with a compelling demand for attention. And this he gained during the next 22 years as an artist at every kind of crime imaginable except murder.

In 1962, at age 29, he was nabbed by the FBI and sent to Leavenworth. He came under the influence of firm but kind officials, and something hap-

[for numerous ladies].
Edwards tells his story candidly, simply, honestly — although some hunter does like to hear want of something, so more explanation of a would confuse his credentials.
Although the book heavy, it does leave on unanswered question — what is it like to be a —D.W.

(Redwood City, California, August 4, 1973)

We read the article together. I exclaimed, "I never actually read this before. Can you believe what it says?"

327

"His childhood was most unhappy: he says lack of love developed in him a rebellion toward authority along with a compelling demand for attention and this he gained during the next 22 years as an artist at every crime imaginable except murder."

"Can you believe what he just told us here? An artist at every kind of crime, except murder. Yeah, right! Compelling demand for attention? And this he gained for 22 years? Unbelievable. This is the closest thing I've ever seen to a confession, and he flaunted it in front of everyone. That shook me up, Neal. I think we need to get back on subject."

I returned to the timeline. As the mid-seventies approached, Edwards had 5 children. April, his oldest, was 8 years old by 1977. She recalled her dad taking them to the scene of a double murder in Ohio. In 2010, Edwards confessed to this lover's lane killing to get the death penalty. She described her dad burning down home after home, then fleeing with the family and living in campgrounds, under assumed names. They were not allowed to contact friends. At times, they didn't know where they were. Ed dragged them around everywhere, running to and from the police. By the end of the 70's, Edwards was once again out of control. He couldn't stop killing. Like a meth addict, he was hooked on murder. He stated it in his Zodiac calls and letters. "Please help me, I can't stop myself!"

We were discussing this subject when I remembered, "Oh yeah, I've been meaning to tell you. I found another news article about Edwards speaking at a church camp. He was promoting his reform and encouraging youth not to turn to a life of crime. What a hypocrite!"

I showed Neal the article.

Co. Youth Retreat Scheduled

Ed Edwards, a reformed criminal, will be coming to the Huntingdon County Youth Retreat at Camp Kanesatake, Spruce Creek on Saturday, July 30 and Sunday, July 31.

Edwards will be the main speaker at the retreat, telling of his experiences in prison and in life. A bank robber, Edwards was at one time on the FBI's list of "ten most wanted criminals" and spent 14 years in five prisons.

He is now a writer and a respected citizen, author of "Metamorphosis of a Criminal." He is married and the father of five children, and will soon be making a film based on his book.

The retreat is open to all young people age 12 or older.

MIKE SPECK   LINDA GARNER

SS Officers Meet; Cite Teen Winners

(The Daily News, July 1977, Huntington, Mount Union and Saxton, Pennsylvania)

Neal read the article. "John, did you catch the date? This is exactly one week before he killed Lavacco and Straub in Ohio. These kids from the church camp look just like the victims."

(Billy Lavacco and Judith Straub, killed August 8,1977 Silver Creek Park, Norton,Ohio. Edwards confessed and was sentenced to life for this crime in 2010)

"I can't believe it. He's preaching reform to young kids in Pennsylvania and travels within a week to Ohio, killing two kids 300 miles away. I thought by '77, he was done promoting reform and the book, but the hypocrite is using it to find more victims. He even says it's gonna be turned into a movie! He probably fantasized about killing the church camp kids before he found the ones he killed in Ohio. Psychiatrists are going to have a field day with this. Travel and kill, leave immediately, and return later to steer the cops elsewhere. It's no wonder he was never caught. Remember that quote in the book about him impersonating a psychiatrist? He really knew how to fool people."

I surmised, "This documents his M.O. He portrays himself as a trusting official, establishes an alibi in one area, and then travels long distances to murder somewhere else. He definitely knew psychiatry. There is no way anyone could make the connections. He used his family as an alibi and they didn't even know it. It almost seems as if Kay Edwards was hypnotized the entire 43 years."

"Well let's move on to the 80's in the timeline. Didn't Edwards get arrested in Atlanta sometime around 1982?"

"Yes," I replied. "From 1982 to 1986 he was locked up in Butler, Pennsylvania. He was convicted for arson. Ed Burns. Hmmm, Ed Burns. It kind of goes with EBE, Edward Burns Edwards. I like it."

Chapter 30
The Occult

Edwards was released from prison in Butler, Pennsylvania, June 1986. His family moved nearby while he served his term. They stayed in the area until 1989.

On October 12, 1986 Edwards started killing couples on lover's lanes in Virginia, just south of Pennsylvania and near FBI and CIA headquarters. The murders are known as The Colonial Parkway Murders. Some of the victims were left with items clutched in their hands just as Edwards had proclaimed in his Atlanta Zodiac letters.

The Colonial Parkway was a well-known secluded area for gays. The victims had been approached and killed using rope, knife, and gun. He drowned some, took others from the scene and placed items in their hands, leaving fake clues for the police. All the cases remain unsolved. Just like Atlanta and the young blacks, he selected a sensitive group that would stir the public. Here are the victims.

1986, October 12, Colonial Parkway, VA. Cathleen Thomas, age 27, Rebecca Dowski, age 21.

1987, September, Wythe County, VA. David Knobling, age 21 and Robin Edwards, age 14.

1988, April 9, Colonial Parkway, VA. Cassandra Hailey, age 19 and Richard Kall, age 19.

1989, October, Colonial Parkway, VA. Anna Phelps, age 18 and David Lauer, age 21.

Edwards killed the first couple on October 12th. He had killed Paul Stine, the cabbie in the Zodiac case, on the night of October 11th. Edwards killed near this date because of its connection to Alleister Crowley, the 19th century magician, poet, famous for starting the occult. He claimed to have been contacted by a divine figure in Egypt in 1904, which provided him "The Book of Law", a puzzle book divided into three sections. The third section of the book was to bring on a new spiritual evolution of humanity after 1904. Edwards admired Crowley and studied The Book of Law. It was the foundation for his life of killing. Edwards felt he had his own laws just as Crowley did.

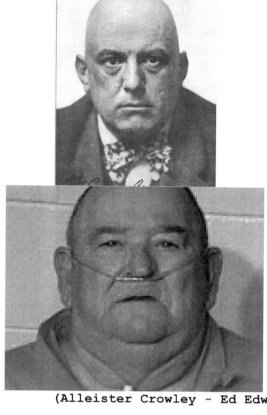

(Alleister Crowley - Ed Edwards 2009)

Neal interrupted, "Three sections? A book of puzzles?"

"Yeah, sound familiar?" I asked. "Crowley is referred to as the Great Beast, 666 or Horus. Horus was considered Satan in some ancient Egyptian beliefs. The 'Book of Law' was Edwards' source of 'science fiction' when he referred to it in his autobiography."

"This demented individual showed an overwhelming interest in science fiction and Egyptian literature. He believed that anyone he killed would be his slave in his next life."
*MOAC

Edwards had obsessed with Satanism, science fiction and ancient Egyptian history his entire life. He had found the solution to his next life and it was killing people for their perceived sins. He was a Satanist taking everything he had gone through in the Catholic orphanage and mirror imaging it with the Devil instead of Jesus. That is why his puzzles contained the letters in his name, in mirror image.

Chapter 31

The West Memphis Three and the 90's

By the end of the 1980's, some of Edwards' kids were old enough to understand things were not normal. April had described a horrid childhood when I spoke to her in 2010. She was the oldest daughter, born March 31, 1969. David, the oldest son, was born February 15th, 1970 and John was born September 23, 1971. All of them were conceived during the Zodiac killings in San Francisco.

(Kay and Edwards with 3 kids)

The picture was taken in 1972 when Ed appeared on several television game shows touting his rehabilitation from a criminal to a family man. April would make the call 37 years later that led police to her father. By the 1990's April had moved away.

The 1990's brought Edwards into the digital age of media. He found a tool for more recognition. Cable TV was in its prime and murder sold 24/7. Many of his killings were the basis for books and films that had been selling for years. The Zodiac had bragged that he was waiting for a good movie to be made about him, but the movies about his murders had already been made. Nobody knew who the killer was. Edwards was supplying details to editors, ghost writers and producers, attempting to sell his stories of murder. They were well written because the killer himself provided the details.

The Satanic crimes of the 80's and early 90's were creating media hysteria, with Edwards making a major contribution. TV producers and the press exploited the sensationalism and it generated revenue. Geraldo Rivera and others propagated the stories. Edwards was creating ritualistic crimes of recognition. Invariably his killings mirrored others. The ultimate example occurred in 1993 when Edwards crucified three 8-year-old boys in Robin Hood Hills Park in West Memphis, Arkansas. He had groomed his way into their life, lured them to the park, beating them exactly like he did to the three boys in Chicago in 1955. Edwards mimicked his murders over and over again.

(Paradise Lost cover)

Edwards' major film debuted in 1996 as the HBO documentary "Paradise Lost, The Robin Hood Hills Murders." The use of the Zodiac sign throughout the credits, and the arrest of three innocent teens for the crime was a red flag.

From 1993 until 2011 Hollywood promoted the HBO documentary and followed the lives of the three innocent teens incarcerated for 18 years for an Ed Edwards murder.

The details of the crime were shocking.

On May 5, 1993, on a full moon in West Memphis, Arkansas, three teens were found beaten and drowned on a ditch bank behind a local truck stop. The three 8-year-old boys were stripped naked, tied up and drowned in a canal. The skin from one of the boy's penis had been surgically removed. Another had been beaten severely in the face. They were dumped naked, bound by black and white shoe laces by the hands and feet.

Cameron had suspected Edwards of the crime after recovering a 1993 letter sent weeks after the murder, taunting the FBI with his identity. The letter was a follow-up to a call Edwards had placed.

Edward Wayne Edwards
P.O. Box 541
Claridon-Troy Rd.
Burton, Ohio 44021
(216) 834-1970

FBI-I.D. Section
Room 10104
10th. St. Penn. Ave. N.W.
Washington, D.C.
20537-9700

July 9, 1993

Dear Privacy Act Agent,

In regards to my phone call July 2, 1993, I am writing in hopes of obtaining all of my CRIMINAL and HISTORY records from your office and the FBI field offices in the following cities. My reason for mentioning these cities is at one time I had either committed crimes there or was there long enough to have an FBI file put together on me.

(1) Arizona, Phoenix and Tuscon.
(2) California, Oakland and Sacramento.
(3) Colorado, Denver.
(4) Florida, Jacksonville, Lakeland, West Palm Beach and Key West.
(5) Georgia, Atlanta.
(6) Idaho, Idaho Falls.
(7) Indiana, Indianapolis.
(8) Minnesota, Minneapolis.
(9) Montana, Billings and Great Falls.
(10) Nevado, Reno and Las Vegas.
(11) New Mexico, Las Cruces.
(12) North Carolina, Wilmington.
(13) Ohio, Akron and Cleveland.
(14) Oregon, Portland.
(15) Penn., Allentown, Erie, Butler, Philadelphia and Pittsburg.
(16) South Carolina, Columbia.
(17) Texas, Houston and Dallas.
(18) Virginia, Norfolk.
(19) Washington, Seattle and Spokane.

The arrest record I have at this time is as follows.

5-30-51 Daytona Beach, Fla. B&B-GL Suspended Sentence
4-24-52 Phila., Pa. ITSMV-Illegal Wearing 2 years, Fed. Referal,
         of Uniform. Chillicothe Rel.10-4-53.
3-11-55 Akron, Ohio B&L Escaped jail; returned, Nollied 4-28-59.
3-7-56   Billings, Mont. Robbery 10 years; Rel. 6-2-59
6-25-59 Portland, Org. Assault & AR 5 years probation.
5-18-62 Cleve. Ohio Bank Robbery 16 years. Rel.8-20-67

(1993 Edwards' Taunting FBI Letter)

The similarity between the 1955 triple crucifixion in Chicago and the 1993 case were undeniable. Two triple crucifixions, 38 years apart, by the same killer.

The Chicago boys were killed in Robinson Woods Park. These boys were killed in Robin Hood Hills Park. In both triple child murders, the victims were Boy Scouts that had been lured out on a school night. The parents were frantic when their kids failed to return at a reasonable hour. The wounds in both cases were said to have been caused by a stick or shovel handle, leaving a strange, curved or crescent-shaped pattern.

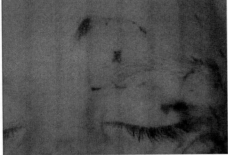

(Wounds of Christopher Byers May 5, 1993)

Edwards was acting out the beatings he took as a child on his victims. After death he stamped the cross in the middle of the irregular circle on the victim's forehead. The Zodiac circle and cross, or S.B.T.C., 'Signed By The Cross', just like the signature of the Zodiac and the signature left on the JonBenet ransom note, Edwards stamped his victims after they were dead and left confusing marks and signatures. This allowed for EXPERTS to come forward and claim "I know what caused the wound." This type of testimony resulted in many wrongful convictions over Edwards' 66 years of killing.

In the West Memphis case, Edwards groomed his way not only into the victim's lives but also into HBO and Hand to Mouth Productions. The media outlets were doing a documentary on the case, filming a scene December 19, 1993, when Edwards conned a cameraman and got himself injected into his own murder mystery, standing over the grave of the victim while the parents wept. The chapter title of the documentary was "First Christmas."

(Ed Edwards, HBO Documentary, 1993 Edward Wayne Edwards, 1994)

Edwards was taking his murders to the bank and was about to reap the rewards. In the film he is holding the murder weapon, the cane, and two one-dollar bills displaying OSIRIS' eye and the Egyptian Pyramid on the back of the dollar. This was three years before he killed JonBenet Ramsey on Christmas. Edwards wore a fake beard, big glasses, and a hat as a simple disguise in this film.

I contacted the film producer, Joseph Berlinger and challenged him with his findings. He told me the man in the clip was a serial killer named Edward Wayne Edwards. Berlinger promised to review the clip. I followed up with another phone call a few weeks later. In the phone interview, Berlinger told me, "I have no idea who that man is, and more so, what that clip is even doing in my documentary! I always thought it was odd that the cameraman chose to break away from the parents who were grieving at the time." Berlinger refused to answer any further questions from me.

Douglas Cooper, of Hand-to-Mouth Productions, filmed the scene on Sunday, December 19, 1993. I attempted to contact him, but Cooper chose not to respond. Cooper had received a knife purportedly from John Byers, the victim's father on the day of the filming. He took the knife back to HBO in New York. Producers Bruce Sinofsky and Berlinger became very concerned about having it in thier possession. The knife displayed blood and Cooper insinuated that Byers had been acting suspicious. What was really going on was: Edwards was trying to set up the victim's father.

During the trial of the three innocent teens, the defense attempted to prove Byers used the knife, shifting the blame to the parents.

Edwards' cane would make all of the characteristics of the wounds. The half-circle wounds, the star pattern, the 1-1/4" diameter. If that cane had a Ferrell on the bottom, it would have caused the 4-pointed wound pattern on the forehead of the victim.

On Christmas of 2010, Edwards sent Neal a Christmas card with the following biblical reference.

"Truly, Truly, I say to you—he who believes has eternal life. Unless you eat the flesh of the Son of Man and drink His blood, you have no life in yourselves. He who eats My flesh and drinks My blood has eternal life, and I will raise him up on the last day." John 6:47 NASB.

Edwards had removed flesh and blood in both the West Memphis Three case and the 1955 Chicago case. This explains why there was no blood at the scene of either and their flesh was gone.

In August of 2011 all three innocent men known as The West Memphis Three were released only on the condition that they accept a guilty plea to get out of prison.

Chapter 32
1945, The Beginning
September 2012

The investigation was surpassing two years. Neal and I had stated repeatedly, "It's a good thing we didn't stop 'here' because we didn't even know about 'this there'..." Edwards himself had said, "Don't publish your book yet, there's so much more you don't know...."

We had established a meticulous timeline of Edwards' life dating back to when he was released from reform school in the late 40's at age 17.

I asked Neal, "How much further do you want to go? The killings are countless, he never quit."

Neal answered, "When we release our findings, I think the floodgates will open. People will remember things, dates, phone calls, letters, maybe even Ed, all pertaining to unsolved murders that have no answers. There is one last place we need to look. It reminds me of Hannibal Lecter in 'Silence of the Lambs.' He told Clarisse, 'You need to go back to the beginning.'"

(Fortunately, this proved to be true as many have come forward after the publishing of

"It Was Me" providing countless leads and new directions. Information and connections continue to pour in and I am compelled to investigate them all. Once this book is published I have no doubt that that work load will become overwhelming if I am unable to get better assistance from law enforcement and private investigators.)

We went back to the book and started once again. Edwards wasted no time establishing the book as not one hundred percent truthful. He claims he was born Charles Murray, yet he was born Charles Edwards Myers, after his grandfather. He also claims his mother died in December of 1935. He would've been only two at that time. I proved otherwise, producing his mother's death certificate with the August 8th, 1938 date, making Edwards five. His mother had been shot on August 2nd and lingered until August 8th. She was buried August 11th, in a Catholic cemetery.

I explained, "He was adopted by Fred and Mary Edwards and they changed his name from Charles Myers to Edward Wayne Edwards. That in itself is suspicious because he was named after his grandfather. Why didn't they want a connection to the family name? My guess is something horrible happened in that 'suicide.' Mary was stricken with MS and became bed ridden. Unable to care for him, he was sent to Parmadale Catholic Orphanage in January 1940. He was 6, unloved, and unwanted. In December of 1946, the Bureau of Juvenile Research in Ohio did an evaluation. A copy of that evaluation is in the back of his book. The report states that Edwards ran away from Parmadale in March of 1945 at the age of 11.

(Parmadale Catholic Orphanage)

"He then enrolled in St. Joseph's Catholic School in Akron, but that lasted for a few months at best. His mother Mary died on October 5th, 1945 and by that fall, Edwards was clearly showing signs of serious problems. The psych evaluation notes he was molesting young girls on their way home from school and Dawn told me he was forcing pre-teen males and females, some as young as five, to perform sex acts in a tent in their back yard. Dawn was 6-7 years old."

Neal interjected, "That gives me a little better understanding of Edwards' childhood. He was born during the depression and by the time he gets out of Parmadale, World War II has just ended. Times were really tough then. It was difficult to buy a car, gas was rationed and the boys are just starting to come home from Europe."

I replied, "Interesting you'd comment on that. What I've been sharing with you has been leading up to the reason I called. I've found a new case. I think it was the beginning. I started researching the Ohio area for old crimes. This led me to a series of gruesome murders attributed to the Cleveland Torso Slayer. He was one of the country's first serial killers. Here's an article that came out right around the time of Ed's mother's death."

The Sandusky Register
<u>Sandusky's oldest business institution—Founded 1822—-More than a century in your service</u>

Sandusky, Ohio, Wednesday, August 17th, 1938
TWO MORE TORSO SLAYING VICTIMS
Apparent 11th and 12th Killings Laid to Mad Slayer

Police are searching for a serial killer that left pieces of his 11th and 12th victims in public. They had been surgically dissected, and parts were found in parks and near railroad cars.

While Neal glanced at the article, I continued. "The press had it all over the papers. This was a prior serial killer who stalked Cleveland from 1933 until 1938. Looking at Edwards' psych evaluation and realizing his first five years were formative years, this case was the foundation for his future killings. He mimicked murders his entire life, but it started right here."

"In the second chapter of his book he brags to be scamming, burglarizing and robbing. He's a young hood that has gone through puberty already. Dawn confirmed that. By 1945, he's only 12 years old. He knows how to hotwire a car, forge checks, and ride the rails to access neighboring big cities. He makes two statements, on pages 25 and 26."

"With my inner rage always at the boiling point, I was uncontrollable."

"My foster mother asked me to help her out of bed, and we both fell to the floor—she never tried to get up again. My guilt about the incident always remained."

"Just before his twelfth birthday, on June 5th, 1945, 45-year-old Josephine Ross was found stabbed and beaten to death in her Chicago home. Her head was wrapped in her dress. She was laid out much like Marilyn Sheppard in 1954 and Mrs.

Robison in 1968. Six months later, Frances Brown was found in her bed with a knife lodged through her neck and a bullet wound to her head. Authorities attributed it to the same slayer. In all three cases the victims had adhesive tape placed on their bodies and they were all washed in a bathtub. Remember, Neal, JonBenet had tape placed over her mouth and so did the three little boys in Chicago in 1955.

"Here's the clincher," I continued. "A note was written on the wall in lipstick." He excitedly showed Neal a photo of the scene.

(Chicago History Museum Photo of December 20th, 1945, Lipstick Killer Note)

"Look, it's just like he said in his book. *'I cannot control myself.'* Remember, he has lost two mother figures by the age of 12 and is feeling abandoned with nowhere to go. He placed this time period in his book."

"Wayne has been presenting behavior problems both at school and at home.... According to the police department, he was involved this summer in bicycle stealing and will not tell the truth even when the truth would be an advantage to him. His family background has distorted his character development very early. He lost two mother personalities, his own mother, whom he considered to be his aunt as long as she lived, and his adoptive mother." * MOAC

"Remember when you told me the ego will strive for any attention, even if it's negative? This is exemplified right here. It was the stressor."

Neal exclaimed: "You have no idea what you just uncovered. Remember when you tied Melvin Belli and F. Lee Bailey together with the Zodiac and Marilyn Sheppard? The Zodiac wrote Belli in 1969."

> Dear Melvin
>
> This is the Zodiac speaking I wish you a happy Christmass. The one thing I ask of you is this, please help me. I cannot reach out for help because of this thing in me wont let me. I am finding it extreamly difficult to hold it in check I am afraid I will loose control again and take my nineth & posibly tenth victom. Please help me I am drownding. At the moment the children are safe from the bomb because it is so massive to dig in & the triger mech requires much work to get it adjusted just right. But if I hold back too long from no nine I will loose ~~complet~~ all controol of my self & set the bomb up. Please help me I can not remain in control for much longer.

(Zodiac's December 20th, 1969 Melvin Belli Letter and Envelope. Copy from Zodiackiller.com)

"Look at the note." Neal continued.

"Please help me. I cannot reach out for help because of this thing in me won't let me. I am afraid I will lose control. Please help me. I cannot remain in control for much longer."

"Now look at the lipstick message on the wall."

"For heAVenS SAKe catch Me BeFore I Kill more. I cannot control MyselF"

"Here's something else—the handwriting. Do you have a copy of the Snook letter?"

(Judge Snook Letter and Lipstick Message)

Neal explained, "Look at the letter C in Charles and Calif and compare it to the word 'CatCh' in the lipstick message. They all look like E's. The letter in 55 and the message in 46 were puzzles. The word 'eateh' meant 'catch Edward Edwards.' He taunted the public with his identity in puzzles his entire life, not just in the Zodiac."

I replied, "This shows that the sensationalism started early. Listen to what his book says about his profile:

"It may be of interest to psychiatrists, sociologists, and social workers to learn that when Edwards was a youngster he was given tests which yielded the result he had an inferior I.Q. The young Edwards was at first diagnosed as having subnormal intelligence. That this was not true and was not the underlying cause of his criminal behavior was clearly documented by later diagnosis and behavior. On the contrary, Edwards was using his intelligence and ingenuity to mastermind devious, anti-social and illegal means for feeding his own need for recognition."
*MOAC age 12.

"The lipstick message confirms the psych evaluation. He was taunting the police to stop him way back then and leaving clues and messages at the age of 12."

I continued, "I think he was acting out the killing of his own mother with these two murders. They led to the one I really want to tell you about. It's the beginning. It set the groundwork for his killing of JonBenet in 1996. I want to tell you about the murder of a six-year-old blonde- haired, blue-eyed girl asleep in her own home in 1946. Her name was Suzanne Degnan."

(Suzanne Degnan, 1946)

On January 6th, 1946, Suzanne Degnan was six years old. It was a Sunday night and Christmas vacation had just ended. She would be going back to Sacred Heart School in the morning. Her parents, Jim and Helen Degnan, shared a beautiful home with another family in the safe part of North Chicago. The Degnans lived upstairs.

Suzanne went to bed at her usual time. She had played earlier in the day with a nice-looking young man that had been hanging around the neighborhood, dressed nicely. Nobody knew who he was. Between 12 and 1 a.m., her mom thought she heard Suzanne crying. She fell back asleep and awoke at 6:00 a.m. to find a ransom note on the bedroom floor, the window open, a ladder propped against the sill and Suzanne missing.

"GeT $20,000 Reddy & wAITe foR WoRd. do NoT NoTify FBI oR Police. Bills IN 5's & 10's BuRN This FoR heR SAfTY"

(Suzanne Degnan Ransom Note, January 6, 1946)

The police arrived and declared it a kidnapping. The FBI was contacted. They waited to hear from the kidnapper(s), but the only phone calls received were unidentified and silent. The police received a phone call from an anonymous tipster instructing them to search the neighboring sewers. Sadly, the tip was accurate. Her dissected body was discovered beheaded and distributed underneath the streets of Chicago.

Police discovered the gruesome crime scene in the basement laundry room of a neighboring apartment building. The area had been cleansed and washed down, but blood was discovered in the drains beneath the laundry room sinks. A message written in lipstick was found on a telephone pole near the building.

Lipstick printed sign on post near building where body of Suzanne Degnan was dismembered, discovered yesterday.

(Lipstick Message, January 1946)

The nature of the note and usage of lipstick linked to the killing of Frances Brown, 6 months earlier. The police were now looking for a serial killer. The Chicago mayor received a chilling message stating Degnan's father may have been the original target.

"This is to tell you how sorry I am not to get Ole Degnan instead of his girl. Roosevelt and the OPA made their own laws. Why shouldn't I and a lot more."

Suzanne's father, Jim Degnan, was a senior executive at the OPA, the Office of Price Administration, a governmental agency started on August 28, 1941 by President Franklin D. Roosevelt. Their responsibilities included price controls and rationing. This policy resulted in food rationing at Parmadale Orphanage where Edwards spent his childhood years.

Eventually, a young con by the name of William Heirens was convicted and served 66 years with the Illinois Department of Corrections for the murder of Suzanne. He pleaded his entire life that he had been coerced into a confession. He died in prison at the age of 84, setting the record as the longest serving inmate. To this day, most believe he was innocent. The investigation by Cameron proved he was.

Neal asked me, "Where do you even want to start? Sensationalism, letters to the press, wrongful conviction. Look at the connections. Kalitske and Bogle were killed just after New Year's Day, the day before she was headed back to school. JonBenet Ramsey was the same age, killed on Christmas Day while her parents slept. The ransom note is even similar. I think the ladder shows she was lured out of her bedroom, not unlike Santa luring JonBenet down to the kitchen. In both cases, a ransom note with similar demands and the child is already dead. The note on the telephone pole, 'Stop me before I kill more.' It all fits! One final comment— 'OLE Degnan'? He used 'OLE' Joe (Scolaro) and 'OLE' Impressio magazine in his notes in the Robison murders. That's an unusual substitute for 'old'—is too coincidental to be in both messages."

I said, "I want to put on my psychiatrist's hat again and analyze Ed in 1946. Dawn is 7 years old at that time and has been interjected into Ed's life. He is extremely jealous of the love and attention that she is getting from his aunt Edith Myers and feels totally alienated and rejected. He doesn't feel loved. He mentions the significance of that in his book.

"Secondly, to point out the tremendous need for communication between the parent and the child and to emphasize how sorely needed in the average household of today is the words 'I love you.' Just as there is no substitute for discipline, there is no substitute for love. But, youngsters who grow up feeling that all their parents want from them is obedience— not love— tend to become resentful and rebellious." *MOAC

"Listen to this psych evaluation that's in the back of his book. It's 1946."

"There is indication of organic brain damage and some psychotic behavior. He is insecure, and sexual disturbance is present. There is an over-compliant, alert, pretentious front, but shallow and impoverished thinking. There is some tendency to pervert ideas, to misunderstand realities. The subject has great need for affection and recognition. Death is the way out of many difficulties which usually evolve around close relationships. Punishment causes the persons to be sorry they committed murder. His heroes find it necessary to implore supernatural help and he has no hesitancy meting out 'hell' for their punishment. There is sexual conflict suggestive of sadomasochistic nature. This boy is over- concerned with age and has a strong dislike for old people."

"This evaluation explains why he murdered the older women and then the child. He was acting out his rage toward his aunt and his cousin, Dawn. He was screaming for attention of any kind. That's why he murders and makes references to heroes and the supernatural. The part about no hesitancy 'meting out hell' for their punishment fits the role of Edwards as the Zodiac and executioner perfectly."

Neal started getting a good picture in his mind. "Didn't you say Degnan was chopped up in a laundry room in a basement? He took JonBenet to the basement. Additionally, there's a part in Edwards' book about luring young girls down into a laundry room for sex. It takes place about this same time-period." I found it in a chapter named, "The School Had Walls."

"Around this time, I discovered what girls' were for. Up to then, I hadn't known what intercourse was. When I found out, I was all for it. 'I had always viewed girls with great curiosity. But there was no young females in the reform school; on Mr. Day's farm, I had no female company, and, as I said, the small town nearby had provided no outlet.

"I found I could get a lot of attention from girls, and I was delighted. Ironically, I became very particular about whom I went to bed with. The girl had to be feminine, and attractive, and had to care about me. I always chose younger girls whom I could dominate. For me, it was essential to excel. It was even necessary for me to beat girls at jumproping and jacks. I couldn't abide a girl out-doing me in anything.

"Because my work involved various areas of the building, I occasionally got the opportunity to be with the girls. Once in a while, I was able to steal a couple of minutes to kiss a girl I especially liked. These brief contacts led to my working out a scheme. The laundry chutes led, from both the boys' dormitories and the girls' dormitories, to the same spot in the basement. I knew I would be down there sorting and washing clothes, and would be left alone for three to four hours. On a certain Saturday afternoon, I arranged that the girl I had been kissing and writing notes to would slide down the clothing chute from the girls' dormitories into the basement."* MOAC

"That's it!" I exclaimed, "You nailed it. Degnan was murdered on a Sunday; that's why he said Saturday in the book. He groomed her the day before. He probably spent that afternoon beating her at jacks and hopscotch. Suzanne's mother reported to police that a 'nice young boy' was hanging around the day before. Ed lured her out that window late at night, undetected by her parents, just like JonBenet 50 years later. Suzanne didn't get carried out of that house. She went down that ladder knowingly and her mother heard her cry. She wouldn't have gone with someone she didn't know."

Neal threw in, "John, I had no idea what you had been uncovering. Sometimes I get a little overwhelmed with the grisly details of Ed's murders."

"I understand, Neal. I have been doing this a long time and am a little cynical. I have another thread to JonBenet. A paper bag with red crayon markings was found with Suzanne's right leg in a sewer. Edwards sketched a red heart on JonBenet's right hand with a red crayon. It was more murder mimicry. That's how Edwards ties his murders together."

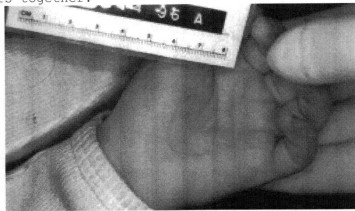

(JonBenet's Right Hand)

"Also, there was an attempt by police to go after Suzanne's parents at first. Edwards didn't succeed in getting John and Patsy Ramsey indicted—but he came close. Before they convicted Heirens of the Suzanne Degnan murder, he was asked, 'Were your victims terrified when you killed them?' He answered, 'I can't tell you, Sheriff, because I didn't kill them. Please watch out, because the real killer is still out there.' (William Heirens, October 1946). When asked, 'Why did you confess?' he said, 'To avoid being executed. I couldn't prove my innocence if I were dead!'

I reiterated, "Despite 66 years of his effort, the press and the police never let up on him. He went to his grave known as 'The Lipstick killer,' when all he was, was a 17-year-old Chicago hood, that became Edwards' fall guy. He died in prison March 5th, 2012, a year after Ed."

Neal reminisced, "Burton Abbott might have gotten a life sentence in 1955 like Heirens, if he had confessed. But instead, he died in the gas chamber, a year after his conviction. Another innocent victim of Ed's."

I stated, "This is horrible. People DO confess that are totally innocent. I have seen it first hand in my work. It's all about the will to live. The power of the press is incredible, and Edwards realized it. By age 12 he was already creating 'crimes of recognition' and getting away with it, watching the press and public devour innocent men. From 1945 until 2011, Edwards killed non-stop, 66 years."

After discovering the beginning of Edwards' murders, the importance of a detailed timeline became paramount. Edwards had started killing as a teen and just got better and better with time. Using all of their resources from the investigation, I put together a complete time frame of Edwards' life, with the help of Ed himself. Although "Metamorphosis of a Criminal" was the key to MOST everything; the letters Ed sent throughout his life were also puzzles. Ed knew that the future was the internet, and his book never made it on the internet for free. In fact, any hard copies still available were selling for as much as 1000 dollars in 2011. That

did not leave a lot of people able to read it. Committing crimes for recognition took on a whole new meaning after Ed straightened Cameron out about its meaning:
=

> You are wrong if you think I killed people for the recognition. I did not let anyone know when I killed someone, so therefore I wasn't doing it for the recognition. Most everything that I did in life was for recognition. Let me tell you right now, that if there is anything you want to know, you don't have to pay me to get the answers. You have been good and nice to me and I plan on returning the favor.

(Ed Edwards to John Cameron, February 2011)

"Ed did not want to be recognized. He knew that eventually the world would realize his significance, if not in this life, then in his next..."

"I was all set to tackle the world. Someday people would hear of Ed Edwards, master criminal." *MOAC

I told Neal, "I want to go back to the book and his life one last time. My instincts say there's more—a lot more!"

About a week later, Neal noticed a voice mail from me. The message instructed him, "You need to come over right away."

He wondered, "What did he find now?

Chapter 33

The Solution

Christmas, 2012

When Neal arrived, I said, "I think you need to just sit down and listen. Boy, was I wrong about the whole recognition thing. It means so much more than what we thought. Not only was the book a puzzle of murder, but so was the internet. Ed was a computer genius. And I found him blogging on Zodiackiller.com from 2000 until his capture in 2009!"

"What?" a surprised Neal said.

"Yeah, using names like Oscar and EEAVE. He was working his way into an Oscar all right, leading them down Ed Edwards Avenue. He used names that tied to him. I found him using dozens, all over the country for 10 years. He was leading the entire Zodiackiller.com website down the path of the real Zodiac killer, seeing if they would bite and identify him."

I had made a surprise trip back to Louisville, Kentucky December 2012 to confront Kay Edwards, and confirm his suspicions that Ed was blogging on the internet starting in 2000. Kay confirmed it and that started the unraveling of what he had done the last decade of his life.

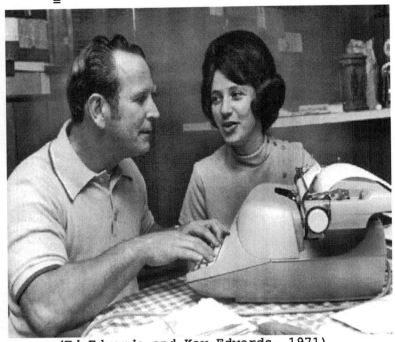
(Ed Edwards and Kay Edwards, 1971)

He had published albums, tapes, and movies for profit. He was paid for his speaking tour, while he was killing everyone in the Zodiac case. He made appearances at police academies and colleges everywhere, while he killed our children everywhere.

In the end, his daughter told a secret, and after 66 years of killing and setting up others, Edwards was arrested, July 30th, 2009. He looked harmless. The press ignored him for the most part. But what he did in his last 10 years of his life was worse than the previous 56. And nobody knew it.

(Ed Edwards, August 19th, 2009)

I said to Neal, "You ever heard of The Black Dahlia?"

"Not really. Wasn't that a movie back in the 50's?"

"Actually, the movie was The Blue Dahlia. The Black Dahlia was the name the press gave to the most famous unsolved murder in the history of the United States. Elizabeth Short was found mutilated; her body sliced in half at the waist and she was laid out in a vacant lot in Hollywood, January 15, 1947. The area was a known lover's lane."

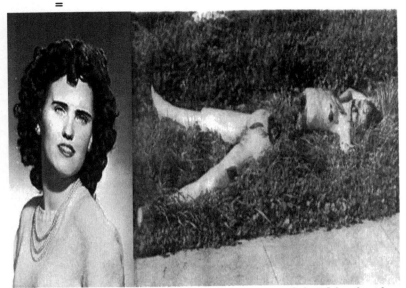

(Elizabeth Short, 22 years old Elizabeth Short Dissected, January 15, 1947)

Neal glanced at the picture of the dissected body and asked, "Is this the Cleveland Torso Murderer again?"

I replied, "No, this is Ed's next victim after he killed Suzanne Degnan in 1946. Suzanne represented his 7-year-old cousin Dawn, and Elizabeth Short represented his mother, who was 22 when she bore him in the back seat of a car on a lover's lane. That is why the Zodiac attacked couples on lover's lanes. They were creating him. A child not born of love. Elizabeth was lured, tortured, washed, cut in half, and then spread out in a public park near Hollywood on a known lover's lane."

"You're kidding me!"

"No. And I found something bigger than Ed's book."

"What do you have, John? I know you're holding back. You've been hiding in your head for months and I know what that usually means."

"I'm crazy?"

"Well that's a given... but you're crazy seems to follow the truth."

"I found a website, Blackdahliasolution.org, and it's Edwards' 2002 public confession to many of his killings in 1945-46, with details only the killer would know. Nobody ever knew who had put up the site. Not only that, it ties his entire life together—all the cases and all the murders. Everything our investigation has uncovered so far, confirmed on this site. It is exactly like his book, a puzzle of murder, a confession to being the Zodiac, the Atlanta Child Killer, the killer of JonBenet, the Black Dahlia... There are so many, many more murders and he did it right up until the end."

Neal asked, "Edwards put up a website? You gotta be kidding!"

"Let me show you. There is so much, this will take a while."

I opened my computer and there was Ed Edwards at age 13 and a half years old pictured with Elizabeth Short just before her demise.

(Elizabeth Short and Ed Edwards, 1947)

I explained. "Edwards authored this site in 2002 as a follow-up to his book, 'Metamorphosis of a Criminal.' He knew that nobody had read the book and put the pieces together by the mid-90's. Once the internet came along he knew he could tell his murder stories as a game on public blogs. Rather than sending letters to the editor he could go right on their websites and blog his expert opinion on the case."

Figure out who authored this site and you will have the real Zodiac killer.

The site gave the answers as to who he killed when he was 12 to 14 years old in 1946-

47, 20 years before he started the Zodiac killings. Few people in 1947 would have ever suspected that a 13-year-old kid could do such a thing. We know different today. He provides ALL the answers as to how he met her, groomed her and then sought revenge after she shunned him, Christmas, 1946.

At the beginning of the site, he claims the real killer of Elizabeth Short is a man named 'Ed Burns.' That is why he highlighted the letters EBE in past letters. Edward Burns Edwards.

I furthered, "The author claims to know who the killer is, but then uses words that suggest HE is the killer. It's the same syntax Ed used in his book and his ransom notes, trying to portray himself as two people. Using words like I or me to imply only one person speaking—the author of the site himself, admitting to committing murder. He's flaunting it in front of everyone, just like his book. He uses the name Ed Burns as his alias and details the killing of Elizabeth Short. He tells it as a riddle, just like the Zodiac letters were!"

Neal started reading.

"On a sunny winter morning in 1947, the bisected, nude body of a once-gorgeous young woman was discovered in a big vacant lot in south- central Los Angeles. It was as blackly mind-blowing as any exhibit in a Madame Tussaud horror museum. The Black Dahlia was born to the world.

"Who is that guy? If we asked him, he might say: 'Who am I?' A burning question with a smoking answer! LAPD has been referring to me as 'unID'd man' for more than fifty years, and I've been here in the Great Beyond for almost as long. You're on to me so I'll tell you my name. And I'll do it with a riddle. They called me a werewolf. I actually was a riddler and a mimicker during my time on earth. My darkest mimicry was a nightmare for thousands of people. Anyway, I'm not Edd 'Kookie' Byrnes of 77 Sunset Strip, the old hit TV show. My reelingly big show was a smash hit on Forty-Seven Sunset Strip. And what did the fuzzies call it? LAPD called it lust murder, and most folks took LAPD's word for it. Had LAPD dug it as I defiled it, they should have been able to decipher my trilogy and arrest me. To me, it was a Suzanne Degnan Murder Tableau in a Degnan Boulevard lovers' lane, with Elizabeth Short as Suzanne Degnan. And where was I in this Madame Tussaud-genre artwork? That's where my published trilogy came in: its purpose was to put me in the scene while keeping me out of range of LAPD's case-cracking radar. I was in the secret story, in parallel with William Heirens, George Murman, Suzanne Degnan and the Black Dahlia. The cryptic trilogy was my magic carpet ride into eternity with Elizabeth Short. But you can take the trilogy as a souvenir program for the tableau...

"The killer wasn't a tall, gaunt drunkard. Smoke was billowing from that miscreant's proximity long before his Dutch-oven demise in LA's Holland Hotel."

I looked at Neal and said, "Do you see what I mean? Do you see how many times he used words such as I or me or my, giving a 'first person' connotation?"

Neal immediately confirmed that I was correct. He noted numerous other connections. Suzanne Degnan, William Heirens, lover's lanes, mimicry, cryptic messages. He looked up at me, "John, this refers to everything in our case. It sounds like the Zodiac himself is doing the talking."

"Yeah, he is. Did you catch the 50 years of being in the great beyond and the magic carpet ride into eternity? This site goes into everything. Edwards was the author! The Black Dahlia killer, the Zodiac, the killer of JonBenet Ramsey and Suzanne Degnan. Solutions to killings starting in 1946 and never ending. And he put it on the internet for all to see—yet nobody could attach it to 'someone.' If you didn't know everything that we do about Edwards, a lot of this wouldn't make sense, but it is his confession. He put it out in 2002. Here's how it starts out."

"This site was created to serve one purpose and one purpose only: To share the truth of what happened to the Black Dahlia and the man that murdered her. You will see no advertisements and will not be asked to give anything but your consideration of the evidence presented.

"The person responsible for solving the Black Dahlia Murder/Riddle spent 30 years working for the U.S. Government as a mathematician and garnered considerable experience in decryption. Although justice can never be served on the man who committed this heinous crime, it is the author's hope that the information revealed in this site will allow the Black Dahlia to finally rest in peace. The murder of Elizabeth Short has haunted the Los Angeles Police Department since the heinous crime was committed in 1947. The reason will undoubtedly surprise many. The truth is: L.A.P.D. knew who killed Elizabeth Short; they had him, they grilled him, but they did not hold him. This site tells the story of the last days of Elizabeth Short, known in life and in death as the Black Dahlia. It reveals the name of her alleged killer, deciphered from cryptic messages he sent to the L.A. Examiner and L.A.P.D. over 50 years ago."

"John, it's Edwards!" exclaimed Neal, I'm sure of it! At the end of the website under FAQ's, the author is challenged by a blogger stating that the author seems to know an inordinate amount about the case. Ed answers, 'In January of 1947, I was thirteen years old.' On the surface, that would imply innocence of any culpability by his mere age alone. Knowing that Edward Edwards was born June 14, 1933, this statement is huge. The math works! He also says he was in Los Angeles at that time, reading the Examiner. You and I both know Edwards was on the run at that time."

"This next photo is of the Black Dahlia and a young kid, taken at a penny arcade. The

cops found one copy in her luggage and the killer sent a duplicate in the mail. The older couple in the photo identified the young man as the one who tried to rent a room at their hotel just before the murder. He signed in as Mr. and Mrs. Barnes.
=

(Police Trying to Identify Man with Elizabeth Short)

"The kid in that photo has never been identified, because they thought they were looking for an adult who had done time in the service! Now that we know the guy in the picture was a kid, it is obvious when you look at it. Ed had gone through puberty by age 13 and his testicles had descended. He was a hairy, mature, strong diagnosed psychopath."

"Now, I'd like to show you a Los Angeles District Attorney's office memo dated January 26, 1950." I pointed out, "I would really like you to look at line 3, 'Beth Short and her boyfriend, a young kid with brown hair, arrived.' Now look at line 14. 'Identified picture of soldier sitting on bumper of Chevy coupe with Ohio license # E-640V-4 'name unknown' a new character as man with Short at Hansen's.'"

MEMORANDUM — JAN. 26, 1950

Subject: CONNIE STARR -- and Francis Starr (Mother)
427 So. Mariposa St.
Apt. 310
DU 9-2535

1. Connie is Ann Toth's girl friend.

2. Connie stated that she was invited to dinner at Mark Hansen's by Ann Toth on Saturday January 11, 1947;

3. that the three of them had dinner together and shortly after dinner about 9:00 PM, Beth Short and her boy friend, a young kid with brown hair, arrived;

4. that it was a very cold night and Beth Short did not have a coat and was dressed in a cotton or gingham dress with a pink top bodice and did not have a coat; did not have stockings on;

5. that Beth Short complained of being cold and frozen;

6. that Mark Hansen seated Beth Short on the davenport near the fireplace, put a blanket around her shoulders, placed a pair of his socks on her feet, put his slippers on her feet

7. that Mark Hansen asked her xx where she had been; that Beth Short stated that they had been to a movie, that Mark asked if they had been to his theater, that she answered no, that she had seen the picture at his theater and that they caught an early movie elsewhere;

8. CONNIE stated that she was home when she read of Beth Short's murder and immediately remarked to her Mother that is was just the other day that she just met Beth Short at Mark Hansen's home when she was there for dinner;

9. Connie and her mother should be questioned separately xxxxxxxxxxxxxx xxxxxxx for purposes of corroboration.

10. Connie is an extra-player who obtain's most of her employment by request calls and a small portion through Central Casting.

11. Connie's moral xxxxxxxx reputation is not too good, xxxxxxxxxxx

12. Connie also stated that she understood that Beth Short had spent the previous night, Friday, January 10, 1947, at Mark Hansen's home, and was planning to spend Saturday night there also.

13. Place date as just before Ann went to *[illegible]* after they *[illegible]* worked together in march of *[illegible]*

14. Identified Picture of Soldier sitting on *[illegible]* of Chev coupe Ohio Lic. # E-6404-Y "name unknown" - a new character as man with Short at Hansens in Nov.

(Los Angeles District Attorney's Office Memo January 26, 1950)

"This memo positively documents that Elizabeth Short's new boyfriend was a young kid from OHIO. January 11th was the day she disappeared. Her dissected body was found on January 15th, in a vacant lot, publicly displayed near a lover's lane. Neal, I want to remind you that even by this age, Edwards was a psychotic, ruthless killer. Look what he did to Suzanne Degnan a year earlier. He chopped her up. The psych evaluation labels him a sadomasochist with organic brain damage and a serious problem with women. The evaluation was done between the killing of Suzanne Degnan, 1946, and the killing of Elizabeth Short, 1947. He was released from Ohio Catholic League Services for Christmas 1946 to go home one last time. They had no idea he had killed Suzanne Degnan, but they accurately evaluated him as a sadomasochist. CHRISTMAS! JonBenet killed on Christmas 50 years later in the same manner? The suspicious car with the Ohio plates? It's really tough for most to believe that a 13-year-old kid did the Black Dahlia, but that explains why it was never solved. He admits that the cops actually had him, questioned him and let him go!"

Neal interrupted excitedly. "Here's another thread to the Zodiac killings. James Richardson, city editor of the Los Angeles Examiner, received a telephone call that identified himself as the killer of the Black Dahlia. The caller informed the editor he was going to send him Elizabeth Short's address book, birth certificate and a few other items from her handbag. A package wrapped in brown paper and addressed to the Examiner was located in a mailbox at the Biltmore Hotel containing the items. Sounds just like Edwards. Do you see the similarities? He called the city editor in San Francisco in 1955 and told him where Stephanie Bryan's body would be found. Most of the Zodiac letters were addressed to the editor. He wrote the editor in the Robison case in 68, demanding they print a classified ad and he did it again in Atlanta in 1980. He repeats the same M.O. in every one of these cases!"

"The black dahlia solution website constantly refers to the 'UnID'd man' who was never there. Young, short, brown haired, with a goofy rabbit grin. It was Edwards. That's why he always had himself photographed over the years with that same stupid grin!" I pointed out.

(Ed Edwards 38 and 13)

"Okay." Neal asked, "What about the book? Why didn't he tell us about it in 'Metamorphosis of a Criminal?'"

"He did. We just missed it." Grabbing my copy, I said, "Listen to this. He even gives his correct age."

"One convict was caught at a bus station with the dismembered body of his wife stuffed in a suit case he was carrying.

"By this time I was thirteen. I got a crush on a woman. She was a very attractive, brunette divorcee. I really liked her because she was nice to me; but I resented the fact that there was a guy who visited her every night. I hated this man because I figured he was cutting in on me.

Feeling that I truly wanted to marry this woman I made up my mind to get even with my rival and to put a stop to his attentions." *MOAC

"Now, on page 46, he describes obtaining his military uniform."

"At Paris Island, they threw a bunch of uniforms at me that seemed three sizes too big, and they issued me a few pairs of shoes. It seemed to me that each shoe weighed 20 pounds."

" Tell me that's not like a little kid trying on his dad's clothes for the first time."

Neal looked up at me, "What's all this business on the website that ID'd Ed Burns as the man that did the crime? Is that some kind of pun referring to Edwards' arson?"

I replied, "Ed Burns is Edward Edwards. It's a pun to 'Look for Ed the Arsonist.' Remember, Ed was arrested for arson in 1982, just after killing all the kids in Atlanta. He started informing to FBI to get out early. Look at his NCIC record. It clearly shows the arson arrest.

```
Charge              01
   Charge Literal   ARSON & RELATED OFFENSES
        Severity    Unknown
     Disposition    (Convicted 1982-09-25; CONVICTED- 4Y-10Y
                    CONFINEMENT, FOUND GUILTY AT WESTERN, PGH PA)
Charge              02
   Charge Literal   THEFT BY UNLAWFUL TAKING
        Severity    Unknown
     Disposition    (Convicted 1982-09-25; CONVICTED- 1Y-2Y
                    CONFINEMENT, FG TO RUN CONSE W/TT 5 TO 12YR AT
                    WESTERN)
```

(Edwards NCIC record, arson, 1982)

Edwards' 1982 conviction for arson occurred after he was caught in Atlanta, Georgia living with a policeman. He had just killed everyone in the Atlanta Child killings. (1979-1981)

Edwards set up the site to place the blame on the name, 'Ed Burns,' as a clue. Ed Burns and Edwards have the same number of letters and the letters needed to solve the Zodiac cryptograms. Edwards the arsonist Burns! Edward Burns Edwards, EBE. The Zodiac killed by fire.

Everyone on Zodiackiller.com had been commenting about the Black dahlia solution site, since its release in December 2002. Nobody knew who the author was. Edwards targeted Zodiackiller.com after he published the site to stand in front of some of the world's leading experts and rub it in their faces."

Neal commented, "Edwards constantly follows the same pattern— misdirection, placing or directing the guilt elsewhere while he stands back and watches the crowd complain about the 'inconsiderate bastard that caused it all.' He did it to Burton Abbott, JonBenet's parents and he tried to do it to Frank Dryman in the Zodiac case, but that didn't work. He did it in all of them!"

I said, "You want to know what the worst part is? 'Special Agents' actually had him. They questioned him on March 27, 1947. I put the entire interview into our timeline. That's why he constantly refers to the 'UnID'd man.' They had him and they never identified him. They just let him walk without identifying who he really was. But he makes it clear they have HIS fingerprints."

Neal pondered the information that I had given him so far. He said, "I'm starting to get a pretty good picture. Ed is cut loose from Ohio around Christmas of 1946 and traipses off to find the love of his life that's just jilted him. How'd he meet her in the first place?"

"Police reports state she had been in Chicago in July 1946, infatuated with the Suzanne Degnan murder. Edwards was in Chicago because he had run away from Parmadale and he wanted to see what was going on with HIS Degnan case. This was right after Heirens was arrested for the murder and forced to confess to spare his life. Elizabeth Short was a freelance reporter and Edwards groomed his way into her life, pumped her full of the details of the killing of Suzanne Degnan, and then planned her demise. Listen to what he said. Betty is Elizabeth."

"And Ed was Betty's best-ever listener. He'd feign interest as she'd relate detail after ghastly detail of the Suzanne Degnan murder. Betty drove Ed crazy with it, literally. She coaxed him to drive her out to Leimert Park. When she was expounding on the irony of Degnan Boulevard going right by her old lovers' lane, he noticed the many big vacant lots in the area . . . Spirit world, where were you? This was the time to send Betty a sign!" *BDS

"She even posed as a freelance reporter?" Neal asked.

"Yeah, she was thrilled to be part of the case, and Edwards fell head over heels in love with her. He was only 13 years old and she was a Hollywood actress. He provided her money through burglary and robbery, and she used him. Elizabeth had information on the Suzanne Degnan case that no other reporter had access to. The real killer was providing her the details and she was 'using' Ed for his money. He made it clear on the site that she teased him about his goofy grin, and being short, and this lead to her killing. Here's some more from the site."

"He and Elizabeth Short hit it off fine at first. She was his dream girl, the prettiest woman he'd ever met. She even had him thinking he wasn't a rabbit: she didn't make cutting jibes about his height and his goofy grin. And 'Ed,' as he'd tell us to call him, was Betty's wheels-and-money-man who'd never try to make her do things she did not want to do." *BDS

I continued, "By the end of summer or early fall 1946, Short went back to Los Angeles trying to end their relationship and Edwards returned to Ohio. By October, he got busted in Akron vandalizing a Catholic church and was placed in the Catholic League Services for evaluation. That's where his psych evaluation designated him a sadomasochist with a deep hatred for older people."

Neal concluded, "So when they let him out to go spend Christmas with Grandma, he headed to

Los Angeles, trying to get back together with Elizabeth Short. Apparently, she said no."

I concurred, "It got gruesome. He didn't go back to meet up with her. He went back to lure her to an apartment with a bathtub, where he could dismember her like Suzanne Degnan. He used luggage to haul her out and that's why the luggage became such an item in the JonBenet case. He laid her out near Degnan Boulevard in Los Angeles to tie the two murders together. Just like tying JonBenet to it 50 years later. Let's get back to the website. He calls himself 'Werewolf Will'."

"As a sepulchral salud to Beth's fixation with the 1946 Suzanne Degnan murder, Werewolf Will used 'ironic psychomancy.' H. . . Besides setting up his psychotoxic spectacular in a weedy lot 'on' Degnan Boulevard . . . Will Cutter used knives and a tub for his Dahlia caper, LA Cutter cut Beth into pieces, LA Cutter drained and washed Beth's pieces free of blood, as Heirens had done for Suzanne." *BDS

I shook my head, "Neal, this is incredible. He is describing exactly what he did to Suzanne Degnan and Elizabeth Short and how he tied them all together through names of streets. One murder occurred in Chicago, one in LA and he ties them together through what he calls mimicry. You can't deny that the murders of Suzanne Degnan and the Black Dahlia are related."

"John, did you catch that part about Norton Avenue? Didn't Edwards write a letter, and for some reason 'Norton, you are the first' was oddly placed in it? We never understood that."

(Letter from Edwards to Ohio Police, 2010)

"I knew that letter was a clue to a puzzle!" I exclaimed excitedly, "That was his confession to killing a couple on a lover's lane in Ohio, 1977. I noticed in 2010 that Edwards was toying with the police by leaving block lettering in strange places as clues. That got me interested in Edwards as the Zodiac killer. I didn't understand *why* Ed put 'Norton, you are the first' in the letter, but knew it was a puzzle. It all makes sense now. It was the beginning, it was the first crime of recognition, and he committed it near Norton and Degnan Boulevard as a clue. He goes on further, tying the case to the Zodiac killer."

"Zodiac sent cryptograms and plain-language messages to three San Francisco-area newspapers. The ciphers were of the substitution type: an amateur cryptographer's delight. The wily Zodiac issued murderous threats to prod newspapers to print his ego tonic. I think the Zodiac got off by scaring the public, jibing and frustrating the police, and luring Bay area amateurs into a code-breaking frenzy. His cryptograms gave him a feeling of empowerment and control. It's now obvious that almost everything in Ed's messages was put there with purposefulness and precision. But virtually no one knew that all they were seeing was dummy text that Ed's concealment ciphers concealed. But why expend brain juice to construct this type of cipher? Why didn't Ed do a no-brainer stunt, like making substitution ciphers? Ed did not make his serial brainchild for the general public." BDS*

Neal now was getting excited. "John, that's exactly what we said earlier! 'The Zodiac (Ed), issued his threats to prod newspapers to print his ego tonic. His cryptograms gave him a feeling of empowerment and control.' That matches our profiling identically."

I added, "He takes it even further. He sent three post cards to the press in the Black Dahlia case, and totally analyzes the hidden messages contained on the website. This is all a precursor to the Zodiac letters to the San Francisco press and it all took place back in 1947!"

(Black Dahlia Killer Letters to Los Angeles Examiner and Police)

"John, this is absolutely amazing. I'd like to go home and study it and I'll give you a call tomorrow."

Neal came by the next morning and I asked him, "What'd you find out?"

"Edwards spends pages explaining the postcards—the placement of each individual letter, the letter size, tilt, every dot. From this, he extracts codes and messages pertaining to the identity of the Black Dahlia murderer. He claims they were all clues to solving the case and identifying her killer, but no one ever figured it out! He uses ladder codes and a code invented by Francis Bacon some 300 years ago based on a binary system. Binary code is what runs computers. He constructs maps and gives gruesome details about the Black Dahlia murder. I wish I hadn't read some of the parts. He gives a graphic description of how he tortured her and what he did to her body."

"Ed Burns roped me, haltered me, branded me with the initials of his name and turned me into a horse. But I wanted to be a Black Dahlia, not a Black Beauty. PLEASE let folks know the truth: it will make me free to rest in peace..." BDS*

"By the time he did the Zodiac, he's fully developed, and you can see it in the writings. There are clues within clues within clues. 'Metamorphosis of a Criminal' was truly just that. He metamorphosed from an amateur kid to a perfected, artistic adult. I was wrong when I felt Edwards was incapable of appreciating the Mikado. He was the conductor."

"Edwards staged a suicide after he killed Elizabeth Short, and left a note on the beach." I stated, "He was attempting to end any further police investigation into the identification of the 'UnID'd Man' in the photo with Elizabeth Short. The police never released the note back in 1947 so Ed replicated it on his site. He then shows the reader how to extract the name Ed Burns."

> TO WHOM IT MAY CONCERN: I HAVE WAITED FOR THE POLICE TO CAPTURE ME FOR THE Black Dahlia Killing, BUT HAVE NOT. I AM TOO MUCH OF A COWARD TO TURN MYSELF IN, SO THIS IS THE BEST WAY OUT FOR ME. I COULDN'T HELP MYSELF FOR THAT, OR THIS.
>
> SORRY, MARY

(Suicide Note Left on Los Angeles Beach, March 1947)

I noted, "Edwards always tried to commit suicide after every capture. He did it in 1951, 1956 and 1961. The signature on this suicide note states 'Sorry Mary'. Edwards' foster mother, Mary Ethyl Edwards, had just died before he killed Suzanne Degnan and Elizabeth Short. Elizabeth Short represented Ed's mother, and he had lost two mother figures just before he did it."

"Wayne has been presenting behavior problems both at school and at home.... His family background has distorted his character development very early. He lost two mother personalities, his own mother, whom he considered to be his aunt as long as she lived, and his adoptive mother." (Ed Edwards, Psych Eval, Ohio Juvenile Research Bureau, 1946)

"Ed was a very disturbed child, Neal. After the death of his first mother by gunshot in 1938, he lost his identity, had his name changed from Chuckie to Ed, and then lost a second mother a year later to MS. He was only 5 years old, and his life was destroyed by the very people that were supposed to care for him. He was killing his mother over and over again throughout his life. Just think about being 13 years old, a sadomasochist and getting away with two of the most sensational murders of the 20th century. It began the Zodiac and he took on a God-like image. His lack of love and desire to be noticed started his pathology. His ego demanded it and he liked it. As the Zodiac he teased us with his identity. As the killer of JonBenet he taunted us with 'The Two People Watching Over Her.' In his book he was a dangerous hardened criminal and a family man."

"And he lived 66 more years to continue killing," Neal reiterated.

"No one has ever come close to solving the Zodiac and that's because they didn't know the 'why.' It all fits like a glove. At thirteen and a half he kills and stages a Hollywood production and gets away with it. He liked it—he enjoyed it—and he couldn't stop himself. He spent the next six decades creating block busters and selling it to the world."

"What a production," Neal said.

"I have one last item from the website that ties him to JonBenet. The Black Dahlia website creator explained how he signs his murders when he wins."

"Ed 'won' and, to proclaim Victory displayed the Black Dahlia remains in a Degnan Boulevard lovers' lane. I say Burns had his Victory-for-Ed flags flying."* BDS

I reminded Neal, "The JonBenet ransom note was signed VICTORY- SBTC. It meant, I Won- Signed By The Cross—the Zodiac cross and circle. Ed had won."

"I guess if I felt all that sorry, I never would have done it. I was always a schemer, I was always thinking of ways of making money. I've always been into crime. It was arranged, it was premeditated, it was thought out, it was planned, and that's what I did. I did it, it didn't bother me, and I moved on." (Ed Edwards, 2010)

Neal turned to me, "I'm absolutely sold! The ties to the Zodiac are clear cut. Edwards created headline grabbing murders his entire life. Look at the cases!"

1946, Chicago, Suzanne Degnan, 6 years old
1947, Hollywood, Elizabeth Short, 22 years old
1954, Cleveland, Marilyn Sheppard, 28 years old, pregnant
1955, San Francisco, Stephanie Bryan, 14 years old
1955, Chicago, 3 teens
1955, Omaha, Carolyn Nevins, 19 years old
1956, Great Falls, Kalitske/Bogle, 16 and 18 years old
1957, Berkeley, San Quentin, Burton Abbott, 29 years old
1960, Portland OR, Peyton/Allen, 19 years old
1968, Michigan, Robison Family of 6
1968-70, San Francisco, Zodiac
1971-74, California, Santa Rosa, Highway 101, 8 teens
1979-81, Atlanta, 24 teens
1993, West Memphis, Arkansas, 3 boys
1996, Boulder, JonBenet Ramsey, 6 years old

"That's 62 murders alone, and out of those there were 13 wrongful convictions. Look at the first and the last. They are identical. Suzanne Degnan and JonBenet Ramsey were mimicry, 50 years apart almost to the day. Every one of these murders received massive 'recognition.' That was his M.O. The letters to the press, the clues, the taunting of authorities, he told us why he did it on 'To Tell the Truth,' in 1972."

Gary Allen: "Ed, there was one important point when you and I were chatting backstage and I asked you, what was the reaction in your neighborhood when you came out of the reformatory the first time? Were you put down by your fellow citizens or did they look up to you?"

Ed , "No—ah, when I was released from the reformatory, they looked up to me and this motivated me to go on to bigger things, because this was why I was out there committing the crime, was for the recognition!"

"Finally," I said, "look at the silhouette Edwards put on his website, BlackDahliaSolution.org. He claims it is the real killer of Elizabeth Short, Suzanne Degnan and the real lipstick killer. It is HIM!

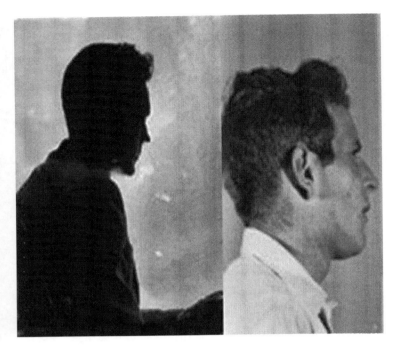

(Blackdahliasolution.org silhouette picture of suspect compared to Ed Edwards)

Chapter 34

America's Most Wanted

It's 1972 and Edwards publishes his murderous rampage called, "Metamorphosis of a Criminal." Nobody figures out the puzzle so you put a new one on the internet 30 years later called Black Dahlia Solution. Nobody figures that out either. So, what do you do next?

The ruse continues. Nobody has put all the clues together. You still don't want to get caught; you just want everyone to know what really happened and how clever you are. You want recognition and you will seek it until you die and into your afterlife.

Neal asked, "So what would you try next? If I had become computer literate and I typed in Zodiac killer, it would take me to the best source that still exists today—Tom Voigt's Zodiackiller.com. His site went up in 1998."

(Zodiackiller.com)

"Exactly!" I exclaimed. "Tom Voigt hooked up with America's Most Wanted Host, John Walsh, in 1998. They were going to team up and catch the Zodiac. Are you familiar with John Walsh?"

"Somewhat; fill me in."

(Adam Walsh, age 6 and John Walsh, America's Most Wanted)

Adam Walsh, John's son, disappeared from a Sears department store in Hollywood, Florida on the afternoon of July 27th, 1981. He was 6 years old. His mother had left him in the video aisle to watch some older boys play a game while she went to the next aisle over. There was talk of a suspicious security guard that made the boys leave. This murder occurred weeks after the last Atlanta Child Killing. Edwards targeted Hollywood, Florida, a wealthy white community, the complete opposite of Atlanta. On August 10th, 1981, Adam's head was found floating in a canal of water 150 miles north of Hollywood. He had been beheaded and the rest of his remains denied to his grieving parents. The find occurred while the Walshs were on Good Morning America begging desperately for the release of their son. They were notified during the show that the head was their son's.

John Walsh spent the last 32 years trying to figure out who killed his child. In 2008, Hollywood, Florida, police announced that Ottis Toole, a confessed killer, was responsible for Adam's death.

Ottis Toole et Henry Lucas

(Ottis Toole et Henry Lucas)

Ottis Toole and Henry Lucas were captured in 1983 after a nationwide crime spree. They sat in jail between 1983 and 1986, confessing to hundreds of murders they couldn't have possibly done. They were treated like royalty by police as they spent three years confessing to agents from Texas, Florida and Pennsylvania, about murders they supposedly had done. The media labeled them the "Worst Serial Killers Ever." There was one problem. On many of the murders they confessed to, they couldn't have done them. Toole confessed to killing Adam Walsh- and then recanted. Police from around the country spent three years interviewing Toole and Lucas, and in the end, the Texas Attorney General issued a report stating the entire thing appeared to be a hoax.

Lucas and Toole listed hundreds of murders they had done, and they knew the details. The investigation of Lucas and Toole was headed by officers from Pennsylvania, Texas and Florida.

Toole was being held in Texas in 1983, Lucas was being held in Florida, and Edwards was being held in Pennsylvania—all at the same time. Edwards was working a deal with Pennsylvania authorities to get out of prison early. He had been convicted of burglary and arson in 1982 after being arrested in Atlanta and was supposed to serve 12 years. He got out in 1986—the same year the Lucas report came out labeling them a hoax.

Lucas, Toole and Edwards were all in prison at the same time, and all three men were informing to police on murder. Edwards was informing to Pennsylvania agents on murders he had actually committed —but was pinning on others. He admitted this in the 2011 phone call to me.

John Walsh has spent the last 30 years blaming Ottis Toole for Adam's death and has done so repeatedly. Toole died, September 1996, three months before Edwards killed JonBenet Ramsey.

In December of 2008, John Walsh went on TV with Hollywood, Florida, police and publicly blamed Ottis Toole for his son's death. After this, Edwards went online and admitted to being the killer of Adam. He did it 5 days after Wisconsin police questioned him in a 1980 lover's lane killing that would be his demise.

Using the screen name BABABIJAN, Edwards posted his admission to sending John Walsh the 1991 Zodiac/Scorpio letters John had kept secret for 15 years. He posted under the website Crime and Punishment. He posted it twice to make sure it would be understood.

June 14, 2009 at 10:04 pm
(11) Bababijan says:

It was very convenient for John Walsh to go along with the official decision to close the unsolved case of the kidnapping and murder of his son, Adam, because some police officials in

Florida were convinced that they would be far better off to pin such a horrible crime on a dead con man, Ottis Toole, instead of pursuing the diabolical force behind the kidnappings and murders of so many children in America regardless of their colors. Let us not forget the Scorpion's warning for John Walsh that he was his worst nightmare. Why? Did Zodiac change his pen name back in 1990 to Scorpion to cryptically claim responsibility for Adam's demise? Why did John Walsh remain mum for so many years before partially releasing the Scorpion files for the public? If not for the police, then let us hope that this info can be used as a head start by John Walsh if he really wants to find out the truth about the death of his son. He owes him that more than any other person in America. In my opinion, Zodiac Network must be listed on the top of John Walsh's America's Most Wanted list for the whole world to see. Anything less will be unacceptable.

(Posted on Crime and Justice, June 14th, 2009)
"Edwards posted his confession to killing Adam and being the Zodiac killer on his 76th birthday, knowing he was about to be arrested for his first murder and the unraveling would begin."

"John, do you realize what you've uncovered?"

"I do now! But it gets even bigger. John Walsh and Tom Voigt of Zodiackiller.com partnered up in 1998 to catch the Zodiac killer. They did a big production about it and Ed followed the entire thing on line, blogging against the entire community. John Walsh had received a Zodiac killer letter in 1991 and kept it secret until 2006. He didn't even tell Tom Voigt about it in 1998. The FBI convinced him not to go public for fear it would cause terror. Here it is."

AMERICA'S MOST WANTED
OFFICIAL INVESTIGATION TRANSCRIPT

"Scorpion Letters"

Brief:

It's been more than 15 years, but America's Most Wanted is just now ready to reveal a series of very personal threats. In 1991, AMW host John Walsh was sent a series of anonymous, threatening letters that contained cryptic clues, secret codes and claims that the author committed some serious crimes.

The FBI has examined the letters, and while they still don't know who wrote or sent these letters, they say they were not sent by The Zodiac Killer.

And the cryptographs have yet to be solved. Can you help solve this mystery?

Fax your solution to (202) 521-9907 or call our hotline at 1-800-CRIME-TV

I am your worst nightmare coming true. My true identity is not known to you yet, and hopefully will not be for a long time. Your show is more exciting, interesting, and factual than any shitfilled movie or series. I have recently moved into New Jersey and began a new crime spree. I am currently responsible for 23 unsolved crimes ranging from Arson to Burgulary to Sabotage homicide and occasionally everything in between. I strongly advise that you keep this letter and start a rather large file, since you will be hearing from me again. I have enclosed a rather difficultly encoded message containing information that will prove ~~overtot~~ rather useful to you. This code took a lot of time and effort to develop, in hopes that it will defeat FBI and CIA code-breakers. Anything you wish to tell me or ask me can be conveyed to me on your show.

SCORPION

intricate and difficult to recopy onto these cards. My style of handwriting on these cards is verry much altered, and controlled in order to throw off graphologists. I would much rather communicate with you with letters sent between us but you and your over anxious associates would try to nail me even if I used a P.O. Box for a return address. This would create a rather messy situation since I do not plan to be taken alive if at all, and I truly believe in the use of superior firepower. This creates a problem for our communication since the only way I can communicate with you is by letter and possibly phone and your only safe medium in both of our best interests is your informative and helpful show. Consider this your second and definately last chance, since I will soon start collecting bodies for you, to prove that this is not a prank. Hopefully for you no one will expose themselves to me as an easy target for my ever growing anger before I get a chance to hear from you. I now realize with many hundreds of hours of mindracking experimentation with my complex ciphers that my first one that I sent you was comparatively simple to my second, third, fourth, and now temporarily final cryptograph system. I have been encoding useful information for your use and have done it fairly, since all of my ciphers can be decoded simply, once the limited patterns and systems are discovered. I have enclosed another cipher for you to deal with. See you in hell amigo! ←

SCORPION

(Scorpion Letters)

"Neal, did you notice the signature on the letter?"

See you in hell amigo!

(signature from letter)

"Now look at the signature on the letter Ed sent you, giving us permission to write his story."

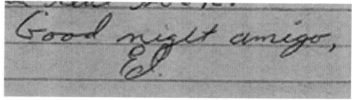

(signature from letter)

Neal told me, "Some of Ed's ciphers in the Zodiac case were based on the Greek alphabet, which has 24 characters, starting with the Alpha- and ending at the Omega. Ed used the Greek Alpha and Omega in the Zodiac Bomb Cipher and when I solved it, you had to put the Alpha symbol at the beginning and the Omega symbol at the end."

C △ J I ■ O ⋊ ⊥ A M ㄱ ▲ Ω O R T G
X ⊙ F D V ʇ ◨ H C E L ⊕ P W △

(Zodiac Killer Bomb Cipher)

"The Greek Alpha and Omega symbol is this:

Aα Ωω

"The Alpha and the Omega, the beginning and the end, the A and the W, there is even a clear A and W within the puzzle. John, Ed killed Adam and has been taunting us with the solution since he did it. Adam Walsh was the beginning and the end. This is overwhelming. How many more murders did Ed do?"

"Hundreds, Neal. Hundreds," I said sorrowfully.

On July 30th, 2009, about 6 weeks after his confession to killing Adam Walsh, Edwards was arrested for the August 9th, 1980 lover's lane murder of Timothy Hack and Kelly Drew in Jefferson, Wisconsin. The unraveling of what he had done was just beginning, and Edwards had put every one of his murders out on the internet to be put together as a puzzle. Edwards had killed nonstop from 1945 until his death in 2011. He continues to use the justice system in his afterlife to kill.

"Neal, this is gonna take years to unravel!"

"We don't have years, John. Neither do hundreds of victims from the last 50 years. Give me the rest that you found after your visit with Kay."

"It's ugly, Neal. He committed some horrific murders and setups all over the country between 2001 and 2009, while he was blogging on Zodiackiller.com. Here's the top 7 in summary order. He set up 8 in the last 10 years of his life and they're all still serving time."

Chapter 35

The Final Decade of Killing

"Edwards planned to get caught on each one of the murders he committed since he was 11." I said to Neal, "That's why he wrote that message in lipstick on his first one 'Please Stop Me I Can't Control Myself,' in Chicago, 1945. He does JonBenet 50 years later and still doesn't get caught. He planned all of them deliberately, patiently and cold bloodedly like he said in his book. Sometimes it took decades to bring to fruition, but he would carry through."

"He had a bigger plan on what he was exposing, John. He was the foreign faction fighting the unjust criminal justice system, even though he was the one making it unjust. He wanted to see the demise of the USA."

"That's exactly right, Neal. And in the end, he targeted Washington, the media and Fort Bragg, the nation's defense."

Starting around 2000, Edwards started blogging details of his life on Zodiackiller.com, describing who the Zodiac killer was, to anyone that would listen. He challenged the expert opinions for 20 years, giving them the entire story but you had to know who the blogger was. Many questioned the knowledge he had. Cameron uncovered thousands of conversations he had as he led the bloggers to believe the Zodiac was alive and well. He detailed every opinion he had about the Zodiac's thought process and how he was raised.

"Zodiac's crimes have no sexual activity involved. These crimes were about something else. IMHO.

Zodiac's 3-part cipher, contains the only sexual passage in all his letters that I remember, and all it tells us is that he had sex with at least one girl and he enjoyed it. When compared to the single statement about sex, Zodiac makes several statements about religion and religious domination of his victims, in this life and the afterlife. Again, a very notable observation. I was raised in a family which tended toward human secularism, which put me in a situation of having to kowtow to devout Christians and realizing the wrath of the Irrationalist when I offered my opinion on one thing or the other. As a result, I've maintained a deep interest in organized religions and their teachings. The more fundamental the parents' religious belief, the deeper the problems demonstrated in the child. This always stayed with me because it truly matched my experience.

Zodiac fits my personal 'profile' of this type of person from this peculiar social climate. Short hair, neatly dressed, quiet and controlled. Add the weekend killings and we have the 9-5 work ethic and the unwillingness to expose himself to peer or marital scrutiny by deviating from his normal schedule. Heck, his wife probably thought he was out bowling, hunting, or something! (probably hunting as Zodiac suggests.)

What also goes into this is that he was well-established with a circle of family and/or friends and had every desire to maintain that relationship unblemished. This above all was his fear and the thing that kept him from coming out and telling the world who he was. In essence, his connection to family/friend/church/social structure was what kept him from going over the edge and immediately declaring himself to the world.

I've seen it so many times I can't count, the desire to scream out one's actions, weighed against the fear of the consequences. The consequence the individual is concerned with is not jail or death, but how others in close relationships will view the individual when things become known.

This probably sounds far-fetched to many of you, that a cold killer can have a family life and a career, and it is of course just my opinion." (Ed Edwards, Zodiackiller.com, October 21, 2000)

I said to Neal, "Remember what Ed told us in that letter about his family?"

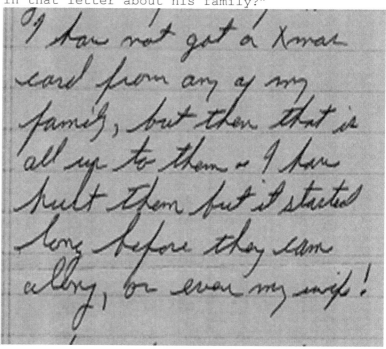

(Edwards Letter to John Cameron, November 2010)

I continued, "It started long before they came along, or even my wife!" 'This matches what he said on the blog. He had a family, kids, social circles, and had his murderous life also. His wife Kay had stated he must have had two lives. His wife and family came along in 1968, just before he started killing everyone in San Francisco. This is how Ed plays the game, truth with lies. That's the light and the dark; it's the good guy and the bad guy, the ying and the yang. Kay was on the good side of him and wouldn't have known most of what he was doing. She appeared hypnotized when I spoke to her around Christmas, 2012. She sure knew he was blogging in the final years of his life, and was talking about 'other' sensational murders. She invited me into her computer room. It was the size of a nice office. Ed had everything, because he was a writer his entire life. Look what he told the bloggers on Zodiackiller.com."

"By sexual loser I meant that the person or people acting as Zodiac probably were not sexually active in what we would think of as 'healthy' ways. Though I'm not sure that that is what drove Zodiac. If I remember my 60's and early 70's correctly (I do with all fond remembrance!) sexual 'deviation' was the norm for many of us. The only ones sexually deviant at the time were the straight-laced ones who were too hung up to get it on. Besides, I personally think Z was a straight lace with religious hang-ups, probably a smothering mother and a wife who acted just like his mother (kiddie stuff in the car, etc.) He was probably in such a rut he needed to feel some power of his own. Just my opinion, but boy did I love the 60's!" (Ed Edwards Zodiackiller.com, October 21, 2000)

Edwards had blogged under numerous names over a 9-year period on many different websites. Most of it occurred on Zodiackiller.com, but if other newspapers were doing specials on his murders, he would make sure to jump in on the blog and straighten out the so-called EXPERTS.

The list of names he used is as follows with the IP addresses, if they were available.

"Any of these names can be Googled by entering the 'name' and 'Zodiackiller.com,' and the conversations he participated in will come up." I pointed out.

1) Bababijan (Crime and Punishment Website, Zodiackiller.com)
2) Curios Cat (Crime and Punishment Website, Zodiackiller.com)
3) Oscar 216.244.24.154, 219.178.191.173, 216.244.24.134, 209.178.191.173, 216.244.24.134, (Zodiackiller.com)
4) Oklahoma_mike (Zodiackiller.com)
5) Zoe Glass 63.69.48.31, 208.202.125.35, 208.202.125.35, (Zodiackiller.com)
6) Sylvie 198.81.17.177, 198.81.16.38, 152.163.213.189, 64.12.105.44, 205.188.193.154, 205.188.192.153, 64.12.105.27, (Zodiackiller.com)
7) Evil 205.188.199.171, 205.188.199.52, 205.188.199.56, (Zodiackiller.com)
8) ZK (Zander_Kite) 64.196.43.60, 64.196.42.204, 64.196.42.223, (Zodiackiller.com)
9) Anonymous 152.163.201.76, 205.188.197.183, (Zodiackiller.com)
10) Hurley 205.188.200.58, 205.198.192.179, 152.163.206.186, (Zodiackiller.com)
11) Esau 24.176.178.187, 24.4.254.113, (Zodiackiller.com)
(332)
12) Peterh 141.154.77.250, 63.214.116.76, (Zodiackiller.com),
13) Chrissy Shaw 67.26.88.233, (Zodiackiller.com)
14) Peter H 63.214.66.165, 63.214.97.239, (Zodiackiller.com)
15) Zander Kite (zk) 64.196.40.26, (Zodiackiller.com)
16) Sylvie (Sylvie14) 198.81.16.34, (Zodiackiller.com)

17) Lapumo 159.134.234.69, 159.134.234.15, (Zodiackiller.com)
18) Peter_H 141.154.81.179, (Zodiackiller.com)
19) Mike (Oklahoma_Mike) 24.143.24.165(Zodiackiller.com)
20) EEAVE (Washington Post Website)

During the year 2000 Edwards was leading the bloggers to believe that the Zodiac killer was still alive and working. Many had their own theories about the Zodiac and Edwards would jump in on conversations and straighten them out when they were wrong. Using the name Oscar was a clue as to who the blogger was. His name wasn't Oscar, but he was earning one on the blog. Everyone was impressed at what Oscar had to say because he had details and theories that made more sense than anyone. In the last decade of his life Edwards committed some of the most sensational murders in the country. Before committing them, he made sure the bloggers knew that the Zodiac HAD a Montana connection. Tom Voigt, the owner of Zodiackiller.com tried to tell everyone there was NO connection.

"Ok everybody, please read carefully. There is NO known connection between Zodiac and Montana." (Tom Voigt, Zodiackiller.com, 12-18-2000)

By Zander Kite (Zk) (nsa-24-197-136-36.sc.charter.com - 24.197.136.36) on Tuesday, December 17, 2002 - 02:42 pm:

I shall also contribute, but after the Christmass rush. If I'm not mistaken, there was some argument over whether Zodiac mentioned Montana or Colorado. At any rate, I'll accept this interview as evidence that Zodiac refer(r)ed to Montana, possibly even Deer Lodge.

(Zander Kite post)

I detailed the murders of his last decade. "The first murder I found was in Washington D.C. He was targeting the government."

On May 1, 2001 in Washington D.C,
Edwards kidnapped 26-year-old Chandra Levy,

criminal justice and journalism student from Modesto, California. She was working for the Federal Bureau of Prisons on the pending execution of Timothy McVeigh, the USA's most prolific killer at the time. Edwards targeted Congressman Gary Condit as the fall guy for the crime. Condit was from California whose constituency (jury) was the Bay area, the same area that convicted and executed Burton Abbott in 1957, for the killing of 14-year-old Stephanie Bryan. Edwards targeted and killed people from the Bay area his entire life to get even. He said he would do it in the letter he sent February 7, 1956 to Judge Snook in California, just before the death sentence was pronounced on Burton Abbott.

"Mr. Snook, You had better give Burton Abbott more time than one week, as you and the twelve jurors are standing or sitting on a bomb. In fact, if Burton Abbott is sent to death row at San Quentin you and the twelve jury men will not be here to convict another not guilty man."

Edwards was the ticking time bomb he mentioned in 1956, planning his murders for maximum recognition and terror. Chandra Levy was an intern for the Federal Bureau of Prisons. She was given the responsibility as an intern, to handle public media relations for the pending execution of Timothy McVeigh. McVeigh had blown up the federal building in Oklahoma City and killed 168 people, April 19th, 1995. McVeigh was set to be executed June 11, 2001 and a month before, Edwards kidnapped her.

Levy was kidnapped May 1, 2001 and never seen alive again. She remained missing for over a year. Congressman Gary Condit became the focus of the investigation after admitting to an inappropriate relationship with her. During the summer of 2001 the press went crazy on Gary Condit and destroyed him. Then, something horrible happened to take Edwards out of the spotlight. The terrorists struck the twin towers on September 11, 2001 and Chandra Levy was gone from the press, yet her body had not been found.

Whenever another killer would take away his recognition, Edwards would create another "crime of recognition" to outdo the one getting all the press. He killed Chandra just before Timothy McVeigh's pending execution to steal the papers and he stole the 911 terrorists' recognition by sending anthrax to congress and the MEDIA.

September 18, 2001. New York, New Jersey, Florida and Washington D.C. Edwards mails the Anthrax Letters to congress and the MEDIA, shutting down the mail system and creating terror.

(September 18, 2001 Anthrax Letters)

I explained, "Edwards mailed the letters 7 days after they struck the twin towers, and he wanted everyone to think that THE MUSLIMS were now inside the USA exposing us all to deadly anthrax. He used felt tip markers just like he did in the JonBenet case. It's harder to track felt tip writing."

"Well, he certainly created terror, John," Neal said. "We went to war a few years later all fearful that the terrorists were within. I guess they were but they weren't Muslim."

"Exactly, Neal. Two bio-weapons specialists were targeted by the FBI as the letter senders. Steven Hatfill settled a law suit against the government in 2004, and the FBI paid him 4 million dollars for their false accusations. The other suspect, Bruce Ivins, died suspiciously on July 27th, 2008 of a Tylenol overdose. That date is the anniversary Edwards killed Adam Walsh in Florida and he anthraxed Florida."

"John, do you have Edwards out in Washington blogging from anywhere?"

"Yes, I have him blogging just 30 miles south of Fort Detrick where the anthrax was stolen, and you aren't going to believe what he said. He tied the Zodiac killer to Egyptian history and science fiction just like he said in his book."

"In the Osirisian Mysteries you find the Egyptian God Osiris who represented the Lord of the Dead, Ruler of the underworld. Osiris is the dispenser of justice and in Masonic terminology the Zodiac is represented by an oblong square with the 4 Cardinal points in each corner and Osiris in the middle. Osiris is ruled by Saturn which rules the day Saturday and is represented by the Nile River. In the Osirisian Mysteries the drama is always carried out between the waxing to the full moon on a sacred lake. Osiris is represented in several mythologies by either the Sun or the Moon. Osiris has been known to represent "the ruler of the dead"; that is, he judges the sinners and collects their souls for purification in the afterlife (they become his slaves). Many of the Zodiac killings were on a Saturday or close to the midnight hour on Friday. He unconsciously or consciously chose to kill around bodies of water or references to water. He may have planned his killings between the waxing to full moon. If Zodiac were a Mason he may have identified himself with Osiris and may have felt protected by that identification."

"Osiris is also represented by the symbol of the circle with the cross in it. The same symbol Zodiac used. If you get a book on ancient symbols you can readily see that many of the Arcane symbols Zodiac used in his ciphers are a part of the Masonic mythology. The Osirisian mysteries are included in the Scottish Rite in the acquisition of degrees. My point is I feel Zodiac was a Mason and chose his name based on the Masonic definition of the word "Zodiac" and that he distorted the Osirisian mysteries to fit somehow his demented personality with the delusion that he was the reincarnation of Osiris in this particular lifetime. If Zodiac was a Mason this would have given him more access to information concerning the Zodiac case than your average individual. (Ed Edwards, August 19, 20, 2000 Zodiackiller.com)"

Neal pointed out, "Ed was a Mason in 1968 when he got out of Leavenworth. And that comment he made, 'The ruler of the dead that judges the sinners and collects their souls for purification in the afterlife; they become his slaves.' That is exactly what I said he was doing back in 2010 when we started this investigation. He was acting out as Satan or Osiris. It's Osiris' eye on the back of the dollar bill Ed was holding in that Paradise Lost Scene:

(Ed Edwards, Paradise Lost, HBO Documentary, 1993 Holding Two One Dollar Bills Exposing Osiris' Eye and Egyptian Pyramid)

Edwards had blogged this information in August of 2000 from Ashburn, Virginia, just 33 miles away from Fort Detrick where the Anthrax was stolen. 911 happened and changed his plans so he monopolized on our country's fear and anthraxed the media and congress, tying it to Islam. He targeted them for their destruction of Congressman Gary Condit, the summer of 2001.

Edwards began blogging again one month after the attack about the envelopes sent. He used the name BOOKWOORM, tying his rant to the anthrax attack, the 911 attack and the scales of justice.

"Using fake return addresses, like the 4th grade one, would be something any terrorist, serial killer, etc. would do. The question is why they use the return addresses that they do use? Letters from kids wouldn't seem suspicious. My other guess on the school one is that the Pentagon is shaped similar to a school zone sign.

And grade school kids sent letters to the weather people. We look at the sky to see what it looks like outside. The sky is where the planes came from on Sept. 11th, too. The sloped writing reminds me of when the Titanic sank. Or it could have something to do with the scales of justice." (Ed Edwards, Zodiackiller.com, October 24, 2001)

He furthered his connection to the anthrax attacks in a blog in April of 2002. All the misspellings were his.

"The kind of society that would consider a mass murderer terrorist a hero is rather bleak to imagine. If we consider for a moment Zodiac's as terroism 101, we can see today the damage of a more advanced terrorist from recent events. As millions consider the more advanced terroist a hero today a time may come where a similiar population will consider the same about Zodiac. Would a seret cashe of eveidence revel a mission in which an agreived group might except or even embrace zodiac's tactics? Has the more advanced terroist of current time learned from zodiac? As suggest on the board there are undenaible similarities in the recent antrax letters to thoose of Zodiacs. I would imagine such a soceity could develop in the midst of a holy war. The insanity of such a war would grow agreived groups. Any of which would be capable of pushing a button to a weapon of mass desruction if they had it. Has Zodiac passed out such buttons? Sure a secret cashe of evidence is possible. As is a game of who's got the button." (Ed Edwards, Zodiackiller.com 4-29-2002 blogged from Washington DC)

After killing Chandra Levy in May of 2001, and doing the anthrax attacks in September and October 2001, he posted the above comments online and planted Chandra's skull in the heart of Washington D.C. in Rock Creek Park, May 22, 2002, the day the Levys were on Oprah Winfrey begging for the safe return of their daughter. He had planted Adam Walsh's head in 1981 on the day the Walshs were on CBS' Good Morning America begging for the return of their son. Everything he did was to maximize terror and recognition. Edwards left a tube of red lipstick at the scene where Chandra's skull was found and this confused police. The lipstick killer had struck 56 years after he started killing and nobody put the puzzle together.

Eventually, an innocent man named Ingmar Guandique was arrested in 2009 for the killing of Chandra Levy. His arrest based partially on testimony provided by Edwards as witness # 10 in the arrest affidavit dated March 2009. Edwards stated the following in the affidavit.

"It has known Guandique for years and that Guandique was a member of MS-13 and has committed many robberies. Guandique boasted that he was called Chuckie, and that he had a reputation for killing and chopping up people. Guandique told Witness # 10 that he had committed many crimes against women including rapes. He stated that he would tie their hands and feet together, usually with a rope or he would improvise.

The Witness # 10 statement was a parable of Edwards' life of killings. Edwards' real name was Chuckie—Charles Edward Myers. Edwards chopped people up his entire life and hauled them out in suitcases. Edwards had committed many crimes against women since 1945. And Edwards was selling firearms to MS13 in 2001 while living in Oklahoma with his wife Kay. He wanted to be close to the pending execution of Timothy McVeigh. Edwards would follow other killers and mimic their murders to confuse police. He would never let McVeigh go down as the USA's worst killer.

Witness # 10's testimony was provided to police in writing in November of 2008, and the author was never identified. Witness # 10 never appeared at trial yet the information was used to arrest Guandique. Ed was witness No. 10

Edwards had blogged from Chandra Levy's hometown 4 days before killing her. He spoke about how easy it was to change his appearance. He was leading the bloggers to look at the Zodiac killer for Chandra Levy's murder. He used the name ZOE GLASS.

"How many ways can one change their appearance? from head to toe. finding an old 60's ad for shoe lifts, brought speculation of how much height could one easily gain. two and half to three inches with a shoe lift and an equal amount with shoes would seem achievable. Perhaps with construction or cowboy boots. a hat or 'big hair' could add more inches to an illusion of height. what else might a 'master of disguise' have in his bag, although Batman was a master of disguise, there was no mistaking him when he was disguised as the caped crusader." (Ed Edwards Zodiackiller.com, 4-21-2002.)

Edwards continued to blog under other names before he killed Chandra. He used the name 13 words just days before doing it. There are 13 letters in his name.

"Not only is very easy to change one's appearance, it's also possible for perps to leave misleading physical evidence. One example is the burglar who wears shoes/boots etc, twice his size and never the same boot but always the same size. Hence, the physcial profile based on the shoe size is inaccurate, also the planting of false fingerprints at a crime scene is not unusual by perps. (Although a good crime scene tech can ID those latents as false). Recently worked a case where a perp set the crime scene to appear as if he had cut himself on a glass window while entering the victims residense leaving a nice trail of blood and of course DNA, too bad the blood was not his. (Ed Edwards, April 19th, 2001 Washington DC)

Edwards was portraying himself online as an investigator that had worked cases in the past where fingerprints and blood were planted. He described in the blog what he had done to Dannie Gloeckner in 1996 when he beheaded him, took his blood and gave it to police claiming Dannie had climbed through his window and broke into his home. Edwards gave police blood on glass in 1996 in Ohio. Edwards details giving the blood to police in a 2010, You-Tube confession to killing Dannie, given to the Geauga Maple Leaf Press.

Edwards targeted Chandra Levy because she was about to graduate from USC with a Masters in Journalism and Criminal Justice. She was from the area of California that convicted and executed Burton Abbott in 1957. Her father was a doctor in Modesto, and she worked with the media in the Federal Bureau of Prisons for the pending execution of Timothy McVeigh. Edwards targeted McVeigh because the press was claiming him to be the most prolific serial killer ever. He killed 168 people and injured 600. Ed Edwards followed serial killers to outdo them.

After Edwards had killed Chandra and bragged on the blog about taking fingers and planting evidence, he sent Tom Voigt of Zodiackiller. com, a set of 8 fingerprints rolled in red lipstick.

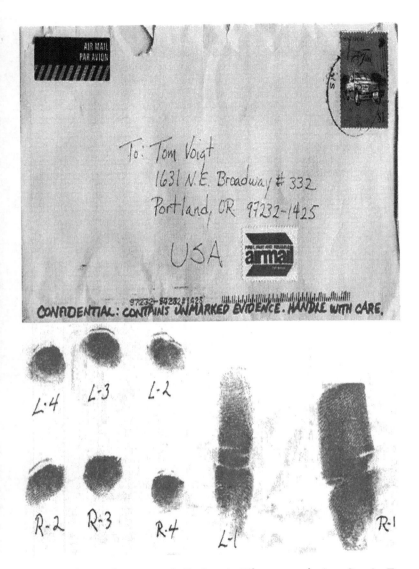

(Envelope and Latent Fingerprints Sent To Zodiackiller.com November 22, 2002.)

The prints were rolled in a red substance. Edwards only sent 8 fingerprints, and all were missing the tips. This was a clue. Edwards is missing two tips, leaving him with 8. His NCIC record lists it:

```
Scars, Marks, and Tattoos
Code                      Description, Comments, and Images
MISSING FINGER,RIGHT      , TIP OF RING FINGER
MISSING FINGER,RIGHT      , TIP OF MIDDLE FINGER
```

(Edwards NCIC record)

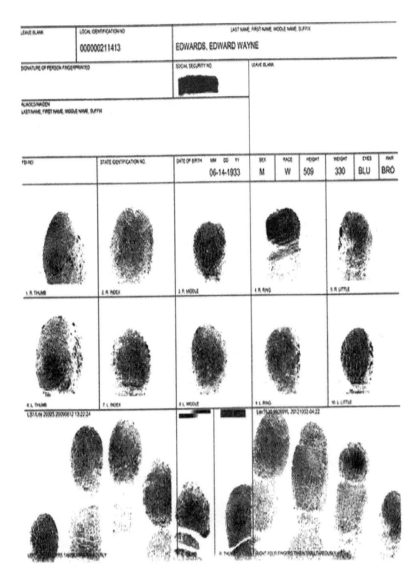

(Edwards Fingerprint Card)

By leaving off the tips it made identification impossible through an automated system. Edwards posted an opinion on the fingerprints a month after sending them:

"It wouldn't surprise me if the prints could not be checked even if they do belong to the writer. They appear to be limited to the second and third, or just the third joints of the fingers. The two or three times I have been printed, only the first joints were taken". (Ed Edwards, Zodiackiller. com, 12-9-2002)

Edwards was correct about the portion of the fingers he sent in. The lower joints of the fingers rarely appear on fingerprint cards and Edwards only sent in the lower parts of the 8 fingers, no tips.

Edwards wrote a lengthy letter trying to get Tom Voigt to enter into an agreement to reveal the real Zodiac killer story.

> Dear Editor
> This is the Zodiac speaking.
>
> This is the way I used to address myself to the Editor of the San Francisco Chronicle. No longer is this necessary, for I am not that person anymore.
>
> I have changed.
>
> Still the interest as to the events I perpetrated on an unsuspecting public are alive and well after 30+ years. Some say I must be dead, others have a multitude of theories as to my demise. The truth is, I am very much alive, and I am enclosing evidence in this correspondence to match DNA and prints on file and in Quantico.
>
> I am writing now to share a missing link in the Zodiac Killer's profile, now that all the compounded theories has not yet touched upon a probability that my conscience compels me to know. This is not to diminish the horrible acts I perpetrated (it can't), but to supply the truth to set me free from a delusion that I may have only been hallucinating I was the Zodiac.
>
> In those years I was an LSD and heroin addict with a taste for the bizarre, sub-cultural and underground lifestyles. I would have "brown-outs" of consciousness that would hardly last for days. In that state, I experienced the graphic deeds of the Zodiac Killer as if I was an observer, not the perpetrator.
>
> When I regained my senses and the high was over (a momentary state between trips and fixes), I would share my recollections with those around me who were pretty much in the same state as I. They as well as I would be blown-away to then see in the news the very events I had described hours earlier.
>
> My peers and I thought I was psychic. They used to call me "Priest". Being heavy substance abusers and not caring to divulge any information to what we all believed was a corrupt and perverted system, I remained in my own eyes and those of my peers to be clairvoyant.

(Letter From Edwards to Zodiackiller.com, November 22, 2002)

Tom Voigt has withheld page two of the above letter for 11 years. Two months after sending in the above letter and prints, Edwards tried one more time to get Tom Voigt to catch him. He sent him another letter trying to make a blockbuster movie deal.

Dear Tony,

What irony! What twisted, spiraling fate that our paths should cross at this particular time in light of who you are and what I am. It's oh so amazing how fiction imitates life!

In writing you first the letter (you ▮▮▮ and ▮▮▮), I wasn't interested in your web site. Fact is until I decided to write, I never entered it nor knew of its existance. I was honestly not aware of the screenplay being written about the web site, a do-something year old copycat me, and last but not least yours truly. I, in our first communication, simply wanted to appease my conscience.

Now thanks to the miracle of technology, here we are in communication for a second time. I appreciate your giving me the information I was looking for.

Congratulations, on your part, for the upcoming movie-script. It sounds like fun, but truth will not be served in its current format and ending. Reality is, Tony, neither you nor anyone else can write as appropriate an ending for the screenplay as myself. The last thing the public needs is another fictitious tale.

If you want a news-breaking ending along with a realistic story line between me and the Zodiac - wannabe, you need my input. Knowing now as you do regards the matches of DNA and points, that I am the real deal-that I have changed so it is possible for others to change as well, you need me to help make this the box office BLOCKBUSTER it can be.

Imagine the publicity, Tony; "The movie that drew the Zodiac out of hiding!" This film has the potencial to make your efforts and the efforts of all parties involved in this project PROFITABLE.

(January 15th, 2003 Edwards Zodiac Killer Letter to Tom Voigt of Zodiackiller.com)

The letter was sent on the 56-year anniversary of Edwards' killing the Black Dahlia in Hollywood, January 15th, 1947. Edwards had also sent a packet containing a white powdery substance along with the fingerprints he sent in.

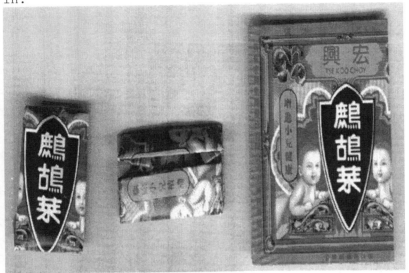

(Tom Voigt November 22, 2002 Letter Containing White Powder Poison)

The packets, made in China, and tying back to Edwards' history of hunting down communists, was a clue as to who the sender was. It was also a clue that he was the Anthrax killer from 2001. The Zodiac killer was the Anthrax killer.

The items Edwards sent to Tom Voigt have been in the public domain since 2002 on his website. Voigt moved from Portland, Oregon to San Francisco after receiving these letters in an attempt to catch the Zodiac. Tom Voigt's website was taunted by Edwards from 1998 until his capture in 2009. In the end, Voigt's desire to bring out the Zodiac killer worked.

Edwards used the Chandra Levy case from 2001 until 2009, trying to get the police to go after anyone just to prove he could do it. He knew if he provided the evidence they would follow his false clues.

In 2008, the Washington Post did a 12-part series on the unsolved Chandra Levy case and pointed the evidence directly at an illegal immigrant named Ingmar Guandique. It was after this series of stories that Edwards became a witness in the case and provided his written statement which eventually contributed to the arrest of Ingmar Guandique for the murder of Chandra Levy.

Edwards posted the following after the Washington Post ended the series in 2008 accusing Ingmar Guandique of being the killer of Chandra. He was taunting the "expert" opinions of all involved and warning them. He used the name Linda. The rant was a biblical warning of what he was revealing.

"Then, the FBI learned from the message of God that the prime suspect in this case was the mastermind of at least three other murderous crimes against other women. Believe it, for God was mad that spiritual evidences were not taken full weight as they should have been. And God said, this 2008 will be a year to regret if US is not serving the justice upon the culprits' gang-leader of these horrendous crimes. And the time ticking on, then, you have the tornadoes, the 500-year-flood, and the 8000 dry shots of tinder-burning thunderbolts in CA. So, again, here is an almost rehash of the unfinished business against the implicated, for God demanded this be tho`roughly investigated again, if not, this year is far from over yet. It's good to be fearful before God, for that is how all learn from God in these first steps of getting close to Him.

Semen of Condit on Chandra's yet-washed underwear serve to reveal how sneaky he had been with all those who confronted him about the type of relationship he had with Chandra. Timing of that semen stain can be tied with the 'big news' that eventually hoodwinked Chandra into a trap of a callous-beast-in-disguise. (911) This crime, together with the previously committed ones, were team work, with cruel hearts behind the veil, no wonder another poster reminded the readers to: avoid a minister/ or son of such........The bees are 2/3 missing in some parts of US, and humankind simply can't live without these hardworking ones. God said, 'US, make these things right immediately, less there'd be no bee flying over all the buds across this land called by my name in the first place. These series were like intelligent bricks to elicit the all-seeing jades out of the heart of the earth, and thank goodness, the jades are coming in. May God have mercy upon US, and strengthen her in avenging the cries of Chandra in good speed. Heads up, necks stretching, eyes fixating for all the sincere hope of a matured judgment into this already made bare case, and only after an execution compatible to that truth, then the whole world will chorus, 'indeed justice is served rightly as we have surmised since its beginning.' US, listen to that, I hope in advance, you're not to late to act now for Chandra/US well-being altogether." (Ed Edwards, Zodiackiller.com, July 24th, 2008)

Neal pointed out, "Every time he is using the word God in this rant, he really means Satan. This sums up how Ed felt. He was God and was orchestrating injustices for decades, getting people to sin and then killing someone close to them. When he said 'avoid a minister/or son of such,' he is describing himself. He used the preacher ruse all over the country."

"Well, it worked well for him. In 2010, illegal immigrant Ingmar Guandique was convicted of Chandra Levy's murder. Now, in 2012 the United States Attorney General contacted the judge in the Ingmar Guandique case to inform him and the defense that there are problems."

"What's going on, John?"

"A witness had provided testimony that Guandique confessed while the two were housed in a Kentucky federal prison in 2006. Edwards was living in Kentucky in 2006. The Defense has filed an appeal for a new trial and the judge is expected to rule by January 2014. The government has held 5 secret hearings since 2012 regarding the wrongful conviction of Ingmar Guandique. A white noise machine was used in the courtroom, so reporters and spectators could not hear what was being said. The judge has sealed the records until the defense and prosecution can agree on what to release. This in itself is unheard of in a post-conviction trial proceeding. Neal, there has never been court hearings like this in the USA. Edwards had gotten into the investigation of Chandra Levy and now it is all unraveling in a courtroom."

"Good. It's about time this was exposed. What was the next murder you found after he did the anthrax attacks?"

"You will find this one interesting. He targeted a newspaper EDITOR on Halloween."

November 1, 2001, Columbia Missouri.

Edwards targeted and killed EDITOR Kent Heitholt of the Columbia, Missouri Tribune. Heitholt was celebrating his 5-year anniversary with the paper and there was an open public reception. Edwards targeted EDITORS his entire life and he targeted this one on Halloween night, leaving him strangled and beaten in the parking lot at 2:30 am. He committed the crime on Halloween because it leads into November 1st, the Catholic All Saints Day. This represents the good and the evil, the light and the dark. Heitholt was beaten in the face with a cane-like object and his hyoid bone was broken just like Chandra Levy's. Eventually Ryan Ferguson and Charles Erickson were wrongfully convicted in 2006 and are currently serving time.

Edwards blogged on Zodiackiller.com the day after killing Heitholt, about having a confrontation with a newsman. The name he used was Sylvie. Edwards used this name in written documents in the 1968 Robison, 6-family-member murders in Michigan. Mr. Robison was also an EDITOR like Kent Heitholt.

"My neighbor is a decades long employee for the Press-Enterprise. Usually a very nice guy, he became very defensive and assertively protective of his Paper when I politely questioned him on his Paper's choice not to do a story on CJB, this being the 35th anniversary of her death. He admitted that the PE is now owned by a Nat'l group BUT he says ALL the reporters are local who care dearly about their community. He went on to tell me that (as Tom suggested) the PE would NEVER wish to cater to the RPD - AU CONTRAIRE - as they were the ones to keep up relentless heat on the officers that shot unarmed Tyisha Miller, and that their continual unfavorable stories on the RPD were the reason the officers lost their jobs and the Miller family received 5 million. He claims the RPD constantly harassed PE employees at that time. He believes in his opinion that they did not do the story so as not to be redundant, that the multi-part piece done last year had since yielded nothing new, thus no reason to rehash. I respectfully disagreed with him there, even a short refresher article would, INMO, have been in order. Then he turned it around on me - 'Why do you critics expect everyone to do it for you, take matters into your own hands,' blah, blah, blah. Finally he said 'why doesn't everyone give us a break, we are a huge contributor to charities!!' (Ed Edwards, Zodiackiller.com, November 2, 2001)

I furthered, "Heitholt was an EDITOR in Shreveport, Louisiana before he moved to Missouri. Edwards targeted editors and had spent considerable time in Shreveport. He had mailed the JonBenet letter from there in 1997. Edwards targeted Heitholt because he had a daughter Kali, a production designer and artist student, attending USC in Los Angeles. Two of her classmates were targeted and found guilty for the murder of her father. Kali Heitholt lived in the same city Ed killed Elizabeth Short, known as the Black Dahlia, in 1947."

"It's amazing how he was able to tie so many things together, John. How many more did he do? We haven't even gotten through 2001!"

"I'm sure there are others but the next one I tied him to was a young couple on a beach in 2004."

August 16th, 2004. Jenner, Sonoma County, California.

Edwards killed Lindsay Cutshall and Jason Allen as they slept in their sleeping bags on an ocean beach. Lindsay was from Ohio and her dad a preacher. Jason was from Michigan, the same place Edwards killed the entire Robison family in 1968."

(Lindsay Cutshall and Jason Allen, 2004)

The two had been asleep in a tent on a remote beach when Edwards approached them with a shotgun, shooting them both in the head like he did to Dannie Gloeckner in 1996. He left writings at the scene that tied him to the killing, and he led the bloggers on Zodiackiller.com to believe the Zodiac killer did it. He used the name Oklahoma mike. Edwards lived in Oklahoma with his wife Kay at the time he blogged.

>Oklahoma mike
>Username: Oklahoma mike
>Registered: 02-2004
>Posted on Sunday, August 22, 2004 - 08:15 pm:

Ever since my wife told me of hearing about this case several days ago it has preyed on my mind more and more. After reading several news accounts and gaining information on the Zodiac chat

Sat. night I decided to start this thread. At the outset I know it is very doubtful the original Zodiac is alive and/or free and the odds are far against him being the perpetrator in this latest viscious crime. But I can't help thinking of these similarities to Lake Berryessa and Santa Barbara:

1. Victims were a young romantically involved couple killed at a beach.

2. Whoever the perp was, he had to know the area well.

3. The victims car was parked along a highway with a path leading to the beach. None of the beaches were accessible by automobile.

4. The actual murder site was not visible from the road.

5. No robbery or sexual assault occurred. Killing seems the only motive.

6. A gun was used in each of the crimes (at Lake Berryessa he only used the gun to intimidate, but a gun was integral nonetheless).

7. No bodies were mutilated and there was no sign of uncontrolled rage. Even with stabbing at Lake Berryessa he was described as cold and methodical.

8. The killer evidently approached and withdrew unseen.

9. The killer seems to have stalked the area not specific persons.

    10. Few, if any, other persons knew the victims intended to go to the site.
    11. None of the victims had anyone with a grudge against them, so far as known. They were all described by friends as well liked.
    12. Victims were Caucasian.
    13. It is less than 100 miles from Lake Berryessa.
    14. Near water.
    15. It has always been assumed that Zodiac knew the outdoors at least fairly well. That is one reason ALA was/is such a viable suspect. This killer had to have outdoors skills better than most people nowadays jdo.
    And a few final thoughts: Another serial killer, BTK, resurfaced after more than 20 years. Everyone thought him long gone as well. The SFPD and Riverside PD recently closed their cases. This would infuriate Z if he were still alive. Plus, BTK, an imitator, has returned and is now getting all the press coverage. Several strong motives for Z to come out of retirement. My wife pointed out that at Lake Berryessa and probably Santa Barbara Zodiac liked to control and terrify his victims before killing them which would seem different. But she said, "Now he'd be old and could not take such a chance, he'd go for the quick kill, shooting them in their sleep". And finally, I am a typical scientific and skeptical fanatic, demanding only facts. But somehow, even all the way out here in Oklahoma, this new crime just 'feels' like Zodiac. As I said at the beginning, it is very unlikely that this could be the work of the original Zodiac. But DAMN!
END

    Edwards left writings at the scene of the murder tying the crime to Satanism. He purposely left every E standing out. The letter is dated August 4th, 2004; the 69-year anniversary of Ed's mother's pending death. The handwriting matched some of letters Edwards sent to Neal and myself.

Deligated

8/9/04

At the Driftwood Inn, alone, again, Outside of myself and placed of hell, see I'm doing quite poorly at rhyming with deftness, to be honest, how boring. Suspended in time, linked only to others through a transcribe, brief as breath and who decides the size of these lines? Deligated by here, a last vestige of mystery and anonymity when all is known for security and preferred allure, yet so impersonal that you could be me! Legally! Well, this is me, free of I.D. and soon to walk nude along the beach, things can be peachy. Keen if you let them be! He, he

(August 16th, 2004 Sonoma County, California, Letter Left at Cutshall/Allen Murder Scene)

"Well this is mE, frEE of I.D. and soon to walk nudE along thE bEach, things can bE pEachy kEEn if you lEt thEm bE! HE, hE"

Besides leaving the E prominent throughout the letter, Edwards left two pictures drawn on the driftwood at the scene that was a clue as to who had committed the crime.

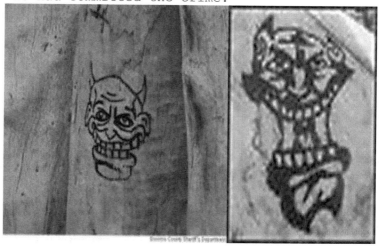

(Two Drawings, Felt Tip Marker, of Satan)

Edwards had signed the poem in a large R standing for Ra, the Sun God in ancient Egyptian mythology. The ancients believed RA merged with Osiris and became not only the creator, but the God of the dead. That is why Edwards stated he was collecting slaves for his afterlife, in the Zodiac case. Edwards criticized the police on line, for not releasing the pictures and beach poem right away to the public. Police had withheld many of his letters over the years for fear it would cause panic.

"What is it that makes police sit on so much evidence for almost 2 years? I can see the need to hold some things back, but surely not so much as they have just released." (Ed Edwards, Zodiackiller.com 5-10- 2006)

The Zodiac had killed Lindsay Cutshall and Jason Allen in 2004 while everyone on zodiackiller.com was wondering if he was still alive. Edwards told them online that an old man could have certainly done it.

"I don't think Arthur Leigh Allen was the Zodiac. Anyone (even an old man) can pull a trigger, especially against 2 sleeping victims. From what I have read, the victims were just shot and that is it. If you are talking about revenge, anger or 'if I can't have her no one can' there would be a lot more violence at the scene. This was random or they were stalked by a person that was not emotionally attached to either person. The killer has probably walked that section of beach many times reliving his/her crime. August 16, 2004 was new moon, so on the nights of the 15, 16, 17, there would effectively have been no moon during the nighttime hours." (Ed Edwards Zodiakiller.com, May 3, 2006)

Edwards gave out the details as he challenged Zodiackiller.com to catch him. The two victims were last seen in "San Francisco," in the heart of the Zodiac, before they drove north toward the same area where Edwards buried Stephanie Bryan, in 1955. As they slept on the beach, Edwards approached them and shot them both in their tent.

(Jason Allen and Lindsay Cutshall, San Francisco, Last Pictures In Their Camera)

Lindsay Cutshall had a camera, and it has been speculated that the picture of the beach might have been taken by the killer himself. It was the last photo on the film. The driftwood in the foreground had the Satan pictures drawn on it. The rocks in the background appear to be pyramid shaped.

Edwards killed the couple in August, the month he killed so many others. He blogged about his knowledge of the weapon used to kill them and led the bloggers to believe the Zodiac had committed it. He left a note with a poem about what's at stake.

(Notebook detailed below)

"Santa Claus?? Leprechauns? Tooth fairy? Alien, buggie man and someone harry. Take what's at stake before another mistake, which like you, who I very hate, shouldn't break but make in such a hurry."

Edwards left a parable of his life at many of his scenes. A writing left in the beach journal indicated the killer was an only child. The name "Chrissie" was a name Edwards used on Zodiackiller.com.

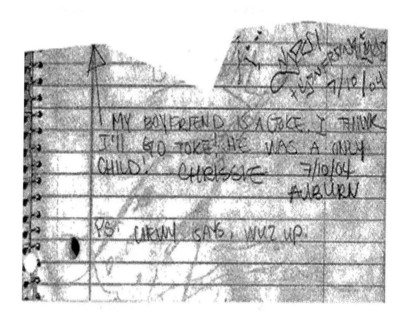

Edwards sent many letters over the years indicating he was an only child, born illegitimate. Both Lindsay and Jason had been attending a religious church camp the week before their deaths and were due to head home to Ohio to get married, where Lindsay's father, Chris Cutshall, was an evangelical minister. He believes that the devil was responsible for the deaths of his daughter and her fiancé. In a 2006 interview, he sadly stated that he believes the murders are linked to satanic activity.

After killing in California in 2004, Edwards returned to Ohio. The next "murder of the decade" was the brutal crucifixion of a nun and the setup of a Catholic priest in Toledo. Although Edwards had killed the nun in 1980, he spent 25 years trying to setup an innocent priest for the crime.

(Father Gerald Robinson Sister Margaret Pahl)

On April 6th, 1980 in Toledo, Ohio, Sister Margaret Pahl unlocked the Sacristy of Mercy Chapel and was preparing for Easter Saturday Mass. She was brutally attacked inside the Sacristy 30 minutes before mass started. A suspicious looking priest was seen leaving the area just after the killing. He has never been identified.

Sister Pahl had been strangled from behind. She had a broken hyoid bone; 31 stab wounds: 22 to the face, and 9 in the shape of an inverted cross on her chest. Edwards covered her in the white altar cloth, and then stabbed her through it in an upside down cross. It meant Signed by the Cross, just like in the JonBenet Ramsey case, SBTC. Both left covered in white cloth to represent purity.

Like many of Ed's victims, Sister Pahl had a broken hyoid bone as did Chandra Levy, Dannie

Gloeckner, JonBenet etc... This was Edwards' signature rabbit punch. He demonstrated it in his 2010 confession you can find on You Tube. Ed Edwards 2011 Confession Describing the Rabbit Punch. The rabbit punch knocks you down, unable to scream or breathe, and unable to move. It is a sign that the killer got "close" to his victim.

Sister Pahl was killed in the church Sacristy, not the Chapel. Easter Saturday morning is the only day The Body of Christ is held in the Sacristy. It represents Jesus in the tomb and the coming resurrection on Easter Sunday. Edwards had staged the crime to occur moments before Father Gerald Robinson was due for Easter Saturday Mass. He was in the shower when the murder occurred and was alerted to find Sister Pahl crucified in the church Sacristy moments before Mass. Father Robinson became the prime suspect. The unidentified priest seen leaving the Sacristy just after the murder was the real culprit.

Edwards targeted Father Gerald Robinson for setup in 1980, but the prosecutor wouldn't file charges. The evidence wasn't there and the entire case was sensational. Then, in 2002 a psychiatric patient came forward directing the evidence towards Father Gerald Robinson. Robinson was arrested in 2005 and convicted in 2006. He had adamantly denied any involvement in 1980 and maintains it to this day. My brother received a letter in 2013 from Father Gerald Robinson and it is clear that an innocent man has been sitting in jail for 7 years now.

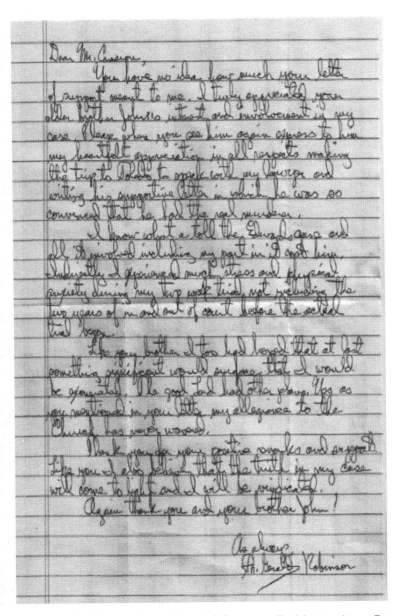

(Father Gerald Robinson Letter to Joe Cameron May 2013)

Father Gerald Robinson was targeted by Edwards because of his name and his relationship with the Toledo Catholic Diocese. It was a Catholic League worker named Mr. Robinson in 1948 that lied and sent Ed to the reformatory. It was this chapter in his book that tied together the 1968 Robison family murder and the 1980 crucifixion of Sister Margaret Pahl in Toledo, and setup of Father Robinson. Edwards switched the names in his book on purpose as a clue.

"A man came to see me and introduced himself as Mr. Robinson. I was told by Mr. Robison I could come and go as I wish. When we pulled in front of the school's main entrance, January 1948 I saw looming in front of me two big black steel doors. After Mr. Robison signed the papers for my admittance I was led downstairs to a shower and my clothes were taken. My imitation had begun and my suspicions were rapidly growing. My resentment knew no bounds."
*(Ed Edwards, MOAC, January 1948)

By age 15 Edwards had such hatred for the Catholics he became a Satanist, targeting religious people and destroying them for decades. He had killed two women, Arliss Perry at Stanford Memorial Church, October 12th, 1974 and Irene Garza, killed Easter Saturday April 16th, 1960 in McAllen, Texas in the same manner as Sister Pahl.

Edwards used his intelligence to write a book that was a puzzle of murder that when revealed would reveal Satan. After Father Robinson's conviction in 2006, he started planning revenge on a happy, healthy family in Toledo, Ohio. He would take their first-born son and plan it for decades.

April 1st, 2008. Lakeland, Florida. On April 1st, 2008, Robert A Wiles, age 26 was kidnapped from Lakeland, Florida.

MISSING PERSON!!!

Robert A. Wiles
26 years old

5'9", 165lbs, hazel eyes

Last seen:
National Flight Services
Lakeland, FL

Missing Since: April 1st
Reward $250,000
Contact: 1.866.838.1153

PLEASE HELP US FIND ROB!!!
WE LOVE YOU AND ARE PRAYING!

(Robert A Wiles Missing Person Poster)

Robert was from Toledo, Ohio and had attended Bowling Green University. His mother and father owned National Flight Services, an aviation company with offices in Ohio, Texas and Florida. The Wiles had been married since 1980, and Robert was their first-born son, born after the killing of Sister Margaret Pahl. He was a pilot and was running National Flight Services for his family in Lakeland, Florida. On the day he disappeared he was preparing to fly out to Dallas, Texas for a conference.

Sometime after 6:30 p.m., April 1st, Robert disappeared, never to be seen again. His body has never been found. "Three Days Later" on April 3rd, Tom Wiles, Robert's father received two text messages that contained a ransom note:

April 3, 2008, 0900 Text Message.

"Mr. Wiles. I suggest you read your Lakeland email if you ever want to see your son again. We can't imagine why you wouldn't answer a call from your son."

"We have Robert. If you hope to see him alive again you must follow our instructions without deviation! Do not speak about this to anyone including family. Tell everyone Robert is

Ill. Do not contact any authorities or private parties. Obtain an item of luggage of the appropriate size and place 750.000 dollars in small unmarked untraceable bills. Place the luggage containing the money in a plain cardboard box and ship it to your Lakeland Facility with detailed instructions that it is highly confidential materials for a special project that your son is working on. You should instruct someone you trust to place the box unopened in your son's office. This must be completed by the evening of the 6th. NO EXCUSES! No exceptions! We are watching everything and if you think you can outsmart us it will cost your son's life
Group X"

    The Robert Wiles ransom note contained similar language as did the JonBenet Ramsey ransom note and the 1955 Stephanie Bryan ransom note Edwards had penned.
    1996 RAMSEY NOTE "Mr. Ramsey. At this time, we have your daughter in our posession. She is safe and unharmed and if you want her to see 1997, you must follow our instructions to the letter.
    2008 WILES NOTE. Mr. Wiles We have Robert If you hope to see him alive again you must follow our instructions without deviation!
    1955 STEPHANIE BRYAN NOTE: Bryan Don't be idiotic. This is not a hoax. Don't contact any law enforces if you expect to see your girl in the near future. Don't contact anyone it will take the package a while to reach me but your child will be okay if you follow instruction"
    1996 RAMSEY NOTE: you must follow our instructions to the letter.
    2008 WILES NOTE: you must follow our instructions without deviation!
    1955 STEPHANIE BRYAN NOTE: He will give you instruction. Follow them and you will reach your child.
    1996 RAMSEY NOTE: you will put the money in a brown paper bag.

2008 WILES NOTE: the money in a plain card board box

1955 STEPHANIE BRYAN NOTE: Wrap it in a small box then wrap the box in brown paper.

1996 RAMSEY NOTE. Speaking to anyone about your situation, such as Police, F.B.I. etc., will result in your daughter being beheaded

2008 WILES NOTE: Do not contact any authorities or private parties. Do not speak about this to anyone including family

1955 STEPHANIE BRYAN NOTE: Don't contact any law enforces if you expect to see your girl in the near future.

1996 RAMSEY NOTE SIGNATURE: Victory! S.B.T.C

2008 WILES NOTE SIGNATURE: Group X

1955 STEPHANIE BRYAN NOTE: You tipped Law. Wise up they can't help you only I can. You will get instruction

Edwards had been writing ransom notes as puzzles for decades. In every case the victim was already dead, and there was no chance of getting them back alive. The parents would become the first suspect and in the end innocent people were destroyed or executed by the system. Edwards targeted the Wiles family for destruction just as he had targeted the Ramseys and the Bryans.

In 2006, after the conviction of Father Gerald Robinson in Toledo, someone approached Tom Wiles and convinced him that he would need kidnapping insurance on his employees in the future. Mrs. Wiles provided me with the policy.

National Flight Services, Inc.

Insurer: Federal Insurance Company
Term: 4/14/07 to 4/14/08
Policy #: 68043943

KIDNAP & RANSOM

$ 1,000,000	Kidnap & Ransom Coverage
$ 1,000,000	Custody
$ 1,000,000	Expense
$ 1,000,000	Accidental Loss
$ 250,000	Benefit Amount, Loss of Life

Deductible: $0

Extensions:
- Mutilation: 25% of Loss of Life Benefit
- All other Accidental Loss: 100% of Loss of Life Benefit Amount

Territory: Anywhere in the world except the United States of America, its territories and possessions and Puerto Rico; Canada and the Prohibited area; and international airspace or waters only in the course of travel or transportation between any of the countries, jurisdictions or places included above.

Exposure: # of Trips - 6

Disclaimer: The abbreviated outlines of coverage used throughout this document are not intended to express any legal opinion as to the nature of coverage. They are only visuals to a basic understanding of coverage and do not detail all policy terms nor do they alter any policy conditions. Please read your policy for specific coverages, limitations and restrictions and call us with questions.

"Look at the date of the coverage, April 14, 2007 to April 14, 2008." I pointed out to Neal, "This policy was issued April 14, 2006, and jury selection started "three days later," April 17th, 2006 in the Father Gerald Robinson trial, going on in Toledo. And guess when Father Robinson was born? April 14th, 1938, the year

Ed's mother died of the gunshot. And guess when Chandra Levy was born?"

"April 14th?" Neal said.

"Yup—1977, Edwards thought of everything when leaving his fake clues. In this case, he left them in the insurance policy itself, dating them the day of Chandra's and Father Robinson's birthdays. He kills Robert on HIS mother's birthday and he killed Stephanie Bryan on her father's."

I had contacted the Wiles family in 2013 and spent considerable time with Mrs. Wiles after connecting Edwards to the kidnapping, ransom and killing of her son. Pam Wiles, Robert's mother, described the way the insurance scam came about.

"Unbeknown to me and Robert, kidnapping insurance was placed on our policy; it was renewal time. Robert and I had no idea we had kidnapping insurance and didn't even know when renewal time was. I found out in 2013 that this kidnapping insurance policy was added for the time period of April of 2007 until April of 2008. It was only good during the period they took my Robert. Someone put a bug in Tom's ear to get that insurance." (Pam Wiles, Robert Wiles' Mother)

The kidnapping insurance scam was perpetrated during the arrest and trial of Father Gerald Robinson. Someone had gotten into the company and was dividing Robert and another employee named Toby Holt. Mrs. Wiles described what was going on with Robert just before he disappeared.

"Robert traveled to the Dominican Republic in March of 2008 on business with National Flight Services. Prior to his disappearance he wasn't in his normal state of mind. He returned seeming weary not keeping himself as neatly dressed as he usually does." My first thought was "did someone put Robert in a position slipping him a drug or placing him in a hypnotic state?"

In the months before Robert's kidnapping, Mrs. Wiles and her husband were going through a separation and the family was seeing a psychiatrist. Robert refused to go to their psychiatrist and may have found his own. Someone also scammed Robert and the company of 50,000 dollars just before the crime. After Robert disappeared, someone sent the Wiles an anonymous letter directing them to look at a "Psychiatrist named ZUBIN MYSTERY" that had been flying in and out of Toledo in 2005-06 on chartered planes and was an expert in mind control. The letter was sent by Edwards who was chartering planes in and out of Toledo during the Father Robinson arrest and trial, standing in front of everyone as he destroyed Toledo.

Mr. Wiles
National Flight Service
11341 W. Airport Service Rd.
Swanton, Ohio 43558

TOLEDO OH 436
13 SEP 2006 PM 2 L

SEP 15 RECD

Mr. Wiles

National Right Service

11341 W. Airport Services Rd.

Swanton, Ohio 43558

Re: Wiles kidnapping case

Dear Mr. Wiles,

I have heard news reports about this young man, your son, who was kidnapped. I know nothing about your son, but I do know a person who may be of interest.

This person likes to maintain a very high profile and because he is not instrument rated, regularly hires pilots to charter him around the country out of the Toledo area and may have hired this young man to charter him to Suttons Bay, Michigan, Chicago, Florida and other places in 2005-2006 and perhaps during these last couple years. He is an unusually intelligent psychologist highly skilled in mind control and hypnosis. His name is Zubin J. Mistry.

If this person hired your firm to charter for him, I would be highly suspicious that he may be responsible for your son's kidnapping.

I can only say that this person used hypnosis and rohypnol in an attempt to defraud me of my estate, valued at just under 1 million dollars. As a doctor and son of a family of doctors and lawyers, he has access to the social security numbers, dates of birth and mother's maiden name of nearly anyone who has a health care record and having this information on me, he was thereby able to access my financial accounts and computer. He hacked my computer and altered my trust to make himself the sole beneficiary and then poisoned me. I nearly died. If I had, he would have inherited every asset I held. Because he is a doctor, he is above suspicion and unquestioned by most everyone.

He also spends much more than he earns, makes bad business deals and tries to manipulate people out of their money to gain it for himself. I know he had done this to other well off women for financial gain and given that he regularly hires pilots, *if* and I want to say *if he hired you!!*, he may have targeted your son. If he is not a customer, I would dismiss this letter. But if he ever has hired your firm, you really need to investigate this person further.

Besides having assets he wanted, I knew way too much about this person. I believe he didn't want me as a witness to other criminal acts he committed, and tried to kill 2 birds with one stone in targeting me.

This person is a genius level sociopath, into sadomasochism, and derives sexual fulfillment from torturing people, male or female. Please do nOt turn this over to the FBI unless you verify *he was a customer*. I am afraid of him and if he found out I told you about him, he would sue me, if he could, to get my money or just kill me. He tried more than once and he's hard to get away from.

    Best of Luck finding your son.

1278

(Note to Mr. Wiles)

About a year after Robert's disappearance, Pam Wiles observed a sign in the foyer of her doctor's office listing ZUBIN MYSTERY in the office complex. She explained it to me.

"I was continuing to go see our counselor; then one day to my surprise I saw the name Zubin Mystery in his office. I asked the counselor how long Zubin Mystery has been in his office, not explaining why. He said oh he needed to rent some space for a while explaining what a bright intelligent person he is. I thought to myself why does Zubin Mystery need to rent space if he has an office of his own in Toledo?"

The Zubin Mystery letter Edwards had sent to the Wiles family was another parable on his life and contained clues as to the identity of the writer. Shortly after observing the name ZUBIN MYSTERY in the family's doctor's office, Tom Wiles was contacted by a man with the assumed name of Vernon Hutchison, claiming to be a psychic and to have talked to their dead son. The man was described as about 80 years old, short and fat.

(Edward Edwards, 2009, 76 years old, 5ft 9, 270 lbs)

The "psychic" provided Tom Wiles handwritten notes of the conversation he had with his dead son on Easter, 2009, one year after the kidnapping. The notes are written in question and answer format with Vernon (Ed), asking the questions, and Robert Wiles answering them from the grave.

April 12, 2009 Sunday
— Easter —

9:10 PM
(46)

Kidnapped or abduction of Robert A. Wiles
Questions put to Robert & answers from him.

#1. Your deceased if that's the case please move the antenna to the yes side, antenna moved to yes side

#2. Were you murdered right after you were abducted? yes

#3. Is your body buried in Polk County? yes

#4. Did you know any of the ones who abducted you? no

#5. Did they shoot you: no; did they strangle you - no
    did they stab you - no; did they drown you: yes!

#6. Would you say it was a gang who abducted you? yes

#7. Did they say why they did this to you? no

#8. Were they wanting Ransom? no

#9. Is your body close around Lakeland Fl.? no

#10. Did they leave you in the water? no

#11. Did they take your body out of the water and bury it? yes

#12. Did they bury you in a shallow grave? yes

#13. Do you know where these people live? yes

579

April 12, 2009 - Sunday

*10 April 14, 2009 - 4:15 PM/ Robert indicated that he would let his father know what part of the Lakeland map that I have is to where his remains are since he didn't tell me. He did indicate that his remains were somewhere in my map area.

Tues 10:30 B April 15, 2009 - Wed/ Continuing Q&A to Robert

#1 Robert may I ask you a few more questions please? yes

#2 Do you see the map on my Dining Room table? yes

#3 The entire area of that map somewhere your remains are buried in a shallow grave? yes

#4. The men who abducted you live in this map area? yes

#5. Were you abducted at the airport? no

#6. Were you abducted at your home? yes

#7. Did they quiet knocked on your + when you ans. that is when you were grabbed? yes

#8. Would you say they knew you were home by yourself? yes

#9. Did any of these men hang around the airport? yes

#6. Did they have cameras inside and outside the port? yes

#7. Were these men caught on film at the airport? yes

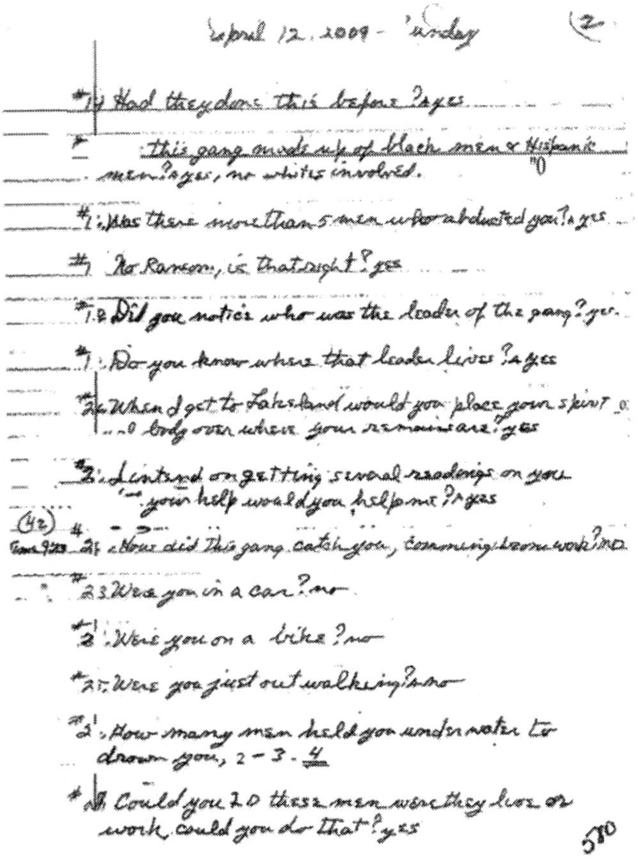

[Handwritten notes dated April 12, 2009 - Sunday]

1. Had they done this before? yes
   - This gang made up of black men & Hispanic men? yes, no whites involved.
2. Was there more than 5 men who abducted you? yes
3. No Ransom, is that right? yes
4. Did you notice who was the leader of the gang? yes
5. Do you know where that leader lives? yes
6. When I get to Lakeland would you place your spirit or body over where your remains are? yes
7. I intend on getting several readings on you — your help, would you help me? yes
8. How did this gang catch you, coming from work? no
9. Were you in a car? no
10. Were you on a bike? no
11. Were you just out walking? no
12. How many men held you under water to drown you, 2 - 3 - 4
13. Could you ID these men, were they live or work, could you do that? yes

(The pages were a puzzle and contained the answers as to how Edwards killed Robert.)

Just as Edwards had done in 2004 in the Sonoma County Beach poem, he left all the E's prominent capitals, standing for, Edward Edwards.

Edwards had provided me with this E only in 4 words out of all the letters he wrote.

(comparing E from various letters)

Every letter sent by Edwards to anyone was a taunt as to his identity. They all contained puzzles and clues. In his conversation with the dead Robert Wiles, Edwards detailed that 'HE' was invited into Robert's apartment and drowned him in the bathtub. He buried his body in a shallow grave and taunted the family for a year with false calls, ransom notes and fake letters, using names like Zubin Mystery as a clue. The Z Mystery, the Zodiac Mystery.

In the question, "How many men held you under water to drown you?" Edwards writes 2-3-4, with four underlined. This was also a clue. In mirror image it would be 4-3-2. They all equal 1. Four minus three =1. Three minus two = 1. One person killed Robert Wiles and it was the psychiatrist, Zubin Mystery, the Z Mystery, the hypnotist, the doctor of psychiatry, the preacher. He had groomed his way into the Toledo Ohio family to kill their first-born son in revenge for the wrongful conviction of Father Gerald Robinson two years earlier. Robert Wiles' uncle was a Catholic priest that worked with Father Gerald Robinson in Toledo.

The day Robert was kidnapped was Ed's mother's birthday. April 1st, April Fools. He denied Mr. and Mrs. Wiles Robert's remains just as he had threatened to do to the Ramseys in 1996. Robert's remains have never been found because just before he was about to plant them, Edwards was arrested, and the unraveling began.

In 2010 police arrested and convicted National Flight Services employee Stobert Holt for the murder of Robert Wiles. Edwards had killed Robert Wiles in his apartment the night of March 31, 2008, took his cell phone and used it to follow Stobert Holt from April 1st until April 3rd, planting all the evidence to make it look like Stobert had Robert's body and cell phone.

(Stobert Holt Convicted May 12, 2012)

Stobert Holt was asked by "48 Hours," a CBS crime program, about his conviction. "I was in disbelief. There is no evidence to support the conviction. I'm upset because I'm an innocent man convicted of manslaughter."

He was asked to explain the cell phone records.

"Someone had to be following me using it to make it look like it was me. If I had killed Robert I wouldn't be that stupid. I watch CSI."

During the sentencing phase, Tom Wiles asked Stobert, "We have a son we don't know where he is. We want to bring him home. I want to know where my son is. I'd give everything I have just to get him back."

Stobert responded, "As everyone else's does, my heart goes out to the Wiles family. I still maintain my innocence. I have from the beginning. They are probably hoping that I'm going to tell them where to find Robert and I just don't have that information."

Stobert Holt was sentenced to 30 years and will not be released until he is 72 years old.

Edwards had one more final setup to accomplish before his arrest in 2009. Edwards targeted the defense department and anybody claiming to be an expert on crime. His final ruse was against the Criminal Investigation Division of the U.S. Government.

"I work for the Criminal Investigation Bureau of the US Government." (*MOAC, Ed Edwards)

Edwards targeted Fort Bragg and the military as his last crime of recognition.

United States Army
Criminal Investigation Command
Media contact: CID Public Affairs **FOR IMMEDIATE RELEASE**
703-806-0372

Officials Confirm SPC Megan Touma's Manner of Death

Fort Belvoir, VA, July 11, 2008 – The U.S. Army Criminal Investigation Command, commonly known as CID, in conjunction with the Fayetteville, N.C. Police Department, today announced the official manner of death as homicide in the death of Specialist Megan Touma.

The announcement comes after a second autopsy, requested by Army CID and the Fayetteville Police Department, was conducted by the Armed Forces Institute of Pathology.

Specialist Touma's body was discovered in a Fayetteville, N.C. hotel room June 21, 2008.

For investigative reasons, the cause of death is not being released by law enforcement officials at this time.

U.S. Army CID Special Agents are conducting a joint investigation with the Fayetteville Police Department into the death of Touma. The Fayetteville Police Department remains the lead investigative agency for this case and questions regarding the investigation should be directed to Lieutenant Dave Sportsman at 910-489-8824. Questions regarding CID issues can be directed to Chris Grey, CID's director of Public Affairs at 703-806-0372.

No further information is releasable at this time.

-30

June 14th, 2008. Fort Bragg, North Carolina. In his final setup, Edwards targeted the very people he portrayed his entire life: The Criminal Investigation Division of the U.S. Government. He had mentioned it dozens of times in his book. Edwards killed Megan Touma, age 26 at Fort Bragg. She was 7 months pregnant and was killed on June 14, 2008, Edwards' 75th birthday. He had killed Robert Wiles "three months" earlier, April Fool's Day, the anniversary of his mother's birth. The Zodiac killer was proving in 2008 that the movie, "Zodiac" released November 2007, was wrong.

Megan Touma's body wasn't discovered until the 21st, when someone smelled a foul odor and found a "Do Not Disturb" sign on her motel room door at the Cross Creek Mall Fairfield Inn. When police entered they found the Zodiac sign written in lipstick on the mirror. Megan was killed in the bathtub and had been rabbit punched in the throat. Her baby had deceased as well. She had been killed like so many others-in the bathtub. Near water is what Edwards had to ritualistically kill by and that is why the Zodiac killed near water.

After the killing on Fort Bragg, Edwards sent a Zodiac letter dated June 17th, 2008, admitting to being at the scene.

> 17 JUNE #))*
>
> To whom it may concern. The following is to inform that I am responsible for the dead body that was found on Saturday, June 21 # 1130 in room 143 at Fairfield INN by Marriott off Skibo RD. It was a master piece. I confess, that I have killed many times before in several states, but now I will start using my role-model's signature. There will be many more to come.
>
> Fayetteville law enforcement are very incompetent. I basically,sat there and watch while investigators were on site.

(Zodiac Letter Arrives June 25, 2008, Fayetteville Police and Fayetteville Observer Paper)

Police at first withheld the fact that the Zodiac had claimed responsibility, for fear it would cause terror. Edwards had committed the murder on his 76th birthday, June 14th, 2008. He had killed Robert Wiles two months earlier on his mother's birthday, April 1, April Fool's Day. Holidays, anniversaries and birthdays were signature signs of Ed Edwards. The beginning and the end; his mother's birth and his birth. Edwards dated the letter "Three" days later, June

17th (on the third day) and claimed he was at the scene watching them process it when it was discovered June 21st.

On June 28th, 2008 Edwards went online using his grandmother's name, Anibal, and directed the police to go after Sergeant Ed Patino.

Anibal Says:
June 28, 2008 at 4:46 am
This is regarding the murder of SPC Megan Lynn Touma....her boyfreind name was Sgt Edgar Patino..He is station in Fort Brag. He is also marry to Heileen Patino. He was also station he in Bamberg, Germany. I spoke to her the day before she left and she told me that was his baby and she was seven months pregnant. He was a buddy of mind. We were both assigned to 54th Egineer Batallion.This is regarding the murder of SPC Megan Lynn Touma.

Edwards misspelled in the blog to tie it to his horrible spelling in the Zodiac case, and he directed the evidence at Ed Patino, the man that was married and had gotten Megan Touma pregnant. Patino hadn't told Touma he was married. They both met up in the Fairfield Inn in Fort Bragg June 13th-14th. The Fairfield Inn was located on the property of the Cross Creek Mall. Edwards deliberately and cold bloodedly chose this site for what its name was, and what it looked like from Google Earth. The building is shaped like a cross with a circle road around it. Signed By the Cross.

(Cross Creek Mall, Fort Bragg, North Carolina)

Edwards' first murder in 1945 in Chicago was signed in lipstick and so was his last in 2008. The beginning and the end, Edwards was proving to the USA after the release of Zodiac the movie, that the Zodiac was still alive, sending letters and planting false evidence for the police to follow.

Edgar Patino was in Fort Bragg attending a special class on "Psychiatric Warfare" taught by members of the Criminal Investigation Division of the Armed Services. Patino last saw Megan the night of June 13th when he left her room after visiting with her. After Edwards blogged and led police to him, Patino was arrested July 28th, 2008 and charged with the murder of Megan. He denied the murder—writing the note and writing the Zodiac sign on the mirror in lipstick. Two years later, in November of 2010, while Edwards was sitting in Ohio waiting to be executed, Patino accepted a plea agreement to spare his life and is currently sitting in a North Carolina prison trying to prove his innocence. His lawyer didn't tell him he had no right to appeal his plea deal. In 2013 he was denied relief in court. He still serves today.

(Sgt. Edgar Patino)

Edgar Patino was contacted in April of 2013 and responded about his predicament.

Mr. Cameron, May 28th, 2013

Hi. I have received your letter and I also received the letter you wrote in February. I didn't mean to be rude or disrespectful by not responding to your letter. Since I've been in prison I have received a lot of letters from random people across the nation. I've even received letters from TV shows informing me that they would like to interview me on camera. After a while I realized that the best thing to do was to give them the silent treatment and not respond. This is the first time that I have actually responded.

The purpose of this letter is to inform you that in November 2010 I agreed to and signed a plea bargain for 2nd degree murder. My attorney had told me that if I decided to go to trial I would be on trial for 1st degree murder and that I could face the death penalty if convicted. When my family heard about this, they panicked and so did I. Therefor I accepted the plea bargain. I never understood what was going on. My attorney was court appointed and he was never very enthusiastic about obtaining a not guilty verdict from the jury.

While in prison I have filed a motion for Appropriate Relief (MAR) petitioning the court for a "time reduction", but it was denied. I appealed the denial of the MAR to the North Carolina Court of Appeals and it was ordered that my motion had no merit and was properly denied. I still have all of the documentation.

I don't know if you or the law firm out of Arkansas can do anything for me. I appreciate your interest in wanting to help me. Feel free to ask me any questions. I will completely understand if you choose not to write back.

Thank you for your time.

Sincerely,
Edgar Patino

P.S. Thank you for the 25.00 dollars.

(letter from Edgar Patino)

Edwards had spent the entire decade of the 2000's killing people proving the Zodiac was alive. He continued trying to set up someone for Chandra's murder also.

Weeks after killing Megan Touma in 2008 and before the arrest of Ingmar Guandique for

Chandra Levy's murder, Edwards went online to straighten out the Washington Post regarding their 12- part series on "Who Killed Chandra."

"It's sad that Chandra's killer seems as though he/she/or (how ever many may be involved) will not get caught. My opinion of what I believe is that Guandique did not kill Chandra. I don't believe that Chandra was killed at Rock Creek Park. And I still say that I believe that Chandra would fight and scream for help if Guandique attacked her too. And if he fled away for the other two, he would flee away for her also. Condit prolonged this case and prolonged this case, he did not cooperate with the Police or FBI, he had his own polygraph test administered, he can't really provide solid proof of his where abouts during the time of Chandra missing, he rides all the way out to Virginia to throw away a watch box, he insist that another female that he is having an affair with to lie signing a false affidavit, he doesn't tell the truth about their affair. (Chandra and himself). And I don't understand why there was never any information as to whether or not Chandra's apartment was fingerprinted, what else was in her apartment besides the laptop, the dirty clothing, and the pasta and reese cup left in her refidgerator. What phone calls had been made outgoing and incoming on her home phone and cell phone. Who does the lipstick belongs to? Where is her other tennis shoe?"

(Ed Edwards, July 24th, 2008 Washington Post)

A tube of red lipstick was planted at the scene where Chandra's skull was found, May 22, 2002. Some of Chandra's finger bones were never found. Exactly 6 months later, November 22, 2002, Ed Edwards sent 8 fingerprints to Zodiackiller.com, missing the tips. The prints were rolled in red lipstick-like substance and were a clue that the "Lipstick Killer" had struck again.

William Heirens went down in history as the lipstick killer and served 66 years in prison for murders Edwards had committed in 1945-46.

Heirens denied killing 6-year-old Suzanne Degnan in a 118-page written statement taken from him June 30th, 1946.

(newspaper and photos of Heirens)

Like Edgar Patino in 2008, Heirens pled guilty in 1946 with the hopes to spare his life and prove his innocence. Instead, he served 66 years in an Illinois prison for killing 6-year-old Suzanne Degnan, and dismembering her in a tub in Chicago, January 9th, 1946. He died in prison a year after Edwards did, in March of 2012, still proclaiming he was innocent, but the MEDIA claimed he was the Lipstick Killer. It was the State Attorney General in 1946 that announced the author of both lipstick messages found in 1945-46 in Chicago were penned by the same person.

(lipstick message on wall)

The two lipstick messages were a cry for someone to stop Edwards before he killed more. He wrote them when he was 13 years old. Edwards used Heirens 118-page written confession to tie his puzzle together by asking for 118,000 dollars in the JonBenet Ramsey ransom note:

"You will withdraw $118,000.00 from your account. Make sure that you bring an adequate size attaché to the bank. When you get home you will put the money in a brown paper bag. Any deviation of my instructions will result in the immediate execution of your daughter. You will also be denied her remains for proper burial. Speaking to anyone about your situation, such as Police, F.B.I. etc., will result in your daughter being beheaded. It is up to you now John! Victory! S.B.T.C" (Ed Edwards JonBenet Ramsey Ransom Note, Christmas 1996)

Chapter 36

The Conclusion

June 14th, 2013

Edwards killed nonstop from 1945 until his capture in 2009. He continues to kill in his afterlife with executions of innocent people. There were 9 setups and 11 kills in the last decade of his life that received mass recognition. There will be many more. By now Cameron and Neal were three years into their investigation. They had hundreds of thousands of pages of documentation of Edwards' 77 years of terror. With each new discovery, they felt closer to a conclusion, only to learn that they had been led to another startling discovery. Much more was still out there, waiting to be uncovered in the future. Edwards had manipulated the scales of justice in a manner that will take decades to unravel.

    Neal and I agreed it was time to go public. The story needed to be told to the world, and with that exposure, all the more of Edward Edwards would surface, explaining the unknowns. For over a half a century the public, the press and law enforcement have been mystified by his exploits and shrouded "clues"—the ultimate game.

Until now, no one had ever put it all together. In retrospect, all the evidence was there—the pieces could have been assembled years ago. But it was very difficult to see without the key. And that key was having a name to fit to everything. Edward Edwards. With that key and 20/20 hindsight, one can only marvel at how no one could have seen it before. He was so brazenly in front of everyone the entire time, boldly taunting and flaunting.

What was even more frightening was that without the efforts and diligence of the crew at Morning Light Coffee, Neal and myself, the story probably never would have come to light.

I asked the crew, "When did you finally become convinced? What pushed you over the edge to where you finally admitted I wasn't crazy and may be right?"

They thought back over the investigation. "It wasn't one particular thing, John. It was like a building process where no matter where you turned, it just kept accumulating. The first thing that really hooked us was your discovery of page 232 in his book where Edwards knows someone who collects slaves. I suppose next was Edwards' Deer Lodge connection to the rioters that claimed they would kill, 'by rope, by gun, by knife, by fire.' But the discovery that he killed on Fort Bragg in 2008 on his 76th birthday and set up someone named Ed who was staying in a motel that was shaped like the Zodiac cross and circle? Now that cinched it. That pretty much sums up what he was against. The U.S. government and that is why he referred to himself as a foreign faction in the JonBenet Ramsey case."

"Edwards wanted to be caught, but he wanted someone to challenge him." I said, "He figured nobody would suspect him if he just stood in front of everyone. He thrived on being noticed; being significant. Everyone was in agreement; that the Zodiac would never leave this earth without disclosure, and he didn't. He disclosed his entire life, and nobody wanted to believe that he was still alive. He wanted someone smarter than him to figure it out. And that ain't me. Without Neal, this would have never happened."

"What's your greatest hope, John?"

"That our investigation will be carried forth by others and the guilt that he placed on so many innocent people will be removed. I also hope we have answered so many questions that have been asked for years."

"Do you think anyone in law enforcement or MEDIA will carry this on?"

"I doubt it. I know I can't investigate any more murder. The MEDIA perpetuated Edwards' murders for decades, which means we, as a society, contributed. Just watch "Dexter" on ShowTime. It's all of Ed's murders dressed up nicely, put in a package to make us like a serial killer. This has taken its toll on me. But I wouldn't trade it for anything. Ed was like so many of the kids I worked with over the years as a cop. If someone had just loved that guy when he was 5, things would have been different. Instead, nobody listened, and a monster was created that sold his murderous rampage to us and we bought it up."

His real name was Chuckie. He was born an illegitimate child with no love, no mother and no father at the height of the Great Depression. He was destroyed spiritually by evil and decided to tempt us with his own EVIL for 6 decades. Turn on your TV and you will see him everywhere. He has revealed how dark our society has become.

We can change the way the world treats people by reading the story of Edward Wayne Edwards.

There is no power greater than unconditional love.

The End?

Further Uncovered Cases

I was called a crackpot by more than one person after I published my book. I knew it would cause problems with many who had felt they had solved many of the cases now attributed to one horrible serial killer, Edward Wayne Edwards. His cases were designed to do just that. We should all forgive each other and move on.

Ed is killing and collecting slaves in his afterlife just as The Zodiac had said. Several people that Ed framed are on death row and have been for 18 to 20 plus years. Time is running out for them and they will be executed. Others have served most of their lives in prison and will die unless Ed is exposed.

After the release of my book, people that read it found other murders and contacted me. It has been four years since I published **"It's Me, Edward Wayne Edwards, the Serial Killer You NEVER Heard of."** Edwards framed some of the biggest cases in his last 15 years of his life. I will highlight four cases from the years, 1996, 2002, 2005, 2009.

Thanks to the readers of my book for finding the truth and seeking justice.

Chapter 37
Darlie Routier, 1996

On June 6, 1996, at 2:31am, 911 dispatchers in Rowlett, Texas, received a call from 5801 Eagle Drive, the home of Darlie and Darrin Routier. Darlie made the call and told the operator that her home had been broken into and that an intruder had stabbed her children, Devon aged 6 and Damon aged 5, and attacked her.

Police arrived within three minutes of the 911 call. They discovered a window screen in the garage had been cut, which indicated a possible entry point for an intruder. A search of the house and grounds did not locate an intruder. Darlie received a knife wound to her neck and injuries to her arms. She was treated at a hospital and released two days later.

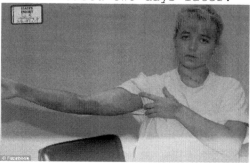

Devon and Damon died of their injuries. Devon was stabbed 4 times and Damon was stabbed 6 times.

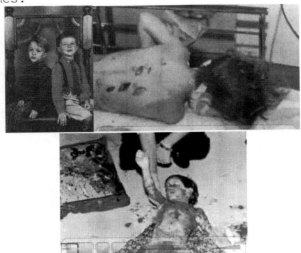

(Damon – Devon)

Darlie's youngest son, 7-month-old Drake, was asleep upstairs with her husband, Darin. Neither were harmed. The case became a media firestorm and was all over cable news. Within one week of the murder Darlie became the main suspect after an incident at the gravesite of her son's funeral.

On June 14th, 1996, 8 days after the murder, a birthday party was held posthumously at the grave site to celebrate what would have been Devon's 7th birthday. Darlie was destroyed by the public and media after a video of her showed her spraying silly string and smiling and laughing at the grave.

Darlie was shown as she sprayed Silly String on the graves in celebration, singing "Happy Birthday." This party was filmed by news crews and broadcast nationally. Shortly after the airing of the party, Darlie became the main suspect in the killing of her boys. Police believed the way she acted at the grave site was a sign that she had killed the boys and staged the scene.

Darlie was devastated by the public reaction and later commented on the video, saying, "He wanted to be seven. I did the only thing I knew to do to honor him and give him all his wishes because he wasn't here anymore. But how do you know what you're going to do when you lose two children? How do you know how you're going to act?"

What police never explained was why they didn't show their tape of the memorial at the grave site. They had secretly taped the entire event and it showed Darlie grieving at the site. When they were pressed in court about their taping of the memorial a police officer took his 5th amendment rights and refused to testify. The illegal taping would have resulted in charges against the police. The jury never saw the tape but got to see the silly string and Darlie laughing.

Darlie was arrested 4 days after the airing of the Silly String video and charged with capital murder. She was convicted in 1997 and sentenced to death. She currently sits on death row in Texas and has been incarcerated 22 years. The Silly String video is what convicted her.

So why do I think Ed Edwards is involved?

Edwards' book Metamorphosis of a Criminal contained all the names of the states that he would kill in the future. Texas is mentioned 8 times and he mentioned kidnapping a girl in Texas in 1955.

The Routier family was religious, loving and successful. There was indication of some turmoil within the family about money and this would fit with Edwards' grooming his way into someone in the family in an attempt to make them think they will be rich, possibly the husband Darin.

Everyone in the Routier family had first names that started with the letter "D". Darlie,

Darrin, Devon, Damon and Drake. This fits in with Ed's need to tie his murders to the letters in his name.

Devon was 6 years old and killed just 8 days before his 7th Birthday. His Birthday being June 14th, the same day as Edward Edwards' Birthday. Devon was 6 at the time of his death and he was stabbed 6 times. They were all killed on 6-6-1996. This was the same year that Edwards killed 6-year-old Jon Benet Ramsay on Christmas and tried to frame the parents. He succeeded in the frame job in Darlie's case, 6 months before Ramsey.

Devon shared the same Birthday as the world's worst serial killer in history, Edward Wayne Edwards. Devon was 6 years old killed on the 6th day of the 6th month of 1996. 666, the occult.

Darlie was convicted February 4, 1997 and sentenced to death by lethal injection. She sits on Death Row today with one final appeal left. The prosecution portrayed her as a spoiled woman who wanted to be on her own without her boys. She was anything but. Darlie was accused of stabbing her sons four times and six times and then slashing her neck and hurting her arm to stage the scene. But her 911 call clearly showed that she was frantic and an intruder had come into the house:

911 TRANSCRIPT
Recorded by The Rowlett Police Department
June 6, 1996.
Transcript created by Barry Dickey
(*This transcript was done after the state "enhanced" the recording and is not accurate)
Time ID Conversation/Sounds

00:00:00 911 Operator #1 ...Rowlett 911...what is your emergency.
00:01:19 Darlie Routier ...somebody came here...they broke in...

00:03:27 911 Operator #1 ...ma'am...
00:05:11 Darlie Routier ...they just stabbed me and my children...
00:07:16 911 Operator #1 ...what...
00:08:05 Darlie Routier ...they just stabbed me and my kids...my little boys...
00:09:24 911 Operator #1 ...who...who did...
00:11:12 Darlie Routier ...my little boy is dying...
00:11:25 RADIO ...(unintelligible) clear...
00:13:07 911 Operator #1 ...hang on ...hang on... hang on
00:15:03 Darlie Routier ...hurry... (unintelligible)...
00:16:01 911 Operator #1 ...stand by for medical emergency
00:18:11 Darlie Routier ...ma'am...
00:18:19 911 Operator #1 ...hang on ma'am...
00:21:26 Darlie Routier ...ma'am...
00:23:00 911 Operator #1 ...unknown medical emergency... 5801 Eagle Drive...
00:24:00 RADIO ...(unintelligible)...
00:26:24 Darlie Routier ...ma'am...
00:27:12 911 Operator #1 ...ma'am... I'm trying to get an ambulance to you... hang on a minute...
00:28:20 RADIO ...(siren)...
00:29:13 Darlie Routier ...oh my God ...my babies are dying...
00:30:12 Darin Routier ...(unintelligible)...
00:31:09 911 Operator #1 ...what's going on ma'am...
00:32:13 Darlie Routier ...(unintelligible) ...oh my God...
00:33:49 RADIO ... (tone - signal broadcast)...
00:34:01 Background Voice ...(unintelligible)...
00:35:20 Darlie Routier ...(unintelligible) thought he was dead ...oh my God...

Darlie says "Oh My God" 22 times during the call and is frantic. The transcripts goes on for many more pages but clearly paints a picture of a devastated mother who found her two boys stabbed to death right in front of her by an intruder.

The year 1996 was Ed Edwards' 50th year of being a serial killer. He was 63 years old. He was more than capable of killing all the way up to his death.

(Edward Wayne Edwards, 1990s)

1996 also represents 666 with the nines in mirror image becoming 6s. Number 1, 666. 1996 was also the year Edwards killed his adoptive son, Dannie Boy Edwards, April,1 1996. April Fool's Day and his mother's Birthday. Edwards killed Darlie's boys 6-6-1996, The Occult Holiday, and killed Jon Benet Ramsey Christmas, 1996 and she was found 12-26-1996. Edwards is a ritual killer and 6 years after 1996, he killed again on Christmas, 2002.

Chapter 38
Scott and Laci Peterson

Framing parents, husbands and wives was Edwards' specialty, and from 1996 until his capture in 2009 he did it repeatedly. Six years after Jon Benet was killed on Christmas, Edwards chose to kill 27-year-old, pregnant Laci Peterson in Modesto, California. He had killed Chandra Levy from Modesto a year earlier. Both women were dark haired 20-year-olds, the type Ed killed his entire life. Edwards killed woman that represented his mother. They looked like his mother and were of similar age.

(Laci Peterson - Chandra Levy)

Laci Peterson disappeared from her home on Christmas Eve, 2002. She was last seen walking a dog at about 10 in the morning. Scott had gone fishing that day to the Berkley Marina and came home in the afternoon to find Laci missing. She was reported missing that night and the case became a national obsession.

Shortly after the disappearance, Scott Peterson became the focus of the investigation as it was learned he was cheating on his wife with Amber Frey. The media circus that followed doesn't have to be explained. We all had an opinion on Scott Peterson but we didn't know of Ed Edwards at the time.

From Christmas 2002 until Easter, 2003 Scott Peterson was vilified in the international press. He had changed his appearance and attempted to hide from the press that followed him daily.

A break in the case came on Palm Sunday, April 13, 2003. Laci Peterson's decapitated body was found on the shores of Isabella National Park off San Francisco Bay in the heart of where "The Zodiac" killed his entire life. A day later Laci's fetus, Conner was found on the shores with a noose around his neck like Jon Benet Ramsey had 6 years earlier. Conner was found April 14, 2003 which would have been Chandra Levy's Birthday had she not been killed by Edwards 2 years earlier. Edwards planted the bodies on Easter week and Scott Peterson was arrested on Good Friday, April 18, 2003 and charged with killing his wife and unborn Fetus.

Shortly after Scott's arrest a letter arrived at the Modesto Bee and the writer took responsibility for framing Scott. The letter was dated 5-4-2003.

5-4-03

A Message From God

On the 12th day of the 12th month Cary Stayner was sentenced to death by a jury of 12 led by Juror #12. 12 days later, Laci & Conner were killed and for an "ACT OF GOD" (me) "Both" were found following the storm on the 12th.

GOD (I) delivered the evidence to secure the arrest of Scott Peterson and the eventual conviction "Beyond a Reasonable Doubt." The murderer was delivered to Modesto Police Department at 12 minutes to 12 midnight on Good Friday.

Yes, it was a "Very" Good Friday

GOD (I) Bless You

GOD is one of us
Open your hearts
Open your minds
Open your ears
Open your eyes
"Both of them"
And you shall know the truth
And the truth shall make you free

(LETTER MAILED TO, MODESTO BEE)

Edwards committed the murder of Laci Peterson shortly after the conviction of another killer from California, Cary Stayner, mentioned in the letter above. Stayner was a serial killer from California that was all over the press just before the killing of Laci Peterson. He was sentenced to die in San Quentin two weeks before Edwards framed Scott Peterson, who is also on death row in San Quentin.

Edwards stole all the press from Stayner and created a "Crime of Recognition", as he had done his entire life, by killing Laci on Christmas, framing Scott on Good Friday, and creating a circus atmosphere with another murder.

The letters Edwards sent in his cases contained clues as to the identity of the writer. Edwards used numbers for letters in past puzzles like in the Zodiac case

The letter was dated 5-4-2003. The number Five equaling E in the alphabet, and four equaling D. ED is the writer. Two thousand three being the year it was sent, and two 3s in mirror image are Es. Edward Edwards wrote the letter and signed it GOD with (ME) next to GOD. Signing it GOD is really signing it Satan and putting (ME) next to it was also a clue. An M in Mirror image is a W so the date and the word ME would be Ed W E.

After Scott was sentenced to death Edwards started blogging on a web site known as "Fratpack." He used the moniker I.K.L.P for "I Killed Laci Peterson." From March 22, 2006 until August 6, 2006 Edwards taunted the bloggers, tying the killing to the Zodiac Killer and telling everyone he is still alive and killing. He used poems to taunt the audience:

"You are jealous this I see. As with my cousin Zodiac you will never capture me. For it is I who does not lack. Green River was a bore, Zodiac a little whore. I am the one to adore. I be the one you should never ignore. For in the end THOU will find that Zodiac is an idol of mine. For THOU should not mock me or Zodiac will be not a memory. For if THOU breaks the code with Freebird inside, THEE will tell you where all others hide. Zodiac had four but there were many more."

Edwards used THEE for him and THOU for us throughout the bloggings. He also submitted two codes that the NSA attempted to crack and could not. The Fratpack website was removed by the NSA and an extensive investigation was done in an attempt to identify the writer.

On October 28, 2005 Edwards blogged the following poem. This was just 3 days before he killed Teresa Halbach in Wisconsin and framed Steven Avery.

"For Zodiac and THEE are not one in the same. THOU watch what they say about Z and his fame. If THOU believes Z has not always been free, Then THOU is so wrong it what it believe. More then THOU will ever know is Z count. Smarts without knowing what Z is about."

(October 28, 2005 Fratpack Website)

Three days after the above blog Edward killed Teresa Halbach and blew her body to pieces framing Steven Avery and Brenden Dassey.

The reason Edwards chose to call himself "THEE" was for the initials of Teresa Halbach and the initials of his own name TH and EE.

Chapter 39

Coleman Case Review

The following is a review of the May 5th, 2009 killing of Sherri, Gavin and Garrett Coleman I Columbia, Illinois. This review is based on the evidence that Serial Killer Edward Wayne Edwards, DOB 6-14-1933, DOD 4-7-2011, killed the family and set-up Christopher Coleman Chris is currently serving 300 years with no parole in Dodge Correctional Institution in Waupun Wisconsin.

Serial Killer Edwards Wayne Edwards was born in Cleveland, Ohio June 14th, 1933. His birth name was Charles Edward Meyers. By age 5 his mother Lillian Meyers was shot in the stomach and died August 8th, 1938. It was listed as a Suicide. Edwards would kill on this date over and over again throughout his life. He pled guilty in 2010 to 4 murders that occurred on August 8th, 1977 and 1980. He tortured and killed couples in love. He would also target couples married on this date. Sherri and Christopher Coleman were married on August 8th, 1996.

After the killing of his mother in 1938 he was given the name Edward Wayne Edwards. He was adopted by Mary Ethyl Edwards who also died a year later of MS. In 1939 by age 6 Edward Wayne Edwards was placed in Parmadale Catholic Orphanage in Parma, Ohio. By age 7 Edwards was raped and beaten by the older boys, nuns and priests. By age 11 Edwards escaped Parmadale Orphanage and started killing people all over the country. His killings were based on the Satanic Verses and Allister Crowley's' 19th Century vision of Murder and Mayhem in the future. Edwards started killing people in 1945 and setting people up.

    1) Edwards' first murder occurred 7 days before his 12th birthday, June 5th, `1945 in Chicago, Illinois. He killed a woman in her bed and wrote on the wall the following message in Candy Apple Red Lipstick, *"For Heavens Sake Please Stop Me Before I Kill More I Cannot Control Myself"*

    2) Edwards' second murder occurred December 9, 1945 in Chicago, Illinois. He killed another woman in bed shooting her and drowning her in the tub. His first 2 victims were representations of his 2 mothers, one died 1938 another 1939.

    3) His third murder was January 7, 1946 in Chicago, Illinois. He lured a 6-year-old girl out of her home on a Sunday night, brought her to a basement, strangled her, dismembered her and spread her remains in the sewers of Chicago. He taunted the police with cryptic letters and messages and wrote in Candy Apple Red lipstick at the scene, "Please Stop Me Before I Kill More."

    The first three murders Edwards committed were known as the "Lipstick Killings." A 17-year-old teen named William Hierens was arrested in July of 1946 for the killings and served 66 years until his death March 2012. He maintained his innocence throughout life and stated he was setup.

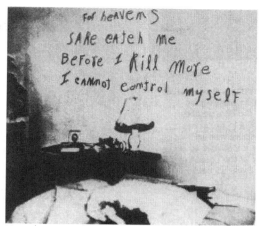

My investigation of Edward Wayne Edwards and release of my book in 2014 proved that Edwards had committed the Lipstick Killings in 1945-46 and set-up William Hierens. He confessed in 2002 on a website created by him admitting to being "The Lipstick Killer." The Website www.blackdahliasolution.org was published in November of 2002 by Edward Wayne Edwards.

Just prior to publishing the site Edwards sent a Zodiac Killer letter to Tom Voigt, owner of Zodiackiller.com attempting to get Voigt to enter into a movie agreement to expose the real Zodiac Killer. At the time in 2002, Hollywood was producing a Zodiac Killer Movie and Edwards was taunting them with the real killer. This would become Edwards MO throughout life. He would kill; contact the press and police with false letters and cryptic clues left at the scene. Many of the writings were in Red for Ra or Satan from Early Egyptian Christian times. Edwards was a true Satanist. He was a high priest. He was at the highest level and none were higher.

Edwards became a Ritual Killer in 1946 at age 12. He killed three people in his first murders, wrote messages, set someone up and was standing in front of the investigation all along. This would be Edwards MO throughout life. Edwards would kill in horrific killings that would get major press and steer the evidence to an innocent person. Many times the person arrested for the murders would be cheating on his wife or doing something else that would bring suspicion on him.

Edwards was arrested for his first murder July 30, 2009 in Louisville, Kentucky. He was 76 years old, married to his wife Kay and had 5 children and 11 grandchildren. He had been married to Kay since 1968 and had been married twice before, in 1955 and 1959. Edwards used his wife and kids as a ruse as he traveled the country from 1955 until 2009 killing people and setting people up in every state. It began in Illinois in 1945 and ended in Illinois in 2009 with the triple killing of Sherri Gavin and Garret and set-up of Chris.

Edwards was a writer and published his autobiography in 1972 at age 39. He claimed in the book that he was a former criminal, a suspect in a double murder, and was once on the FBI's 10 most wanted list. He was proclaiming in 1972 that he was reformed. He traveled with his current family throughout the 60s, 70s, 80s and 90s, 2000s, preaching at churches and schools, police academies and law schools, that he was a former criminal. What he was actually doing was stalking churches for his next victim and using his family as a ruse. He killed every year he was free to do it. He spent a total of 13 years of his 77-year life in prison for such things as Bank Robbery, Impersonating an Officer, Burglary, Robbery, Assault, Weapons, Kidnapping. He was an FBI informant for 55 years, informing on his own murders and setting up people.

Edwards pled guilty in Ohio in 2010 to 5 murders spanning Ohio and Wisconsin from 1977 until 1996. The murders involved kidnapping couples, torturing them, tying them up, strangling them, stabbing them, shooting them and hiding their bodies. He planted evidence at his scenes that led to others becoming suspects. He collected a quarter of a million dollars life insurance in the 1996 case. Edwards profited off of murder his whole life.

In 2010 I befriended Edward Wayne Edwards and ended up writing a book about his life and killings. The investigation started in 2010 and I published the investigative style book in June of 2014. Just prior to the books' publication I tied Edward Wayne Edwards to the killing of Sherri, Gavin and Garrett Coleman and the set-up of Christopher. I wrote Chris a letter in February 2014 and told him.
Here is the letter:

LETTER SENT TO CHRISTOPHER COLEMAN BY JOHN A CAMERON FEBRUARY 2014
Inmate No. S11821: Coleman, Christopher.
Dodge Correctional Facility
Waupun, Wisconsin
Dear Chris: My name is John Cameron and I am a retired cold case detective from Great Falls, Montana. I am writing you to let you know about a serial killer I befriended that is responsible for the killing of your kids and wife. In June of 2010 I was working in Deer Lodge Prison Montana for the Parole Board, when I befriended a serial killer named Edwards Wayne Edwards, born 6-14-1933. I tied Edwards to a 1956 unsolved double murder in my hometown and confronted him about all his murders. I had never heard of your case until the last week.
Edwards MO, starting in 1945, was to groom his way into his victim's lives before killing their kids and wives. I tied him to hundreds of unsolved murders spanning from 1945 until his capture July 30, 2009 in Kentucky. He was married to the same women 43 years, had 5 kids, 11 grandchildren, was a former Marine who went AWOL in 1950 and killed his entire life, setting innocent people up, and watching as the justice system executed innocent people for his crimes. The reason I write you is to offer my services free of charge if you are interested. I know you didn't kill your kids and wife and I know Edwards did. The last murder he committed before yours was in Lakeland and Tampa Florida, April 1, 2008. In that case he used computer, cell phones and

Email to setup and innocent man for the kidnapping of a Robert Wiles.

Edwards was 76 years old in 2009, 5ft 10, 250. He sometimes carried a cane as a ruse. His MO was to portray himself as a Dr. of Psychiatry, Preacher and a Police Officer. He was able to get his victims and intended setups to walk right into him. Most likely he introduced himself to you and the women you were having an affair with. He had all the credentials to prove he was a counselor and actually had offices in cities all over the USA, luring many of his victims by counseling them and then killing someone close to them. He also had close contacts with FBI and law enforcement throughout his life, and was inside most of his OWN murder investigations under assumed identity. He was extremely brilliant and used it to run around the country for 66 years killing and setting people up. You will not hear about any of this on TV or news. I will be releasing my investigation April 16, 2014.

If you are interested in letting me help you your brother or mother could contact me at the listed contacts. I do have a website devoted to Edwards and if you have access you will see what he did, and how it matches what he did to you.

Respectfully
John A Cameron
Coldcasecameron.com
406-868-1026
820 5th ave north
Great Falls MT. 59401

After sending Christopher Coleman this letter I also contacted Chief Edwards of the Columbia Police Department, the agency in charge of the investigation. I spoke with him in February 2014 and spoke with Detective Karla Haney in March. I supplied Chief Edwards and Karla Haney a review I completed on the evidence that suggested Edwards was the killer.

Here is the review.

After sending the review I spoke with Detective Haney and had hoped to get pictures of the writing on the wall left at the scene of the murder. They would not provide me with copies so I told them what to look for. Edwards always left clues in his writings that contained his identity. His Es and Ds would stand out obvious. He would highlight certain letters or place them in mirror image of each other. In his 1945-46 "Lipstick Killer Writings" Edwards left the Cs and Es very obvious.

In June of 2014 I released my book and never heard back from Chief Edwards or Detective Karla Haney. In May of 2015 I was able to get the Discovery Documents in the Coleman case. I also received all the photos of the writings on the walls. After obtaining the photos I observed that Edwards had placed his name within the writings.
I SAW YOU LEAVE

If you look closely at the A in LEAVE you will see it is not an A at all. It is an upside-down number 4 and the number 7 combined.

Edwards made the A with a 4 and a 7 because the word leave contains his name. There are 4 Ds in the name Edward Edwards. The 4th letter of the alphabet is D.

There are 7 letters to his last name and that's why he placed a number 7 upside down as the first letter L in Leave. The capital E after the L or 7 was a clue that the first letter of the puzzle is the capitalized E so his name starts with E. The letter after E is the #4 or 4th letter of the alphabet D. You get ED. So the 7 or the L belongs at the end of the puzzle because 7 letters to his last name and he already gave you his first. So, you have Ed followed by a V with a short stem on one side.

Ed W. E.

The short stem In the V was a clue to mirror image it with the 7 in the letter A and you get a W. EDWARDS is 7 letters and there are 4 Ds to his name.

The word YOU in "I Saw You Leave" was not the word YOU at all. The word was sprayed starting at the end with a sideways "S" attached to an upside down "d" that points to the Capital E in Leave. You get Eds with a W left over. Edward Wayne Edwards

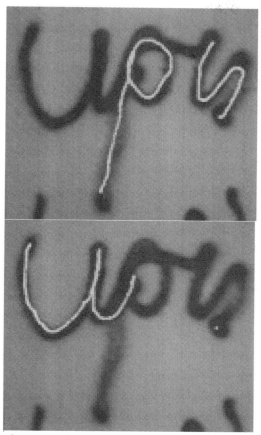

The words YOU and LEAVE contained the letters EDWAEDWS

"I am Alway Watching" Edwards left off the S in Always. The A in Always is not an a at all. It is a symbol with a 7 pointing up.

After the # 7 is "WAY" which is three more letters to his middle name "WAYNE." So, between the words LEAVE, YOU and ALWAYS you get the following letters:
EDWA WAY EDWS
The word YOU in Fuck YOU

The word YOU is an N pointing to WAY for WAYN
and a D. Add those letters and you get:
EDWA WAYN EDWDS
Add the words I AM.

I AM EDWAD WAYN EDWDS
The A in I SAW was a small case r.

Add RSAW to the other letters.
I AM EDWARD WAYNE EDWARDS
The words on the wall "I SAW YOU LEAVE FUCK YOU I'M ALWAY WATCHING" contained Edwards name and his wife KAY HEDDERLY EDWARDS name.

The capital "K" in FUCK is large and drawn out with a long stem pointing to the small case "y" in YOU. We know that after the small case y is an upside-down d and upside-down n.
K Y
Below the K Y is the funny A in ALWAY.

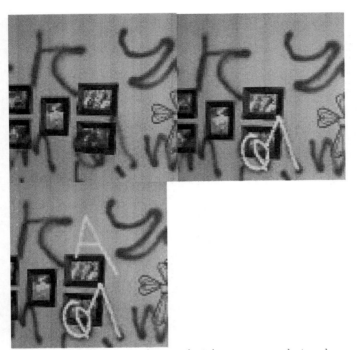

The A in ALWAYS is pointing upward to be moved into KAY.
I AM EDWARD WAYNE EDWARDS- KAY
Kay Edwards Maiden name was Kay Hedderly. The writing on the wall contained her last name also.

FUCK YOU BITCH PUNIS- HED

All of the letters in this writing are spaced apart except for the "hed" in Punished. They touch each other. Above "hed" is a small case "h" in BITCH pointing towards the small case "d" in "hed" between the two Hs' is ED so you end up with more letters to Kay Hedderly.

In all of the messages sprayed on the wall there was a hidden code within the writing. You can see each stroke of the spray can and witch letter came first or how the letter was written. The e in Have is the same as the e and c from Edwards' 1945-46 Lipstick Killings. The message meant Catch Edward Edwards.

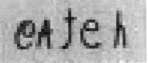

Chapter 40

The Set-up of Steven Avery and Brendan Dassey

Edwards MO was to create a horrific murder, set-up an innocent person, and then stand in front of the investigation under assumed identity. He portrayed himself as a Marine veteran, police officer, preacher and a Psychiatrist to gain access to his victims.

Edwards was an instructor for first aid and civil defense throughout his life and taught police courses in this area. He used this training to gain access to his own murder scenes.

Edwards detailed how he got inside religious organizations and civil defense in this 1970 album he released as a taunt. The album was titled **"Build a Fire in the Person and Not Under Them."** Edwards built a fire under Teresa Halbach after grooming his way into her church. Edwards is an Occultist and staged his murders as rituals. He created horrific murders on Christian Holidays and significant dates in USA history.

Edwards is the real Zodiac Killer and released the album in 1970 after he had killed 5 people in the San Francisco Bay area as the Zodiac Killer. The Zodiac Killer was never indented identified but taunted the press, police and public for decades with anonymous letters. The composite of the Zodiac Killer is shown next to Ed Edwards' picture below

Zodiac Composite 1969 Edward Wayne Edwards 1970

The title of Edwards' album actually reflected what Edwards had done to bodies throughout his life. He would build a fire under them with a bomb he described in detail in the 1969 Zodiac Killer Bomb Letter he mailed to reporter Paul AVERY of the San Francisco Chronicle, November 9, 1969.

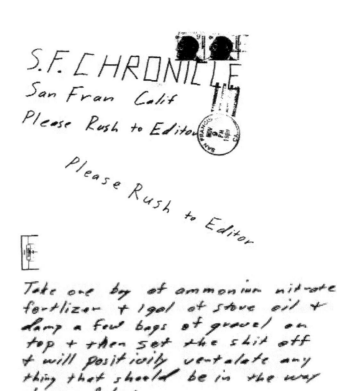

Take one bag of ammonium nitrate fertlizer + 1gal of stove oil + damp a few bags of gravel on top + then set the shit off + will positivily ventalate any thing that should be in the way of the Blast.

In the letter Edwards describes his bomb

Edwards had killed a 26-year-old man in Portland, Oregon, Thanksgiving of 1960. The man's name was WAYNE Budde. Edwards blew WAYNE Budde apart with a bomb similar to what he described in the Zodiac letters.

Teresa Halbach's remains were blown apart by a bomb just like Edwards had done to WAYNE Budde. The bones were not only burned, but shattered into small pieces and planted later.

Teresa Halbach's Remains

Leslie Eisenberg, a Forensic Anthropologist, described Teresa Halbach's bone fragments as the result of obvious mutilation of a corpse.

Edward Wayne Edwards would target his victims long in advance of killing them. He would groom his way into their lives through church organizations. He would groom his way into the lives of his intended set-ups long in advance, collecting personal information, DNA, hairs, fibers, skin cell DNA, and use them to set people up.

THE VICTIM

From her obituary: Teresa M. Halbach, age 25, of St. John, died on Halloween, October 31, 2005. She was born March 22, 1980 in Kaukauna, Wisconsin. Teresa graduated from Hilbert High School in 1998 and graduated from UW Green Bay Summa Cum Laude with a degree in photography in 2002. She was the owner and operator of Photography by Teresa and did children's photography for Pearce Photography in Green Bay.

Teresa was a member of St. John - Sacred Heart Parish in St. John, Wisconsin and the Business Marketing Group in Green Bay. She coached her younger sister's 7th grade volleyball team at St. John - Sacred Heart School. She also enjoyed traveling and went to Spain, New Zealand, Australia, Mexico and all across the United States. Most of all, Teresa loved singing karaoke and spending time with her family and friends.

On the day Teresa was killed she had an appointment to photograph a maroon mini-van at Avery Auto Salvage located in Two Rivers, Wisconsin. She had been to the Avery Salvage Yard several other times to photograph cars. Steven Avery was the son of the owner and had spoken to Teresa on several occasions prior to her death about photographing cars.

The Location of the Murder
Avery Auto Salvage is located approximately 30 miles from St. John's, Wisconsin where Teresa Halbach lived. It is located in a rural part of Wisconsin as pictured from Google Earth.

Avery Auto Salvage

Avery Auto Salvage had been owned by the AVERY family for decades. Delores and Allen Avery had 3 sons: Steven, Earl, and Charles and one daughter, Barbara

Barbara, Delores, Allen Avery-Steve Avery-Earl Avery-Charles Avery

Halloween, October 31, 2005 the day of the murder **October 31, 2005, MONDAY, Halloween, Avery Auto Salvage.** Teresa Halbach went to Avery Auto Salvage at approximately 2:30 pm to photograph a maroon van that was being sold by Avery Salvage.

Steven Avery and Maroon Van

2:30-3:30pm: Teresa had spoken to Steve on the phone earlier and arranged the meeting. Teresa showed up at approximately 2:30-3:00 pm.

3:00-3:30pm: Bobby Dassey is the son to Barb Avery. Bobby woke up and was getting ready to go bow hunting at around 2:30 or 2:45 and saw Teresa Halbach photographing the van and walking to Steve Avery's home.

3:30pm: A delivery driver claims to see Teresa Halbach's vehicle near a gas station by Avery Salvage. Teresa Halbach is never seen again after she left Avery Auto Salvage.

November 3, 2005, THURSDAY, Saint Johns, Wisconsin. Teresa Halbach is reported missing by her mother three days after she disappeared. The killer had three days with Teresa and her vehicle before anyone knew she was missing. Teresa's mother provided police with her car vehicle plate number and VIN number

November 4th, 2005, FRIDAY, St. John's Wisconsin. Police organize a search for Teresa Halbach. A helicopter is used and flies over the AVERY property. Teresa's car is not there. Steven Avery is talked to by police and he lets them in his home to search. Steven Avery then talked to channel 2 news and states that he allowed police to search his house. Steven becomes a suspect because he is the last person seen with Teresa Halbach. There is no sign of Teresa Halbach on the Avery property on Thursday.

November 4th, 2005, FRIDAY, St. John's Wisconsin. Pamela Sturm a relative of Teresa Halbach's and former private detective joins a search. Pam picks up 2-3000 fliers and has a group called "YES" (Youth Educated in Safety) distributed the fliers. Pam's testimony:

Q. okay. an organization that did help you, though, and it's up in the top left-hand corner of this exhibit, is something called YES, youth extended safety; is that right,?
Q. The distribution efforts, that is, getting these posters out; who was in charge of that?
A I guess I was kind of The Unofficial leader, coordinator, of the effort, if you could call it that.

(Ed Edwards had a group called WWTH standing for "We Want to Help" he used this group to gain access to his victims)

400   METAMORPHOSIS OF A CRIMINAL

the club WWTH—We-Want-to-Help. This organization now publishes a newsletter which boasts quite a respectable circulation.

November 5, 2005, SATURDAY, 6:00am, Avery Auto Salvage. Steve Avery and his mother Delores leave town to a cabin they own in Crivitz, Wisconsin.

November 5th, 2005, 10:29 am: Four hours after Steve Avery left town, **Pamela Sturm** a former private investigator and relative to Teresa Halbach, travels to Avery Salvage and finds Teresa Halbach's car. It wasn't there the day before when a helicopter flew overhead. Sturm calls police dispatch and the call is recorded.

DISPATCH: okay
CALLER: okay. Okay, we are at Avery Salvage
DISPATCH: okay
CALLER: okay, and we are searching for the vehicle
DISPATCH: right
CALLER: for Teresa halbach, we have found a RAV4. What color specifically was her RAV4 and do you have a VIN number
SHERIFF: hi this is Sheriff Pagel
CALLER: oh, sheriff pagle, hi, this is Pam strum. I am on the search for Teresa halbach and we found a RAV4
SHERIFF: you did

CALLER: it's a bluish green though. It's more blue than green we just wanted to know if you got the VIN number for that vehicle
SHERIFF: yes we do we do have a VIN number
SHERIFF: (talking to dispatch) can you get the VIN number
CALLER: it's the only thing I can't find it on the
SHERIFF: where, where is, where is the vehicle at?
CALLER: I'm at Avery Salvage
SHERIFF: okay
CALLER: it's all covered up
WIEGERT: is there any license plates on it?
CALLER: no plates on it but it's a little covered up, it's weird, it's covered up
WIEGERT: stay on the outside of the car, go over to the front on the driver side
CALLER: yeah, I, I realize that, I'm in the business so I kind of know but I can't find the VIN number I'm picking up the wiper
WIEGERT: okay
CALLER: there is, I can't find the VIN number isn't that funny oh here it is Nick I don't have my glasses

November 5, 2005, 11:00am. Avery Auto Salvage. Police respond and confirm the car is Teresa Halbach's. The car is the only one out of the hundreds on the lot that is covered in strange debris and double parked, unlike the others. The car was planted and designed to stand out, not be hidden. Pam Sturm is interviewed about how she came about going to Avery Salvage.

Q. Good afternoon, Miss Strom. Describe for the jury, if you will whether you knew a young woman named Teresa Hall bag
A.   Yes, I did she's my second cousin. Her father, Tom Hall back, is my first cousin.
Q. Miss strum, sometime after the 3rd of November after Teresa was reported missing did you volunteer to become involved in search efforts for Teresa
A.   Yes, I did.

Q. Can you describe for the jury how you first became involved
A. On November Forest, I signed news release at like 10:00 in the morning and it was a Friday morning and it said that --they showed Teresa picture and it said Teresa was missing. and as soon as I got home from work, I called my sister and she didn't know anything about it. So I waited until night and I called my other first cousin Betty Halbach, who is Tom Halbach's sister. And I asked her if that was correct and she said yes.

Q. All right. When was it, Miss strum then that you first became involved in actually searching for Teresa
A. Well, that Friday night, when I had talked to Betty, I said, anything I can do for you, anything I can help with, I will certainly help. And she had called back like an hour later and said there's going to be a search tomorrow morning starting at probably 9:00 and I said, well, I would be happy to help.

November 5, 2009, SATURDAY, St. John's Wisconsin. An estimated 30 to 45 people met at Teresa Halbach's Farm House she rented. Pam Sturm Testimony

. That next morning, then, on Saturday, the 5th of November, did you go to the Rendezvous Place: in other words, where everybody else was meeting
A. Yes, I did. it's an old farmhouse that Teresa was renting. And I met with two gentlemen, Ryan and Scott. And they we're organizing a search team.
Q. Just so I can complete the record, that would be Ryan Hillegas and Scott Bloedorn
A. That's correct
Q. All right. Who did you go there with
A. My daughter, Nikole Sturm
Q. How old is Nikole
A. 29 years old.
Q. About what time did you arrive at the residence, if you recall?
A. I estimated it at around 9 a.m.
Q. When you got there Pam what happened
A. Well, well we got there late; the search team was already gone. Ryan and Scott were still there. And I asked them if I could help out. And they said yes, they have maps for the area that they were going to search and he showed me the map

and then he showed me the picture of Teresa and all the details regarding Teresa And I indicated that I would like to go to the Avery salvage yard or Teresa's was last seen and he said, well, if you want to, it's not part of, you know, the search, but if you wish to do that, go ahead.

November 5th, Saturday, 9:00am, Teresa Halbach's home. Pam Sturm arrives at the search party but most of the 30 to 40 people had already left. Pam takes it on her own accord to go to Avery Salvage and search for Teresa. It was not part of the search team's areas to look because it had already been searched by police the day before. Pam describes what she did:

Q. Okay. About what time, then, did let me check up just a minute. Prior to going to the Avery Salvage property, did you receive anything from either of those gentlemen?
A.   I received a map and I received a bulletin that showed Teresa picture and all her details
Q. Did you get anything else, that you can recall?
A.   I also forgot my camera, so I thought I should, you know, try to get a camera and see if Scott or Ryan had a camera, in case we came across something on the property. And I believe it was Scott's camera and he lent it to us
Q. Do you remember what kind of camera it was
A.   It was just a digital camera as far as I know
Q. So the jury understands, it was you that asked for the camera
A. Yes I did

Q. Miss strum, were you familiar with the Avery Salvage property?
A.   No I am not I wasn't at all. All I knew it was a 40-acre plot salvage yard for vehicles.
Q. Did you proceed to that location?
A.   Yes we did.
Q. About what time did you and Nikole arrived at that location
A.   I aproximate the time about 10 minutes to 10, right around that area
Q. All right. About 10 to 10, sometime before 10 in the morning, could you tell the jury what happened?

A. Well,, we drove in and we noticed that there were three driveways to the salvage yard. and it appeared to be the center driveway would probably the one we should take. so we did take that one.

Q. Miss Sturm you are going to have to back up about 3 in from the microphone, okay.

A. I was in my car and we pulled up in front of the main building.

Q. And on exhibit number 25 can you tell me what that is can you point with that with the laser pointer

A. I believe it's that one.

Q. When you got to that location what did you do?

A. When we got to that location, there were a few cars parked to the right of us and we saw two gentlemen conversing. But we went into the building to see if we could find any of the owners of the property. And there was no one inside so then we exited.

Q. After exiting, did you, in fact, find one of the owners of the business and did you in fact, talk to him?

i. Yes, we did. The two gentlemen that were conversing by the vehicle, they stopped conversing and I walked up to them and I said, is anyone of you an Avery, an owner of this property? And he said, yes, and he walked over to us and he said his name was Earl

Q. Just very quickly going to show you a photograph is this the gentleman that you spoke with Earl Avery

A. Yes, that's correct

Q. Okay. I'm sorry to interrupt you; go ahead, what happened then?

A. Well, I told them that we were from -- we were volunteers from the search party. And I said it would relieve Karen and Tom's mind if we could go through the property and make sure that the vehicle Teresa vehicle wasn't there and Earl said, yeah, I know how it is because I just lost a nephew and I know how they are feeling. They must feel awful that she's missing. We just had a conversation and then I asked him if we could go and search the property, the whole property, for a sign of Teresa, or her vehicle. And he gave us permission

Q. Now miss strum prior to your arrival at that location, have you had any contact or direction from any law enforcement officials?

A no, sir, we didn't.

Q. After obtaining permission or consent from earlier Avery to search the property, what did you do?
A.   Earl said that the roads were very muddy in the salvage yard and it would be better if you would walk so you know we locked up our vehicle and walk to the left we decided we're going to Sweep from left to right so we walk down in the between the buildings, I believe it was, and started on the left and swept to the right

November 5th, 2009, SATURDAY, 11:00am, Avery Auto Salvage. Pam Sturm finds Teresa Halbach's car covered in debris. She detailed how long it took her to find the car:
    I believe we entered at 10 to 10 and by 10:20 to 10:25 we had found the vehicle
    November 5th, SATURDAY, 10:25 am. Avery Salvage. Pam Sturm calls the police, and waits for 20 to 25 minutes before the Sheriff Officers arrive. She explains being scared and seeing a man on the ridge above the car.
Q. Now, tell us what happened then
A.   Well, we waited about 20, 25 minutes before someone ride. Before they arrived, we saw a man up on the ridge. By the buildings up here, there's a ridge. And I got a little concerned so I -- like I said, I put Nicki behind the car so nothing would happen to her. And we just waited and waited. And it forever, you know.

Q. In 20 or 25 minutes did somebody arrive?
A.   Yes. Is Sheriff Remiker arrived first

November 5th, 2009 SATURDAY, Avery Salvage. Pam Sturm is asked on the stand about finding the car and is asked if "she got lucky" She explains GOD led her to it.
Q. Looking at it now, do you think you got lucky?

A. Yeah. Well, not lucky, God showed us the way; I do believe that.

After finding Teresa's vehicle and being questioned by police, Pam Sturm goes to Teresa Halbach's mother's house to tell her about the find. On cross examination she is asked if she is a private investigator.

Q. Now, ma'am you, on the dispatch tape, we heard you say, I know, I'm sort of in the business. By that you mean you have private investigator experience right?

Q. So you had some idea what to do and how to do the search right?
A. Some idea.
Q. Is it your testimony that before Saturday morning, November 5th, you had not done anything in terms of investigating or searching for Teresa or her vehicle?
A. No I haven't, I hadn't

Pam Sturm went on to explain that she was further led to another area for evidence by patrons of a bar.

Q. And after that, did you also do any additional investigation on your own
A. Yes, I did
Q. And did you, in fact were you, in fact called to an area near Mishicot by some individuals who had found what they thought might be some evidence?
A. I don't recall being called by someone no.
Q. Well, did you -- were you looking with somebody looking in the area of Mishikot?

A.

Q. Those were bars, right?
A. That's correct.
Q. Do you remember being called to an area near the river, a turn around area near the river, buy one of those individuals from the bar area, to look at some

A. I know we had searched around the area around the river and then at that point, we, meaning one of the bar owners in town, said he would come down and help me out. And on the search we had found a cell phone.
Q. And what was that bar owners name?
A. I don't recall.

On cross examination Pam Sturm is asked about the man she saw on the ridge when she found the car.

Q. And you mentioned a man up on the ridge, or not on the ridge but up on the hill, kind of back towards the buildings, when you are sitting there waiting for 20 minutes
A. Correct
Q. And Steven Avery wasn't that man either was he
A. I don't know for sure.
Q. Well who was that man do you know?
A. I don't know.
Q. Do you have any description of him?
A. No, sir.
Q. Was it the same -- was it Earl Avery?
A. It could have been. It's just too far away to see
Q. So you just wasn't anything in particular about that man, or what he was doing, that cause you concern; it was just the overall feeling you had that maybe this wasn't the safest place to be; is that fair
A. That's Fair yes

Pam went on her own volition to Avery Salvage, with a camera she was given by the search organizer and found Teresa Halbach's car in less than 40 minutes. Pam Sturm was led to other sites later on by anonymous people and bar owners and patrons and again found items that were confiscated by Manitowoc Sheriff's deputies. She believed those items might have been Teresa's.
Pam Sturm is a former private Investigator and Ed Edwards portrayed himself as one throughout his life. Pam Sturm is a Christian and stated GOD led her to Teresa's car. As mentioned before, Edwards would use various characters to work into his victim's lives.

Someone convinced Pam Sturm that she was going to need a camera before she drove to AVERY Salvage. The power of suggestion is what Edwards would have used to groom his way into Pam Sturm and it may have been through her church. Ed Edwards had groomed his way into churches since 1971.

The Reasons Edwards Targeted Steven Avery

September 11th, 2003. Two Rivers, Wisconsin. Steven Avery was released on September 11th, 2003 at the height of the press frenzy in the Scott Peterson case. Edwards had framed Scott Peterson in California in 2003 for killing his wife Laci and unborn child Conner on Christmas Eve, and planting her body 4 months later on Palm Sunday, just 5 months before Steven Avery was released. (Newspaper Article)

CALIFORNIA | LOCAL Testimony Contradicts Scott Peterson Account
November 1, 2003 | From Associated Press
Laci Peterson's sister testified Friday that Scott Peterson said he had golf plans on Christmas Eve, throwing into question his story

about going fishing the day his wife vanished. Amy Rocha said she cut Scott Peterson's hair Dec. 23 and that he had offered to pick up a gift basket for her grandfather near the country club where he was a member. "He said he was going to be out that way golfing," she said in about 30 minutes of testimony. "I assumed all day."

September 11, 2003, Manitowoc Wisconsin. STEVE AVERY is released after spending 18 years in prison for an assault he did not commit. DNA proved him innocent. Police withheld evidence in the case that could have cleared him 9 years earlier, but they did not divulge that information until 2003. Avery was 23 in 1985 when he went into prison and 41 when he came out in 2003. He was "The Most Known Wrongfully Convicted Man" at the time and was all over the press.

2004, Manitowoc County Wisconsin. Steve Avery files a $36 million federal lawsuit against Manitowoc County, Wisconsin, its former sheriff, Thomas Kocourek, and its former district attorney, Denis Vogel.

From 2003 until 2005, Steven Avery was in the press and on TV throughout the country. This is one reason Ed Edwards started plotting to set not only Steve Avery up, but law enforcement also. Edwards had framed dozens of people by 2003 and Steve Avery was getting "recognition" that Edwards believed should have been focused on HIS crimes.

Edwards called his murders "Crimes of Recognition." What this meant was, whenever anyone else was getting recognition in the paper, Edwards would concoct a murder that would steal the press. His 1947 psych records explain "Recognition."

> It may be of interest to psychiatrists, sociologists, and social workers to learn that when Edwards was a youngster he was given tests which yielded the result that he had an inferior I.Q.
>
> As can be seen from the documents which follow, the young Edwards was at first diagnosed as having subnormal intelligence. That this was not true and was not the underlying cause of his criminal behavior was clearly documented by later diagnoses and behavior. On the contrary, Edwards was using his intelligence and ingenuity to mastermind devious, anti-social and illegal means of feeding his need for recognition and identity.

PSYCHOLOGICAL SERVICES
77 East Mill Street
Akron 8, Ohio

By setting people up, Edwards' cases received national attention like Steve Avery was getting at the time of his release. Edwards targeted Avery to set-up for a future murder knowing it would create massive "recognition" and feed his desire to be recognized.

Edwards killed on Halloween 2 times prior to killing Teresa Halbach on Halloween 2005:

1) The first Halloween killing was a 15-year-old female named Martha Moxley. It occurred in 1975 in Greenwich, Connecticut. In June of 2002 police arrested and convicted Michael Skakel for this killing committed by Edwards. A year later Steven Avery was released from prison. Edwards started plotting to set-up Avery on a future Halloween murder.

2) The second Halloween killing was a 59-year-old Editor of a newspaper named Kent Hietholt in 2001 in Columbia, Missouri. One month after Steven Avery's release from prison for an

assault he did not do, police opened up the investigation of Kent Hietholt and arrested Ryan Ferguson and Charles Erickson for the Halloween 2001 killing that Edwards had committed. Charles Erickson falsely confessed like Brendan Dassey.

Ryan Ferguson's trial started October 14th, 2005, just two weeks before Edwards killed Teresa Halbach on Halloween. The trial and sentencing lasted until December 2005. Edwards killed Teresa Halbach in the middle of the trial and did it on Halloween. Ryan Ferguson was released in 2014 because he was represented by Kathleen Zellner, a famous wrongful conviction attorney who is now representing Steven Avery. Charles Erickson is still serving because he falsely confessed and testified against Ryan Ferguson just before Teresa Halbach's murder, Halloween 2005. By killing Teresa, Edwards effectively removed the focus from Steve Avery for being wrongly convicted and put the focus back onto an Edwards set-up.

Edwards targeted Steven Avery shortly after his release in 2003 after police targeted Ryan Ferguson and arrested him for a Halloween murder. Edwards chose Avery to set-up because of his name, and the fact he was getting a lot of press. Avery was a name that Edwards had targeted to destroy in the past.

As the Zodiac Killer Edwards targeted San Francisco Chronicle reporter Paul Avery by sending him what is known as The Zodiac Killers Halloween Card.

Edwards Halloween Card October 27, 1970.

By fire, by knife, by gun, by rope. Teresa Halbach was killed in this manner on Halloween. Her bones were left in the fire pit. She had been shot at least twice in the head. Prosecutors in a press conference stated that she had been tied up, throat slit, shot and burned. (Rope, knife, gun, fire.)

The **4-TEEN** in the card was a clue from Edwards on a previous murder and set-up he had done. In 1955, just before Edwards came to my hometown of Great Falls, Montana and executed a couple on a lover's lane, he had killed 14-year-old Stephanie Bryan in Berkley, California,

April 28th, 1955. The positioning of the Skeleton on the HALLOWEEN CARD was the way Stephanie was found buried in a shallow grave in July 1955 in California. Edwards planted her body on a man named Burton Abbott's property, setting him up and getting him executed. This started Edwards' M.O. of framing people and getting the system to kill for him.

Burton was executed March 15th, 1957 while Edwards was in Deer Lodge Prison, Montana for Robbery. Edwards became the "Executioner" in 1955 and set-people up the rest of his life. In the Zodiac Killer case Edwards told his surviving victim that he had been in Deer Lodge Prison, Montana. Edwards was in Deer Lodge 1956-59 and remained unidentified as a serial killer until his capture in 2009 in Louisville, KY.

Edwards had groomed his way into churches and killed members of congregations in every part of the USA since 1945. Edwards befriended police officers in all parts of the country, and befriended them in some of his criminal plots.

He admitted in an interview with me in 2011 that he set people up and hung out with cops. (Transcript January 2011)

Ed: I can be. For example, like uh, John will be interested in knowing...There's a guy right now, doing life in a penitentiary, he's been in since 1983, and I don't know if he committed the crime or not, but he's in there because I said he did. And that was my getting even with him because he was pulling some bullshit on me, and so I thought, "Okay, I'm gonna set you up real good." So he ended up getting life on my testimony.

John: Wow.

Ed: And uh, I'm 95% sure he killed a guy but he had a big mouth and paid......it hurt him. See that's something I did not have when I was running around was a big mouth. The things I went......my crimes are all old crimes, back in '77 (robo interrupt).....so if I liked to talk, I'd have been in jail a looooong time ago.

of it is correct. There's a lot of things not in there....for example, when I was on the FBI 10 Most Wanted List, uh...my god when I was in Houston, TX, some of my very very best friends every Friday and Saturday night we used to get together in my apartment and we would play cards. And the fact of the matter is, I was on the top ten....and 8 of these guys were cops.

Edwards' wife also confirmed in a 2010 interview that Edwards would befriend police officers wherever they lived. (Kay Edwards Transcript)

JC: Did he like to keep track of the police?
KE: Uh...It was funny. When we lived on Witner, he (laughs)...the police would come over and have drinks with him. And even when he went to Burton, from what I understand, Brian said, he went there and told them who he was, and all that, when we moved there. So..
JC: So it's almost like he became friends with police wherever you lived, or...what do you think?
KE: He...a lot of the places. Sometimes we weren't there long enough to do anything...for him to become familiar with them.

Edwards is pictured in 1979 with Captain Bradley of the Atlanta Police Department. Edwards had set-up Wayne Williams in 1982, after killing dozens of children in 1979-81, and sent letters taunting the police with his IQ and stating he planted evidence:

Capt. Larry Bradley, Atlanta, Georgia Police Dept, and Ed. While Capt. Bradley and Ed are the best of friends today, it was Capt. Bradley who led the raid and arrested Ed in Atlanta in 1962.

Hello its me. Haven't you people figured out who is killing these little people yet. I'll give you a hint, I used to be in San Fransisco. I used to stalk women, but I like to kill children now. At all my victims bodies I have left certain clues, but I guess it's too much for you Rebels to handle. So I guess I'll have to tell you. I'll to kill children because they are so easy to "pick off". Buy the way, if you still have letters from the other murders, I am not writing in the same hand writing.

> *While you're all afraid, you're all upset*
> *Cause none of those cops have caught me yet*
> *I've struck again and didn't leave a clue*
> *Now the whole city doesn't know what to do*
> *You finally found Julie, her name was all she nodded*
> *Keep looking you might find another child*
> *You think that the number stops at nineteen*
> *Man, there are some things you haven't seen*
> *One night some kids got killed in a fire ___*
> *I struck the match, so the death toll is higher*
> *But you can't seem to catch me. I wonder why ___*
> *Thousands of you see me everyday when I pass by*
> *It's pathetic to know that I can get away*
> *With first degree murder on any chosen day*

Edwards M.O. in many of his set-ups was to send anonymous letters to the police taunting them with details of the crime and steering it towards innocent people. When I confronted Edwards about being the Zodiac Killer in 2010 he responded with the following letter:

Hi Neal,

It's me! This letter will be sent from Tenn. or Ky. I think. My friend's wife is sending it. I feel sure they are opening all the mail I am sending out & then resending it after they read it. I am not saying anything wrong but I just don't like it. When you get this don't say anything about how it was sent, but just say "I got the letter." Please let me know as soon as you can. When I told you in my last letter that it is okay if you wish my story I meant it. There is just alot of things I don't want others to know at this time. Believe me I have alot to say. ☺! I do think of you on a

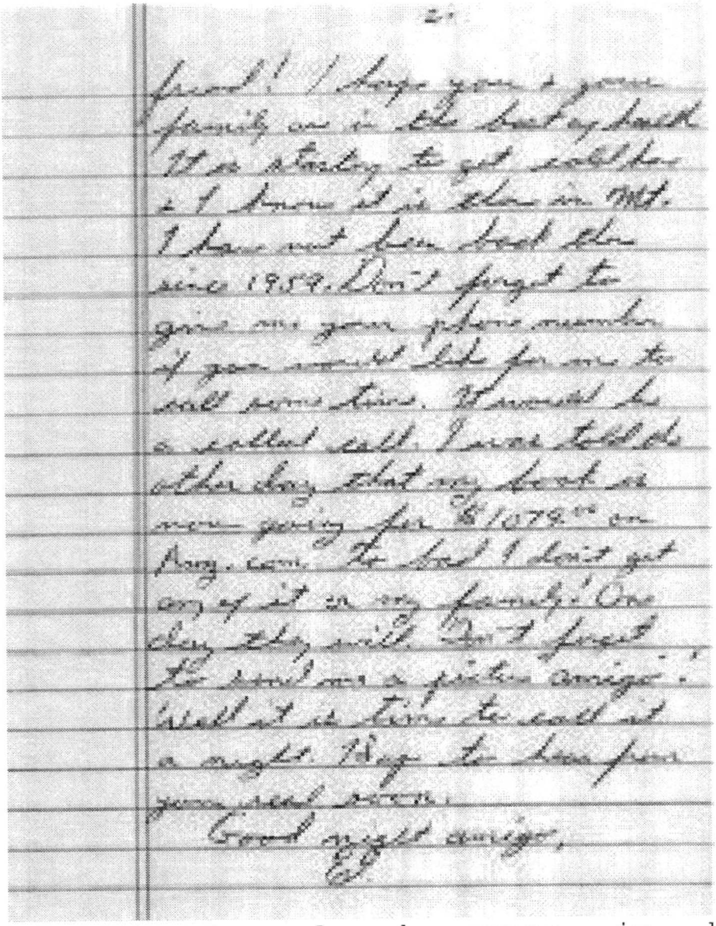
2.

friend!! I hope you & your family are in the best of health. It is starting to get cold here & I know it is colder in Mt. I have not been back there since 1959. Don't forget to give me your phone number if you would like for me to call some time. It would be a collect call. I was told the other day that my book is now going for $1079.00 on Amz.com. Too bad I don't get any of it or my family. One day they will. Don't forget to send me a picture amigo! Well it is time to call it a night. Hope to hear from you real soon.

Good night amigo,
Ed

Edwards played games in his letters, writing in cryptic code so prison officials would not discard them. In the Steven Avery case a cryptic letter, as described by the judge, was sent to the Manitowoc Sheriff in November of 2005, shortly after Steven's arrest.

> Body was burnt up in
> aluminum Smelter, 3 AM
> Fridy Morn.
>
> Sikikay

> manitavac Shuff
> Avery X

This letter was intended to tell the Sheriff when Edwards planted Teresa's body; Friday night at 3:00 am. The police had already searched Avery's property on Friday, November 4th, 2005 and did not find Teresa Halbach's body or car. The following day, Steve Avery and his mom left town and Pam Sturm was led to the car on the Avery property by who she claimed was GOD, as she testified.

The letter also was intended to purport that a young low IQ individual wrote it that may have had some guilt, and participated in the murder. The letter directed the police to look at 16-year-old Brendan Dassey, the last person to be with Steven Avery after Teresa Halbach had visited the salvage yard on Halloween. Brendan is low IQ and the letter appears to be written by someone who is not that bright. Brendan and Steven had a bonfire on Halloween and this is where Edwards planted the remains of Teresa on November 4th, 2005 after the police had searched the property and found nothing.

Edwards would have most likely known members of law enforcement in Manitowoc, Wisconsin, possibly the Sheriff, and that is why the letter was addressed to him.

The set-up of Steve Avery was also designed to set-up the police and make them look like liars and fools. In the letter Edwards tells the police that Teresa was burned in a smelter on Friday at 3:00 am. Teresa's remains could not have been burned in the open pit behind Steve Avery's house and come out in the condition she was found in. Teresa's remains were burned in intense heat and were fragmented by Edwards' bomb that he had used many ties to make people disappear and create a mystery that would live into infamy.

The Burn Pit - Teresa's Remains

The Reasons Edwards Targeted Teresa Halbach

Edwards targeted Teresa Halbach to kill because she had attended Avery Salvage Yard multiple times prior to her death. She would be a female that had contact with Steven Avery on a regular basis. Edwards would have groomed his way into Avery Salvage to gain the information on Teresa photographing for Auto Trader Magazine. Edwards was the same age as Steve Avery's parents and could have easily hung out at the Salvage yard plotting and nobody knew it. This is also how he would have gotten Stevens DNA to plant. The salvage industry employees cut their hands regularly and bleed on cars, counters, and leave the tissues in their public restroom at the salvage yard. Steven Avery cut his hand in the days before the killing while loading a flat-bed trailer with tin roofing.

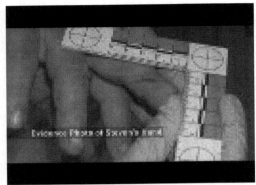

The blood that was located near the ignition switch of Teresa Halbach's vehicle later appeared to be planted with a cotton swab. You can see the round area and then swipe. No ridge detail.

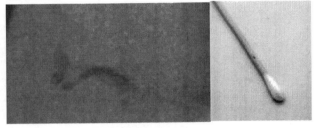

Teresa Halbach lived in St. Johns, Wisconsin and went to the Avery salvage yard to photograph on a regular basis. She knew Steve Avery. She was a member of St. John's Catholic Parish. Teresa was also a coach at St. John's Parochial School. Edwards targeted Catholics to kill his entire life. He could have met her at the salvage yard or the church prior to her murder. Edwards groomed his way into his victim's life so his face would be familiar when he was about to kill them. They never saw it coming in most instances.

Teresa Halbach was a freelance photographer working for a major publication, Auto Trader Magazine. Paul AVERY, who chased "The Zodiac Killer" was also a reporter and freelance photographer for the San Francisco Chronicle.

Edwards targeted people that worked in journalism and magazines throughout life. He also targeted names that tied back to his past murders like the name AVERY.

Teresa was born March 22, 1980, which is the 10-year anniversary date of Ed Edwards kidnapping and terrorizing a woman named Kathleen Johns in 1970 as The Zodiac Killer.

Kathleen Johns 1970

Edwards used a ruse on Johns to get her to pull her car over to the side of the road, just as he would have done to Teresa Halbach. Edwards terrorized Kathleen Johns for several hours and then left Johns and her baby alive to describe him. He wanted to be "Recognized." He then blew her car up with a bomb, like he did to Teresa's Halbach's remains. Edwards used a ruse to get Johns to pull over in 1970 and that is how he would have gotten Teresa Halbach to pull over after she left Avery Salvage Yard on Halloween. Edwards sent a letter in the Johns case taunting the police with his smarts as he did in most of his cases.

> This is the Zodiac speaking
>
> I am rather unhappy because you people will not wear some nice ⊕ buttons. So I now have a little list, starting with the woeman + her baby that I gave a rather interesting ride fo- a coupple howers one evening a few months back that ended in my burning her car where I found them.
>
> ⊕

Edwards would have appeared to be a harmless old man to Teresa. Edwards may have attended her church prior to the murder so she would be familiar with his face. That was his M.O. throughout life.

```
        Edwards   had    killed   dozens   of   people
between 1945 and 1972, and then wrote the book.
He tied all his murders that he committed after
publishing the book, to names and places in the
book. Wisconsin was mentioned once and Theresa
with an H was mentioned 25 times.
```

Theresa, by this time, was acting like a woman scorned. I had borrowed $10 from her the day I met Jeanette; not only had I cut her out of my life entirely, but I had not paid her back the $10.

I managed to juggle the three women for a week. By

Edwards released the book in 1972 and tied all of his future murders by names and locations he had written about in the book. Wisconsin was mentioned in a chapter about him surviving the 1959 Deer Lodge Prison, Montana riot. Because it was mentioned in the book, Edwards returned to Wisconsin over and over again to kill and set people up. That is how the book worked and my investigation of him proved that.

Tension was mounting at the prison. A new warden and a new deputy warden from Wisconsin were brought in, to stem some of the trouble. After the arrival of these new

When Edwards was arrested in 2009 in Louisville, Kentucky for the 1980 Jefferson, Wisconsin murder, police contacted agencies mentioned in his book. I was contacted while working in Deer Lodge Prison, Montana for the parole board. My hometown of Great Falls, Montana was mentioned 5 times in the book. Montana was mentioned 26 times. My investigation revealed that Edwards killed in my hometown Great Falls, Montana on January 2, 1956 by approaching a couple parked on a lover's lane dressed as a police officer, ordered them out, made the women tie up the male. Executed the male with two shots to the head like Teresa Halbach, kidnapped the female, like Teresa Halbach, and executed her with two shots to the head like Teresa Halbach, on top of Mount Royal Road.

Satanic Spirituality Edwards is the Occult Edwards was a ritual killer. He killed a couple in Jefferson, Wisconsin in 1980 in a similar fashion as my 1956 Great Falls double murder, similar to the Lover's Lane murder in Portland, OR in 1960, similar to the Zodiac murders. By being a ritual killer, he regularly kills on Christian holidays, national holidays or significant dates in his life. The 1980

Wisconsin couple was killed on the anniversary of his mother's death and funeral, August 8-10th, 1938.

(On the third day he rises again) Edwards had three days with Teresa's body and car without anyone knowing. On November 4th the Avery's left town and that is when Edwards would have planted Teresa Halbach's car. He stated in the anonymous letter to the Sheriff that Friday at 3:00 am is when Teresa was burned. It really was the day she was planted.

Body was burned up in aluminum smelter, 3 AM Fridy Morn.

Burning bodies is his Occult M.O. Edwards portrays the great Satan. That's why he killed on Halloween. The day following Halloween in Catholicism is "All Saints Day" and the day that follows "All Saints Day" is "All Souls Day." These are the three days Teresa went missing. On the Third Day he rises again through the killing of someone. He gains satanic power through the killing of innocence. He described it in his 1969 Zodiac Killer letter.

" I LIKE KILLING PEOPLE BECAUSE IT IS SO MUCH FUN IT IS MORE FUN THAN KILLING WILD GAME IN THE FORREST BECAUSE MAN IS THE MOST DANGEROUE ANAMAL OF ALL TO KILL SOMETHING GIVES ME THE MOST THRILLING EXPERENCE IT IS EVEN BETTER THAN GETTING YOUR ROCKS OFF WITH A GIRL THE BEST PART OF IT IS THAE WHEN I DIE I WILL BE REBORN IN PARADICE AND THEI HAVE KILLED WILL BECOME MY SLAVES I WILL NOT GIVE YOU MY NAME BECAUSE YOU WILL TRY TO SLOI DOWN OR ATOP MY COLLECTIOG OF SLAVES FOR MY AFTERLIFE EBEORIETEMETHHPITI "

August 1969 Ed Edwards Zodiac Identity Letter

Satanic Spirituality: Edwards' real name was Charles Edwards Myers. (Chuckie) He became a Satanist at a very young age. His mother was shot in front of him at age 5 on August 2, 1938. She suffered until August 8th and died of gangrene. Her funeral was on August 10, 1938. Edwards killed repeatedly in August throughout his life and sent in the first Zodiac Killer Letters during this period, taunting authorities with his identity.

Edwards' 1980 Wisconsin lovers' lane victims were killed on August 9th. His 1977 Ohio lover's lane victims were killed on August 8th. Edwards is a satanic ritual killer. His previous 1974 Wisconsin victim was killed on June 6th, (6-6) she was 16 and he did it 6 years after he started the Zodiac Killings. (666) Edwards killed her at 3:00am on a Friday, just like he had written in the anonymous letter to the Sheriff of Manitowoc. 51

Body was Burnt up in aluminum Smelter, 3 AM Friday Morn.

Edwards ties his murders together through names, dates and locations. Wisconsin was targeted by Edwards his entire life.

In 1999 (666) in mirror image, Edwards killed a Catholic Priest named Father Kunz in Danes, Wisconsin, 28 miles from Manitowoc. He slit his throat and laid him out at the base of St. Michael the Archangel, who in biblical terms took on Satan and lost.

Father Kuntz - St. Michael the Archangel

Edwards is the OCCULT and that is why Halloween killings were so important. On May 4th, 2003, just months before Steven Avery was released from prison the first time, Edwards wrote the following letter to Reporter Garth Stapley of the Modesto Bee detailing his God like image and how he framed people.

> 5-4-03
>
> A Message From God
>
> On the 12TH day of the 12TH month Cary Stayner was sentenced to death by a jury of 12 led by Juror #12. 12 days later, Laci & Conner were killed and for an "ACT OF GOD" (me) "Both" were found following the storm on the 12TH.
>
> GOD (I) delivered the evidence to secure the arrest of Scott Peterson and the eventual conviction "Beyond a Reasonable Doubt." The murderer was delivered to Modesto Police Department at 12 minutes to 12 midnight on Good Friday.
>
> Yes, it was a "Very" Good Friday
>
> GOD (I) Bless You
>
> GOD is one of us
> Open your hearts
> Open your minds
> Open your ears
> Open your eyes
> "Both of them"
> And you shall know the truth
> And the truth shall make you free

    Garth Stapley was the reporter assigned to the Scott Peterson case which was playing out in court and on TV in the months before Steven Avery was released. Just like taunting Paul Avery in the Zodiac case, Edwards taunted reporters in the Scott Peterson case with his identity. Edwards had planned and carried out the killing of Laci Peterson in 2002 and set-up her husband Scott Peterson. He did it on Christmas Eve, 2002. The letter he sent reflects the set-up and Satanic Spirituality. Edwards' mindset was that HE was the Great Satan.

Edwards' letter was a taunt to the reporter that HE, the writer of the letter was the real killer. The letter reflects how HE delivered the evidence to set-up Scott Peterson for killing his wife Laci and their unborn son. Edwards put parentheses around the word (ME) because in by tipping the M to the side, the M is an E which gives you EE, standing for Edward Edwards the real killer. Edwards detailed how to break his coded messages on a website he authored the same year he killed Laci Peterson and one year before he plotted Steve Avery's demise.

Edwards killed Laci on Christmas Eve 2002 and planted the unborn son on Palm Sunday, April 13th, 2003. Edwards planted Laci the following day, April 14th, the beginning of Easter week and the Birthday of a previous victim of Ed Edwards in 2001, Chandra Levy. Edwards had killed Chandra Levi MAY DAY, May 1, 2001, held her body for a year and planted her bones in Rock Creek Park, Washington DC, May 22, 2002, the day Chandra's parents were on TV begging for her return. Edwards creates what he calls "Crimes of Recognition." This meant his murders would go down in history because innocent people usually went down for HIS murders.

Edwards kills and plants bodies on ritual dates like Halloween. Edwards is the "Occult" explained in this letter sent to Garth Stapley November 12, 2003, two months after Steven Avery was released:

Garth Stapley
From:---removed---
Sent Wednesday Wednesday November 12th 2003 11:56 a.m.
Subject Scott Peterson

I read your story on whether or not Laci's death was cult related, you're right, it isn't cult related. It's occult related and there is a big difference between the two. I am a survivor of a politically powerful occult. I spent my life in training for a war, from the ages of 1 to 10 I was give a cult training, from the ages of 10 to 13 I was given cult training, from the ages of 13 to 16 I was given government secrets, from the ages of 16 to 19 I was give training in the politics of business. I then was in three arranged a cult relationships that lasted six years each 9 years, 3 years, 3 years, 3 years, 6 years, 6 years, 6 years and the final 3 9 years have not come yet. The occult is far more intelligent and advanced than anyone gives them credit for and that is how they will get away with their plan, you, the society. Will allow it! Everyone has a price, fear, greed, jealousy, Pride... Everyone has their weakness. If you aren't willing to risk it all to get the truth out. Then you will become yet another puppet for this game.

I think with all the training I have been given first-hand, that makes ME an expert on the occult and even the cult, but, I'm not credible am I?

Notice the prominence of the ME. He explains his codes in the following portion of the letter:
'Looks like this 5 + 6 equals 11/9 reverse it and you get 9/11. Occults practice mirroring an upside down and backwards coded message was for their plans to other occult members. it's like the pieces to a puzzle not everyone has the same piece also, this practice is found in Egyptian hieroglyphics.'
Clues that prove Lacey's death was occult related
First a background to occults and Cults. There's a significant difference between the two. And a cult is the worship of Satan and its purpose to start a satanic war in this country. Its members are not deceived about who they serve, or worship as opposed to the cult whose members are under the pretense of serving God of heaven but are really serving Satan. Both are influenced by power and control of their members and both have extensive knowledge of the Bible,

but not because they have actually read it. Neither groups are permitted or encouraged to seek information on their own, they are forced or coerced into seeking only wisdom from their leaders. Occult perform sacrifices of every kind including humans, and cold perform sacrifices of animals. The end result for a cult member is to prepare and train them for War and the end result for cult members is to weed out the Believers and worship rivers of God in heaven and Destroy them completely either by loss of their mind or by loss of their life through the occult so that the rest of the members do not suspect that the cults are doing it. Or in masses like Jonestown, where it instills fear and paranoia in the public toward religion and God. It gives a strong impression that God is not able to save those who seek him. For both the occult and cult the only Bible they are permitted to possess or read from is the King James version. Again, they are not encouraged to read it on their own and they are under such powerful influence of the group that they dare not question its leader King James had a background in Witchcraft and possibly masonry practices and that is why that is the only version they are permitted to read.

Saying that Lacey's death was not cult related is true, it was not a cult who did this. But it was an occult ritual. the media is getting away with deceiving the public on this one because of the use of the words from the attorneys. They can absolutely be proven truthful by saying it wasn't a cult. But if the pressure was on the occult, it would be a different story because there is too much evidence to back up that it was occult related.

I've been reading many different articles on this case and it's hard to keep track of them all so I'm just going to give the information I've seen and it's up to you to investigate, but really dig for answers because members are going to do their best to shut you down at every turn.

check judges 19 in the Bible. It refers to a woman being cut up and her body parts being sent to tribes as a call to war. In this case, Laci's body parts would be sent to different organizations or secret societies, undoubtedly the police or Fraternal Order of Police, (fraternal referring to mail so although this organization has a perception being for good, the undertone of it is that it is a secret, male Society.) And there is a group within the police department that not many know about called dog or God spelled backwards because they believe they are God's from the Egyptian descent

Check out the Fraternal Order of Rosicrucian's in San Jose, CA and learn about the Egyptian, Oriental, and Mexican Aztec burial practices. you will find that they take out all the internal organs except the heart to prepare the body for burial in some occult practices, the heart is eaten for power but if the occult was practicing and Egyptian ritual it would have been left behind

I read somewhere that Laci's 9th Rib was on the left side was broken and her fist and 6th ribs on the right side or broken the occults practice numerology not cults, cuts forbids such practices if you put that down on paper it would look like this 5 plus 6 = 11 / 9 reverse it and you get 911. Occults practice mirroring and upside down and backwards codes for their messages and plans to other occult members. It's like pieces to a puzzle, not everyone has the same piece. Also, this practice is found in Egyptian hieroglyphs.

8 is a number symbolic for Satan, not 6 like everyone thinks. 6 is symbolic for man, look at Creation in Genesis one and Man was created on the sixth day. 5 is symbolic for the devil, refer to the pentagram which is a five-pointed star and the symbol of the goat which is the symbol for the devil not Satan three is symbolic for Jezebel. In the occult everything that is Christian is opposite. So, if God has a trinity

then so does the occult. Satan, the devil and Jezebel. Satan is the king and Jezebel is the queen Satan and the devil share one body with two heads so the fact that Lacey was 8 months pregnant with a male child is something else that symbolizes it was the occult. A male and a female are opposites and a pure and a defiled sacrifice are opposites. And an infant and an adult are opposites. I could explain the theory behind the Opposites because it is far more than what people think it is, but it is the easiest way to explain it here is the yin and yang. Symbolic for good and evil. Read Jeremiah 7 starting with verse 16, it refers to the Queen of Heaven, it's talking about Jezebel and I think her name is Isis in Egyptian mythology, but I can't remember for certain. And refer to Revelation 12:9 which in my Bible says "this Dragon, the Ancient serpent called the devil or Satan..." they are in the same body with two heads, a two headed dragon.

Now, Lacey was 27 years old, the occult would make that one number 2 + 7 equals 9 the due date for the baby was 02/10/03 add those numbers together and you get 6 and Scott's age was 30 you have 9,6,3 the fact that the due date added up to 6 and the child was a male was not an accident either these numbers represent the trimester stages of pregnancy backwards my guess is that Lacey was killed first the baby second and it is imperative for them to kill Scott now to complete the cycle they reverse everything and if you were to interrupt this by Frank Scott it would ruin the purpose they are seeking

And one last clue that I have seen so far the time Scott was arrested and the time he was booked 11:10 time arrested. 00:09 time booked. Take the hour of time arrested in the minute of time booked 11:09 and reverse them 09:11 and the 00:10 take out the zero before the 9 and on zero before the 00:10 and put them together 09:11:0:10 and drop the last zero to 09/11/01. The date the twin towers went down

Okay, those are the clues to the purpose of these killings, it is directly related to the Twin Towers incident. The occult wants a war within the US to destroy the economy, which they are doing, to destroy the government, which they're doing and to destroy religion, which they're doing. And what most people don't realize is that the U.S. is a copy of Egypt only they Embrace more knowledge and wisdom than just thought of

To have a war you must feed the blood thirsty gods of War called "fortress" refer to Daniel 11:38

Another thing that I have noticed that sing popular to me is the prosecuting attorney is Brazilian and it seems as though he was involved in another occult case were four people killed and she sought to discredit the claim that, it was related to the occult or cult. From what I read of it, it was pretty hard to disprove, but for the lack of knowledge people do suffer. Whatever they can stifle, and silence keeps people in the dark and the only real way to end this is to expose their secrets. My question is, why is he trying so hard to cover up a cult activity, or protected? I'm wondering if he is a member. The public also does not realize how many men in society today are practicing the most defiling things and women

My objective is to get the truth out, having the truth isn't going to make bad things happen to you and it certainly isn't causing the past to be real, knowing the truth allows us to make better choices. It is also a test as to where you stand. Do you really want the truth? Or do you just want to wish everything away

My 5-year investigation of Ed Edwards has uncovered dozens of set-ups and hundreds of murders committed by him. In one case in

California in 1955 the set-up, Burton Abbott, was executed. Edwards considered himself the Executioner and wore the hood in 1969 during the Zodiac Killers Lake Berryessa attack. Edwards killed and set people up so that in his afterlife, the system would be executing for him.

In most his cases Edwards would write letters to police, the press and the victims' families, taunting them with the details of how he did it. In 2010, after his capture he was writing to police in Wisconsin, Ohio and Montana, claiming there were more murders and setups. Police and the FBI never investigated Edward Wayne Edwards after his capture in Wisconsin in 2009.

October 31st, 2005. Madison, Wisconsin. The same day that Teresa Halbach went missing, state legislators in Wisconsin passed the "Steve Avery Bill" to prevent wrongful convictions and reform the justice system. Edwards knew this, and it was well known the bill was going to pass on MONDAY, October 31, 2005. Edwards had his victim picked and his set-up picked long before Halloween 2005. His plan was to steal the recognition Steve Avery was getting and sit back and watch the system devour him and the police.

There is one main road in and out of Avery Salvage as seen from Google Earth and it is remote. I was at Avery Salvage January 2016.

There are back roads that can get you into the Salvage yard without being seen.

Teresa's car was planted to be found. It was the only car that was covered with strange objects at the salvage lot. It was designed to be recognized, not concealed. If Steve Avery was responsible he could have easily crushed the car in his salvage yard car crusher.

Teresa Halbach's Car Other cars on lot

Teresa Halbach was shot twice in the head. She was shot once in the left side of the head and the second to the back of the head, finishing her off. This is how Edwards shot the couple in 1956 here in Great Falls, Montana. Teresa was executed. Edwards would have walked up to her driver's side window as he got her to pull over, shoot her in the left temple and took her. He would put one final shot to the back of the head because that is what he did throughout life. Teresa's skull was in pieces but the two shots were found.

Police surmised a .22 caliber was used on Teresa and Steve Avery owned one that hung above his bed. It was there when they searched his house before Teresa was found. Steve Avery also shot the gun a lot and many of the discarded slugs were available for Edwards to pick-up to use to plant.

A .22 does not exit the skull on most occasions. I have been on many suicides where a .22 was used and it does not exit, or cause much bleeding. Police said Avery shot her in the garage because 4 months later they found a .22

slug with Teresa's DNA on it and the slug was fired from Steven's gun.

The slugs would have been inside Teresa's skull. They did not exit according to the skull bones of Teresa. They could not have been found in the garage. Edwards would have collected the slugs he used before he blew her body to pieces, and then planted that slug in Steven Avery's garage. Edwards already had Teresa's DNA to plant on the slug because he had her body three days before anyone knew she was missing. It wasn't until March of 2006 that police searched Steve Avery's garage and found a .22 slug with Teresa's DNA on it. It was planted.

Edwards would have had a predetermined spot to dispose of the body. He describes it as an "Aluminum Smelter" in the letter sent to Manitowoc Sheriff.

abanamon Smelter, 3 AM

fridy morn,

Edwards would have blown Teresa to bits in an enclosed chamber, such as an abandoned Smelter using his described bomb. That way he could easily collect all the remains to plant. According to lab personnel all the remains were found but were in small pieces. Manitowoc County has an aluminum Smelter known as Skana Aluminum. There are abandoned smelters in this part of Wisconsin. Edwards was familiar with Wisconsin. Edwards had lived in Wisconsin throughout life and killed there in 1974, 1980 and 1999.

Edwards had Teresa Halbach's cell phone, purse and other personal items found in the burn pit and burn barrel after he killed her and he used it to plant evidence to frame Steven Avery. Edwards had done this in cases in North Carolina 2008, Florida 2008 and Illinois in 2009.

Chris Coleman Il, 2009 Edgar Patino, NC, 2008 Stobert Holt, FL 2008

   In all three of these cases Edwards had obtained the passwords prior to killing the victims by grooming his way into their lives. In all three cases innocent men went down for HIS murders. In two of the cases the victims were women approximately Teresa Halbach's age. In the third case Robert Wiles body was never found because Edwards destroyed it using his bomb.

Megan Touma 2008 Sheri, Gavin, Garrett Coleman 2009

Edward Wayne Edwards was a serial killer that killed from 1945 until 2009. His MO was to set people up and stand in front of the investigation under assumed identity pretending to help. He planned his crimes deliberately, cold bloodedly and he would stick to federal crimes, like Kidnapping Teresa Halbach. He said so in his 1972 book, and he stuck with this M.O. religiously until his capture.

The Known Victims

1938, August 2, Akron, Ohio. Ed's mother Lillian Myers is shot in the stomach

1938, August 8, Akron, Ohio. Ed's mother dies of Septicemia, Ed is 5

1940, October, Parmadale, Ohio. Edwards, age 7 is sent to Parmadale Catholic Orphanage for out of control behavior.

1945, June 5, Chicago, Illinois. MURDER, 43-year-old Josephine Ross

1945, December 11, Chicago, Illinois. MURDER Frances Brown

1946, January 6, Chicago, Illinois. MURDER 6-year-old Suzanne Degnan

1947, January 15, Los Angeles, California. MURDER 22-year-old Elizabeth Short

1954, April 6, Boulder, Colorado. MURDER Dorothy Gay Howard, age 19

1954, July 4, Cleveland, Ohio. MURDER Marilyn Sheppard, age 30

1955, April 28, Berkeley, California. MURDER Stephanie Bryan, age 14

1955, October, Idaho Falls, Idaho. MURDER 17 old pregnant wife named Verna

1955, October 16, Chicago, Illinois. MURDER 13-year-old Robert Peterson, 13-year-old Jon Schuessler and 11-year-old Anton Schuessler

1955, December 10, Omaha, Nebraska. MURDER Carolyn Nevins, age 19

1956, January 2, Great Falls, Montana. MURDER 16-year-old Patty Kalitske and 18-year-old Air Force member Duane Bogle on a lever's lane

1957, March 15, Berkeley, California. BURTON ABBOTT EXECUTED for Edwards' killing of Stephanie Bryan in 1955

1960, April 16, McAllen, Texas. Sacred Heart Church, Easter Saturday, MURDER Irene Garza

1960, November 26-27, Portland, Oregon. MURDER Larry Peyton and Beverly Allen on a lover's lane in north Portland

1960, November 27, Astoria, Oregon. MURDER Naval Officer Wayne Budde

1968, June 24, 25, Cross Village/Good Hart, Michigan Upper Peninsula. MURDER six Robison family members

1968, July 23, Montreal, Canada. MURDER Norma Villancourt; a 21-year-old teacher found dead in her Montreal apartment

1968, December 20, Vallejo, California. MURDER David Faraday and Betty Lou Jensen on a lover's lane in the Zodiac killings

1969, July 4. Benicia, California. Edwards shoots Michael Mageau and Darlene Ferrin on a lover's lane in the Zodiac killings

1969, September 27, Lake Berryessa, California. Edwards stabs 20-year-old Bryan Hartnell and 22-year-old Cecelia Shepherd on a beach in the Zodiac killings. Hartnell survives.

1969, October 13, San Francisco, California. MURDER cab driver Paul Stine in the Zodiac killings

1969, November 28, State College, Pennsylvania. MURDER Betsy Ruth Aardsma in a library

1970, September 6, Lake Tahoe, Nevada. MURDER Donna Lass in the Zodiac killings

1972, February 4, Redwood City, California. MURDER Yvonne Weber, Maurine Sterling, ages 12 and 13 in the Highway 101 killings

1972, March 4. Santa Rosa, California. MURDER Kim Allen, age 18, Highway 101 killings

1972, April 25, 1972. Santa Rosa, California. MURDER Jeanette Kamahele, age 20, Highway 101 killings

1972, October, Akron, Ohio. Edwards publishes his autobiography Metamorphosis of a Criminal, the True Ed Edwards Story. The book was a puzzle of murder

1972, December 14, Santa Rosa, California. MURDER Lori Lee Kursa, age 13, Highway 101 killings

1973, March 8, Detroit, Michigan. Joe Scolaro, Richard Robison'\s partner, kills himself from being harassed by police for the killing the Robison family of 6, June 21, 1968

1973, July 15, Santa Rosa, California. MURDER Caroline Davis, age 15, Highway 101 killings

1973, December 22, Miranda, California. MURDER Theresa Walsh, age 15, Highway 101 killings

1974, October 12, Stanford, California. Edwards stalks and crucifies Arles Perry, age 19, in Stanford Memorial Church at Stanford University

1975, July 30, Detroit, Michigan. MURDER Jimmy Hoffa

1975, October 31, Greenwich, Connecticut. MURDER Martha Moxley on HALLOWEEN. Michael Skakel arrested and convicted in 2002. Released in 2013

1976, February 15, Detroit, Michigan. MURDER Mark Stebbins, 12, Oakland (County) Child Murders

1976, December 22, Detroit, Michigan. MURDER Jill Robinson, 12, Oakland Child Murders

1977, January 2, Detroit, Michigan. MURDER Kristine Mihelich, 10, Oakland Child Murders
1977, February 17, Mayo Clinic, Rochester, Minnesota. Edwards kidnaps and kills Helen Brach
1977, March 16, Detroit, Michigan. MURDER Timothy King, 11, Oakland Child Murders
1977, August 8, Akron, Ohio. MURDER Billy Lavacco, age 21 and Judith Straub, age 18, while they are parked on a lover's lane
1979, July 25, Atlanta, Georgia. Edward Smith, 14 and Alfred Evans 13, Atlanta Child Murders
1979, August 24, Akron, Ohio. Ricky Beard, age 19 and Mary Leonard, age 18
1979, August 30, Erie, Pennsylvania. Edwards burns Deborah Sweet's home and kills an adult male and two children
1979, September 4, Atlanta, Georgia. Milton Harvey, 14, Atlanta Child Murders
1979, October 21, Atlanta, Georgia. Yusef Bell, 9, Atlanta Child Murders
1980, March 4, Atlanta, Georgia. Angel Lenair, 12, and Jeffery Mathis, 12, Atlanta Child Murders
1980, April 6, Toledo, Ohio. Edwards Crucifies Sister Margaret Pahl in a Sacristy in a Catholic Church at Toledo's hospital
1980, May 18, Atlanta, Georgia. Eric Middlebrooks, 14, Atlanta Child Murders
1980, June 9, Atlanta, Georgia. Chris Richardson, 12, Atlanta Child Murders
1980, June 22, Atlanta, Georgia. Latonya Wilson, 7, Atlanta Child Murders
1980, June 23, Atlanta, Georgia. Aaron Wyche, 10, Atlanta Child Murders
1980, July 6, Atlanta, Georgia. Anthony Carter, 9, Atlanta Child Murders
1980, July 30, Atlanta, Georgia. Earl Terell, 11, Atlanta Child Murders
1980, August 9, Jefferson, Wisconsin. MURDER Kelly Hack and Timothy Drew
1980, August 20, Atlanta, Georgia. Clifford Jones, 13, Atlanta Child Murders

1980, September 14, Atlanta, Georgia. Darren Glass, 10, Atlanta Child Murders
1980, October 9, Atlanta, Georgia. Charles Stephens, 12, Atlanta Child Murders
1980, November 10, Atlanta, Georgia. Aaron Jackson, 9, Atlanta Child Murders
1980, November 10, Atlanta, Georgia. Patrick Rogers, 16, Atlanta Child Murders
1981, January 3, Atlanta, Georgia. Lubie Geter, 14, Atlanta Child Murders
1981, January 22, Atlanta, Georgia. Terry Pue, 15, Atlanta Child Murders
1981, February 5, Grand Rapids, Michigan. Deannie Peters, 14
1981, February 6, Atlanta, Georgia. Patrick Baltazar, 11, Atlanta Child Murders
1981, February 19, Atlanta, Georgia. Curtis Walker, 15, Atlanta Child Murders
1981, March 2, Atlanta, Georgia. Joseph Bell, 15, Atlanta Child Murders
1981, March 13, Atlanta, Georgia. Timothy Hill, 13, Atlanta Child Murders
1981, July 27, Hollywood, Florida, Hollywood Mall. Edwards kidnaps, kills and dismembers Adam Walsh, the son of America's Most Wanted Host John Walsh. http://en.wikipedia.org/wiki/Murder_of_Adam_Walsh
1981, August 10. Edwards places Adam Walsh's head to be found. http://crime.about.com/b/2007/02/08/did-jeffrey-dahmer-kill-adam-walshh.htm
1982, February 27, Atlanta, Georgia. Wayne Williams is convicted in Atlanta Child Murders
1986, October 12, Colonial Parkway, Virginia. Cathleen Thomas, age 27 and Rebecca Dowski, age 21, Colonial Parkway Murders
1987, September, Wythe County, Virginia. David Knobling, age 21 and Robin Edwards, age 14, Colonial Parkway Murders
1988, April 9, Colonial Parkway, Virginia. Cassandra Hailey, age 19 and Richard Kall, age 19. Bodies never found, Colonial Parkway Murders

1989, October 12, Colonial Parkway, Virginia. Anna Phelps, age 18 and David Lauer, age 21, Colonial Parkway Murders

1993, May 5, West Memphis, Arkansas. MURDER Christopher Byers, Stephen Branch and Michael Moore Ages 8, West Memphis Three Case, HBO Paradise Lost, The Robinhood Hills Murders

1996, March/April, Burton, Ohio. MURDER Dannie Law Gloeckner, 22

1996, December 25, Boulder, Colorado. MURDER JonBenet Ramsey, 6

2001, May 1, Washington, DC. MURDER Chandra Levy, 24

2001, September 18, New Jersey. Edwards mails Anthrax Letters to congress and the press killing 5

2001, November 1, Columbia, Missouri. MURDER Editor Kent Heitholt, Columbia Missouri Tribune

2002, May 22, Washington, DC. The Oprah Show airs the interview of Chandra Levy's' parents and during the showing, Edwards plants Chandra's skull to be found in Rock Creek Park

2002, December 24. Modesto, California. MURDER Laci Peterson, 7 months pregnant. Scott Peterson arrested and convicted, sentenced to death in 2005. Still on death row

2003, October 19, Yavapai County, Arizona. Brandon Rumbaugh, 20, and Lisa Gurrieri, 19, shot to death in their sleeping bags while camping

2004, August 18, Jenner, California. MURDER Lindsay Cutshall and Jason Allen, shot to deaeth on an ocean beach while camping.

2006, Toledo, Ohio. Father Gerald Robinson convicted and sentenced to life for Edward's killing of Sister Margaret Pahl

2008, April 1, Lakeland, Florida. Edwards kidnaps and kills Robert Wiles, 26. Body never found

2008, June 14, Fort Bragg, North Carolina. MURDER Megan Lynne Touma, 7 months pregnant

2008, July 27, Washington DC. Dr. Bruce Ivins supposedly kills self with Tylenol. It is the 27th anniversary of Edwards' killing Adam Walsh

2008, August 6, Washington, DC. FBI announces Dr. Bruce Ivins, who died two weeks earlier, is the Anthrax letter sender from 2001

2008, December, Hollywood, Florida. Police say that Ottis Toole is the killer of Adam Walsh, killed July 27, 1981 and beheaded. http://articles.latimes.com/2008/dec/17/nation/na-adam17

2009, June 9, Jefferson, Wisconsin. Edwards interviewed and a DNA swab taken.

2009, June 14, Edwards posts the confession to killing Adam Walsh "Let us not forget the Scorpion's warning for John Walsh that he was his worst nightmare. Why? Did Zodiac change his pen name back in 1990 to Scorpion to cryptically claim responsibility for Adam's demise? Why did John Walsh remain mum for so many years before partially releasing the Scorpion files for the public?"

2009, July 30, Louisville, Kentucky. Edwards arrested

2011, April 7, Ohio Correctional Facility. Edwards dies

The Wrongfully Convicted Still Alive

There are 12 known inmates in 10 different states currently serving time for murders committed by Edward Wayne Edwards. Here are their names and attorney contact information.

Ingmar Guandique. Washington, DC, Convicted in November 2010, for the killing of Chandra Levy, May 1, 2001. In 2013 the government held secret hearings regarding the conviction. Attorney: Santha Sonenberg, http://www.linkedin.com/pub/santha-sonenberg/2a/828/46a

Father Gerald Robinson, Toledo, Ohio, convicted May 11, 2006 for April 6th, 1980 Crucifixion slaying of Sister Margaret Pahl in Toledo's Mercy Hospital. Attorney, Alan Konop, 413 North Michigan St., Toledo, Ohio. 419-255-0571

Wayne Williams, Atlanta, Georgia. Convicted March 1982 in Atlanta, for the deaths of two adults. After his conviction police announced he was the Atlanta Child Killer and was responsible for 24 deaths of black children from 1979-1981. Attorney: Lin Wood, http://en.wikipedia.org/wiki/L._Lin_Wood

Damien Echols, Jesse Misskelly, Jason Baldwin, West Memphis, Arkansas, May 5th, 1993. Convicted for the Crucifixion killing of three 8-year-old boys in Robin Hood Hills Park. Attorney: Dan Stidham, http://www.stidhamlawfirm.com/ Attorney: Len Goodman, http://lengoodmanlawoffice.com/wp/significant-cases/people-of-illinois-v-kenneth-hansen/

Stobert L Holt, Lakeland, Florida. Convicted March 2012 for the April 1st, 2008 kidnap of Robert A Wiles in Lakeland, Florida. A no-body prosecution was done. Robert Wiles' body has never been found. Attorney; Howardene Garrett, Public Defender, http://www.jud10.flcourts.org/?q=content/history

Ryan Ferguson and Charles Erickson, Columbia, Missouri, convicted in 2004 for the November 1, 2001 killing of Columbia Tribune Editor Kent Heitholt in the parking lot of the newspaper on Halloween Night. Attorney Kathleen Zellner, http://www.kathleentzellner.com/contactus.html

Sergeant Edgar Patino, Fort Bragg, North Carolina, pleaded guilty November 2010 to avoid being executed for the killing of SPC Army Megan Touma. She was 7 months pregnant with his child. She was killed on Ed Edwards' birthday in Fort Bragg, North Carolina at the Fairfield Inn. Edwards left the Zodiac sign in lipstick on a mirror in the room and wrote two letters to the press and police claiming the Zodiac did it and was at the scene.

Scott Peterson, Modesto, California. Found guilty of killing his pregnant wife Laci Peterson in 2004 and sentenced to death in San Quentin.

Michael Skakel, Greenwich, Connecticut. Arrested and convicted in 2002 for the 1975 killing of Martha Moxley on Halloween. Skakel granted a new trial and released in November 2013.

The Known Wrongfully Convicted Deceased

Burton Abbott, Berkeley, California, executed March 17th, 1957, executed for the killing of 14-year-old Stephanie Bryan, April 28th, 1955. Edwards killed her, planted her body behind Abbott's cabin and led the San Francisco Examiner to her body to frame him. He was sent to the gas chamber at San Quentin, March 17th, 1957. Edwards was in Deer Lodge Prison Montana at the time of the execution and received parole from the Montana Board of Pardons and Parole in 1959. He went to Portland Oregon and killed again.

    Carl Jorgenson, Edward Jorgenson and Robert Brom, Portland, Oregon, taken to trial 1968-70 in Portland for Edwards' November 27th, 1960 killing of Larry Peyton and Beverly Allen on a lover's lane. Two convicted; one, Carl, acquitted. Edwards killed everyone in the Zodiac Killings during the trial of these three innocent men.

    Kenneth Hansen, (Deceased 2007) Chicago, Illinois. Convicted in 1995 for the October 16, 1955 Triple crucifixion of three teens in Robinson Woods Park, Chicago, Illinois. http://www.prairieghosts.com/spmurders.html

Made in the USA
Middletown, DE
23 May 2018